MW00960255

La Cave:
Cleveland's Legendary Music Club and the ‘60s Folk-to-Rock Revolution

Steve Traina

This story is lovingly dedicated to my big sis Rosalie, who opened up a new and strange world to me, from which I have never strayed.

JKL, Inc., Publisher

Copyright © 2023 Steve Traina

All rights reserved.

Introduction

La Cave (pronounced "la-KAHV") was a dingy, dilapidated, underground cavern where magic happened six nights a week.

Going to La Cave was like going to your best friend's basement for a loud, rambunctious all-night party if your friend's basement held three hundred people and his parents didn't care how loud the music was or how fucked up you got. In fact, they encouraged it.

Long before the days of arena and stadium concerts, before the Eagles and mega-tours, even before (and during and after) The Beatles redefined pop culture, live music was consumed in small venues in front of oftentimes smaller crowds. At the Café Wha? in Greenwich Village and Coral Gables' Flick Coffeehouse back east, or at the Troubadour in Los Angeles and the hungry i in San Francisco out west, folk (and later, rock) music fans could sit mere feet from an unknown David Crosby or an equally anonymous Lou Reed, Joni Mitchell or Judy Collins, unaware and unconcerned that they were living through historic times in likewise historic places. They were there for the music.

But of those countless clubs, only a couple handfuls survived and prospered long enough to become iconic venues. One such club was Cleveland's "House of Folk Music," La Cave.

In the mid-Sixties, Billboard Magazine – the bible of the music biz - called nine such clubs "trend-setters." Of the ninc, seven were on an east or a west coast, and only two were marooned inland. One of those two clubs was La Cave. What Billboard noticed in real time was the prescience and persistence of these clubs to recognize, sign, nurture and promote the temporarily unknown superstars-to-be of modern popular music – often before the unwashed masses had even heard of them.

There was no template for success, no "how-to" business model to be followed. What was needed for success couldn't be taught or learned. It took luck, timing, a few bucks, and most of all, an innate sense of where musical tastes would be in the near future. These clubs, and the men of vision who guided them, became the vanguard that alchemically turned musical lead into gold records. And along the way, an entire generation grew up with new values, wisdom, and an abiding love for the music that was chosen for them by these visionaries to serve as the soundtrack for the explosive societal change of the Sixties and beyond.

The entrance to La Cave

Acknowledgements

This story is for us, the cave dwellers. Mostly, though, it's for Nelson Karl, the visionary who set it all in motion, and Stan Kain and Larry Bruner, the two Resident Wizards of La Cave, without whose mutual support, friendship, and packratting of all the old records, this project would have been impossible. This story is, and always will be, theirs.

Table of Contents

Chapter 1: Setting the Stage

"Folk music" has always been around, but rarely has it become the dominant popular American music genre - with one glaring exception. In the late 1950s, after incubating in small clubs, coffeehouses and summer camps for nearly twenty years, the New Folk Revival burst into mainstream listening. And for a few wondrous years, the sound of banjos and acoustic guitars behind simple vocal harmonies, sung by clean cut Ivy League young men and pretty, young women with prettier voices, told the stories of Everyman, and sold millions of records in the process.

In the mid-Fifties, anti-communist fervor swept away a lot of "radical" lefties, many of whom were singer/musicians like Pete Seeger, who was convicted and blacklisted. The conviction was later overturned, but the damage had been done. "Folkies" largely went silent. But then, on 3 February, 1959, when Buddy Holly's Beechcraft Bonanza airplane crashed near Clear Lake, Iowa, "the music died." In short order, Elvis was drafted, Jerry Lee was disgraced, Little Richard found Jesus, and Chuck Berry went to prison. Rock & roll wouldn't begin to recover until February of 1964 when the British, in the form of The Beatles, invaded and conquered America, musically speaking, and opened the door to a completely new sound with which to captivate the next decade of listeners.

But in 1959 that was OK. America already had rock & roll's replacement. Folk music, having survived and even transcended the uber-patriotic '40s and the repressive '50s, filled the black hole left by the supernova of those first rock and roll superstars. The Kingston Trio sold tens of millions of records. This success paved the way for acts like Peter, Paul and Mary, The Limeliters, the Brothers Four, The Chad Mitchell Trio, The New Christy Minstrels, and many more acoustic folkies. Record companies began clamoring to sign and promote their own stars. Vanguard and Folkways became the preeminent folk music record labels. Columbia and the other big boys scrambled to catch up.

Hard on the heels of The Trio were stars-to-be like Joan Baez, whose debut album reached the Top 10 in late 1960 and remained on the Billboard charts for over two years. And in 1961, the bard of Hibbing, Minnesota, future Nobel Laureate Bob Dylan made his first recording. Acts like the Kingston Trio played small clubs, colleges and coffeehouses, but by 1961 they and their peers had outgrown these tiny venues and needed larger clubs in which to perform. "Cleveland's House of Folk Music," as La Cave came to be known, was ready to be born. The only thing missing was a man of vision.

Enter Nelson Karl.

Nelson Karl

Nelson Karl and a Cast of Dozens

Nelson Karl was a good and dedicated lawyer, by all accounts. Later in life he was named lead- or co-counsel in many American Civil Liberties Union (ACLU) actions and his passion for civil rights became legendary. As 1962 commenced he was also an old man by the yardstick of the times. He was all of 35.

Nelson was captivated by music in general – not coincidentally, he had married jazz singer Alice Einstein – and acoustic folk music in particular, and took guitar lessons from a man, a prodigy of sorts, named Stanley Heilbrun. Stanley, a student at Cleveland's Institute of Music, was able to play 30 musical instruments, or so he claimed. What is undisputed is that Stanley *owned* 30 instruments. This was several years prior to a pretentious Time Magazine article titled The Psychedelicatessen, which called Stanley the nation's first proprietor of a new sort of business, something called a head shop. But we're getting ahead of the story.

One day, at the end of a guitar lesson, the story goes that Stanley let a small piece of adding machine tape fall to the floor. Nelson asked what it was, and was told it was nothing, just some numbers, his $712 calculation of capital cost to open a coffeehouse/nightclub in the University Circle area, where students from nearby colleges Case Tech and Western Reserve University congregated. Nelson took the bait. Perhaps he was drawn into the novel beatnik idea because of its cultural fantasy, but more likely it was because of the lure of the music.

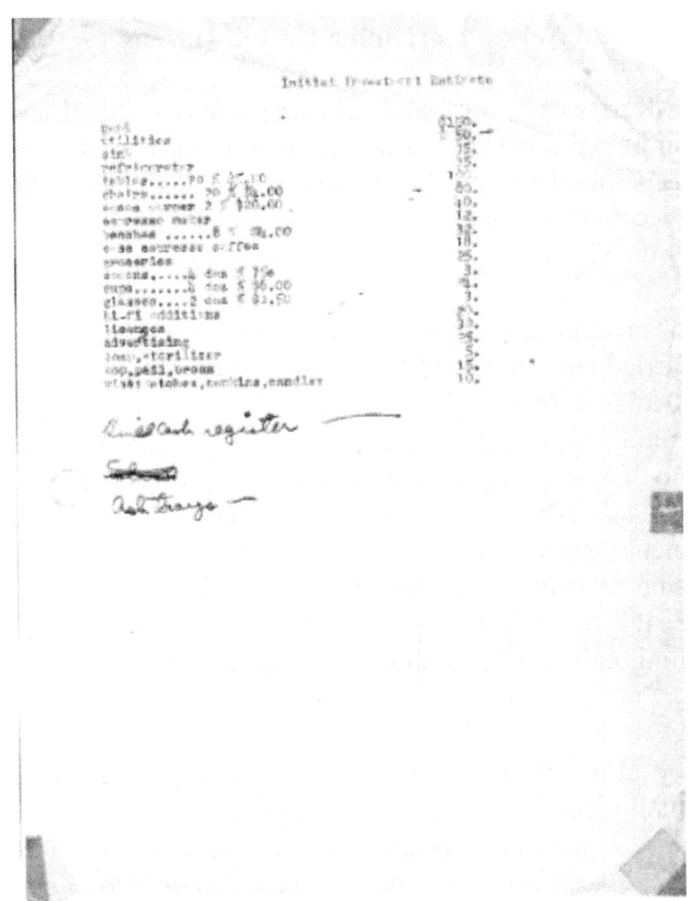

"Initial Investment Expenses" February 1962

Stanley had the place picked out: an empty basement at 10615 Euclid Avenue in the once-bustling theatre district known as Doan's Corners, that had once housed, among other less than savory establishments, a pool hall where a young Leslie Townes Hope hustled a little 9-ball on his way to becoming international movie star Bob Hope. Above it at ground level was a similarly dilapidated Social Security office. By the '60s, streetcars and vaudeville shows were just memories. The two-level Alhambra Theatre at 10403 Euclid remained open, but the bright lights of other marquees like The Keith's 105th, The Circle, and The University were all gone. Scattered around the neighborhood were more gin mills and local watering holes than a determined drunkard could frequent in a week's time. Peppered in amongst the flotsam and jetsam of society were the prostitutes, the panhandlers, the pimps and the police who daily danced a dangerous interaction that often ended in violence, arrest, and other examples of civic misbehavior.

The local college students in the area - and there were many – couldn't have cared less. There's a time in life when a person knows that he or she is immortal, and for these youths this was their time. The fact that they operated in droves helped the appearance of safety and, in reality, there really was less danger on the mean Cleveland streets in the early '60s than there were in the years to follow.

Doan's Corners

The geographical location of what was to become La Cave was an oddity. It stood hard against the southeast corner of the Hough neighborhood, which would explode into the flames of racial unrest in just a few years, and at the same time hovered on the western edge of a relative urban Eden of parks, museums, colleges and other, more refined, landmarks.

It also was home to thousands of more or less well-to-do college students away from home and on the hunt for their next good time. Nelson Karl was nobody's fool and besides, at $150 a month, the rent was right. On 21 February, 1962, he drew up Articles of Incorporation, enlisted fellow guitar student and local lawyer Lee Weiss and Heilbrun as a couple of nominal stockholders, and a few days later signed a year's lease to commence March 1st. In a flurry of activity, he lined up a vendor's license, a fire and theft insurance policy, a food service permit, an admissions tax permit and, since this was to be a coffee house, an espresso machine. He also hunted down a liquor license that a local businessman by the name of Nick Lanese wanted to divest himself of, hired Heilbrun to act as club manager for the lofty sum of $75 per week, and called up Cleveland's daily morning newspaper *The Plain Dealer*, which ran an article on March 23rd detailing the grand opening of La Cave de Café. Four days previously, a scruffy young lad who had recently changed his surname to Dylan had just released his debut album on the Columbia label.

La Cave, threadbare and bereft of most of the amenities of a college hangout, was born. It would quickly become Nelson's folly and struggle to survive. Until, that is, 25-year-old Stan Kain chanced upon the cellar club and waved his magic wand. The La Cave saga is largely the story of Stan Kain.

Stan Kain's Beginnings

Stan was born 1 May 1936 to Allen and Dorothy Kain and missed the worst of the Depression and World War II. He grew up in a close-knit middle-class Jewish family in Cleveland Heights, a quick hitch-hike up Mayfield Road through the Murray Hill neighborhood known as Little Italy. "The Heights" truly was the heights, as you needed to climb Lee Road hill from the north or Cedar Road hill from Cleveland to the west to get there. Quite literally, people escaping the inner city moved on up when they settled in The Heights.

The Heights boasts more than its share of music clubs and even a wonderful outdoor venue, Cain Park, that seats 3,000 and brings in national and international acts during its short summer season. In 1938, Dr. Dina "Doc" Evans co-founded Cain Park, an outdoor amphitheater situated in a natural ravine in The Heights. As its director, she mentored many students who later became well-known in entertainment.

One of her projects was young Stan Kain, who found a home in the drama department of Heights High, where Doc Evans taught. Stan's dedication to his new craft caused Doc Evans to offer Stan an intern's position at Cain Park. Young Stan, still in high school, had arrived at the bottom of the entertainment totem pole. And so his real education began, a course of study that would serve him well over the next decade and into his chosen profession of audio-visual production. Stan's focus on the technical aspects of show production activated an entrepreneurial spirit that led him to imagine himself promoting local shows.

Cain Park ca. 1950s

Stan graduated from Heights High in 1956 and his internship at Cain Park became a full-time position as a jack-of-all-trades: building sets, repairing broken a/v equipment, and maintaining the increasingly complicated backstage infrastructure that supports theater activity. Eventually, he moved into controlling lights and sound for shows.

A portion of Stan's station at Cain Park

Stan's debut as stage manager was somewhat less than auspicious. In fact, it's hard to imagine things going any worse for the young man, whose exuberance still overshadowed his talents. "This one show," Stan relates, "you know, the stage lights were supposed to go up and down, but just as Bob [Hope] came out, the one right in front of him at the microphone got stuck and wouldn't go down, nearly blinding him. So I ran out on stage, right in front of Bob, facing him, and got the light unstuck. Bob said something about me and the crowd laughed, but I was way too nervous to even hear what he said. I just ran offstage."

Stan's embarrassment didn't end there. *The Plain Dealer* had a bit of fun at Stan's expense in describing the event for its readers. Critic W. Ward Marsh described the antics that ensued when the audience roared at the mishap.

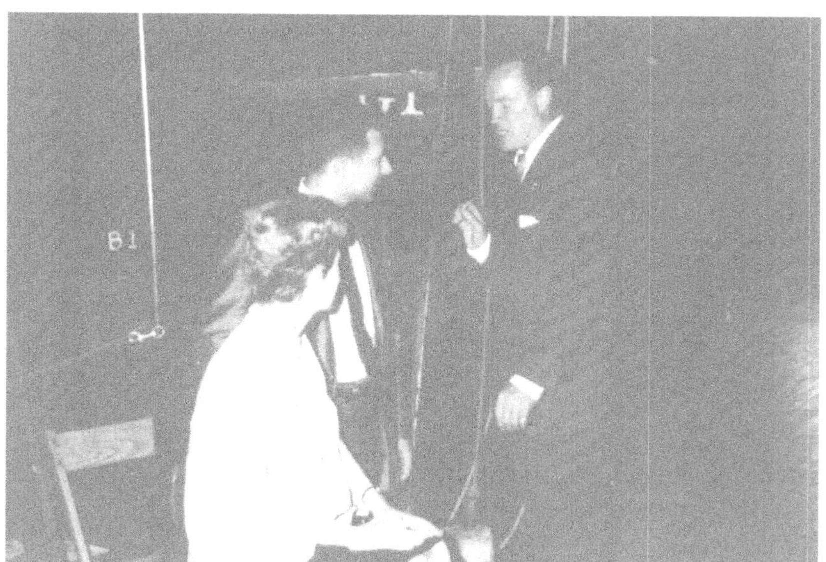

(L to R) Carol Kain, Stan Kain, Bob Hope

But the die was cast. Stan said, "The feeling of watching the audience from the wings, being a small part of the presentation, was amazing. I learned a lot from those high-pressure shows in front of packed houses, and I realized that if I could handle this, I could maybe have a place in, you know, putting my own shows on someday."

"Someday" was going to arrive sooner than Stan imagined. It took Stan less than six weeks to pick up a couple of financial partners, Don Jay and Ralph Sanders, and sign an agreement to bring a hot act to town.

Stan Kain at his side hustle, 1961

Stan Kain was always a humble, self-effacing man, but for the better part of the 1960s he was one of those few special people who had no idea they were writing history with their deeds. In the sixty years since Josh White, Sr., got on stage to a sold-out room in mid-1962, La Cave has earned true cult status. People all over the world grew up at least in part at La Cave. Musicians, waitresses, and the unnamed masses of baby boomers now scattered through time and space, still speak of their days, or rather, nights, at La Cave as if those nights were among the most important parts of their entire lives. Probably because they were.

La Cave was an urban university of sorts. Music was its curriculum, but social interaction was every bit as important. The likes of Bob Gibson, Ed McCurdy and Dave Van Ronk were the professors, and the dean of this institution of higher learning was the little Jewish fellow with the quick smile, twinkling eyes and gentle manner. But, like so many overly dramatic stories, this tale would have ended quickly and painfully and neither the myth nor the effect of La Cave on its graduates would have happened without the Dean, Stan Kain.

Meanwhile, Back at Cain Park

Stan Kain had settled in to his position as stage manager at Cain Park. In August of 1959 he boldly signed a promotional agreement to host the Kingston Trio, America's hottest act at the time with three songs in the top five of the Billboard charts, to an October appearance at Cleveland's venerable Masonic Auditorium, a 2,100-seat venue at Chester Avenue and East 36th street. The Masonic boasted acoustics so superior to any other venue outside of New York City, that the internationally-acclaimed Cleveland Orchestra chose it as its recording home for many years.

The show was successful, so much so that in 1960 Stan decided to emulate his mentor, local theater impresario Max Mink, and begin booking shows of his own. Along with his partners he hosted Erroll Garner to tinkle the ivories at suburban Musicarnival in July. When the final accounting was submitted, the 1,400 show attendees netted Garner a cool $2,500 while Stan, the neophyte promoter, lost $178.04. The disappointing financial result only served to whet Stan's appetite for success. By the time 1960 had receded into history, Stan had promoted half a dozen concerts, and set his sights on the stars, literally. When the 1961 season concluded, a slightly older and somewhat wiser Stan Kain received a $203.16 invoice for monies owing the venue. The puny amount didn't bother him in the least. In fact, it presaged a career during which Stan's distaste for any kind of financial calculations played a significant role in his future bookings.

Chapter 2: 1962 - Beginnings are Delicate Times

1962 came into this world on shaky ground. Across the pond, Decca Records celebrated the new year by rejecting a Liverpool rock-n-roll quartet in favor of signing the immortal Brian Poole and the Tremeloes. Further east, Nikita Khrushchev was busily extracting all he could from President Eisenhower in exchange for downed U-2 spy plane pilot Francis Gary Powers, who found his way home in February. Khrushchev settled for getting back former Geordie boy and super spy Rudolf Abel in return.

Significantly, on 20 February, Ohioan John Glenn found permanent hero status by doing something no other American had even attempted, boarding space capsule *Friendship 7* and orbiting Earth as the entire nation watch mesmerized. In a probably meaningless coincidence, La Cave would forever shutter itself within a week of yet another Ohioan's heroic interstellar achievement, when Wapakoneta's favorite son, starsailor Neil Armstrong, took one small step on 20 July 1969. From blastoff to touch down, La Cave's journey through time and inner space mirrored the national effort in outer space.

But by the end of May, when regiments of students abandoned University Circle and returned home, dad's pocket money extinguished, La Cave instantly fell on hard times. Nelson decided to pull the plug. But how? He had nine months left on his 12-month lease. Nightly receipts somewhat south of fifty dollars just didn't cut it.

Luckily, Nelson's bad news traveled so fast that Stan Kain would soon transform it into everyone's good fortune.

La Cave as Coffeehouse – March to September 1962

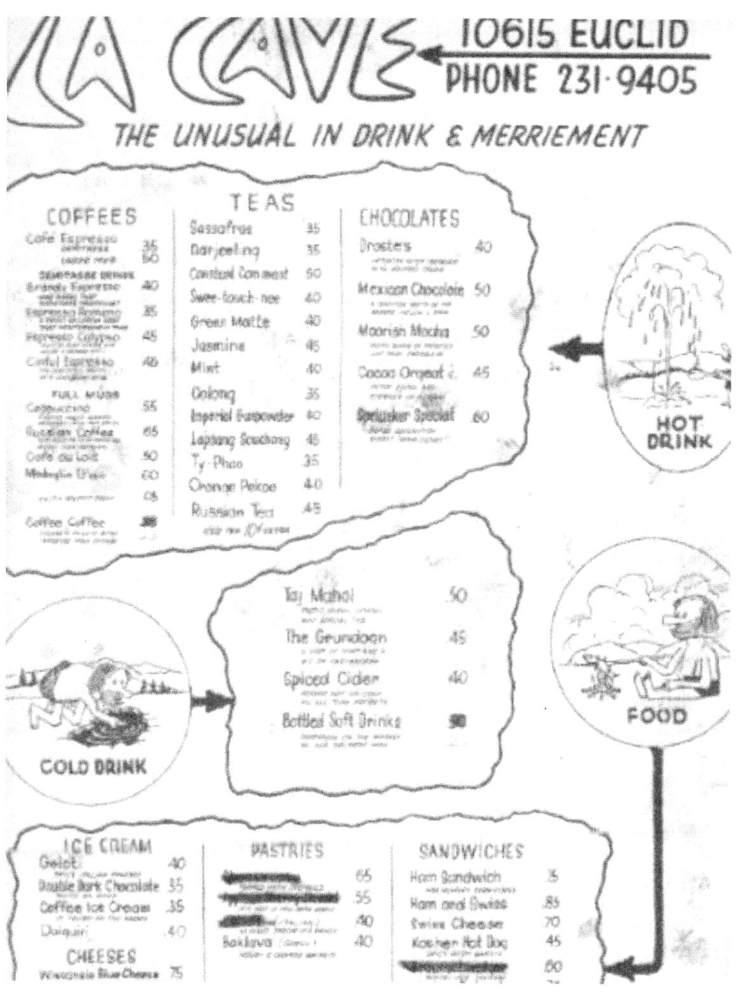

La Cave's first menu

Once Nelson Karl decided to dive into the shallow water of bohemian coffee sales, there was no turning back. Always a man of action, the icy drafts of February that blew off Lake Erie brought with them a whirlwind of heated action. He hit the ground running. He calculated the further costs of furniture, kitchen equipment, and the like from a handful of local supply houses, settling on the Harris Company as the "Best Place."[i] He also priced used draperies to be used as a stage backdrop, dividers between the kitchen area and the main floor area, and eventually to create a "green room" behind the stage for performers.

In February, Nelson sat down with an agent of White Properties, Inc., owner of 10615 Euclid and they hammered out a two-year lease agreement. Among some its more interesting points besides the monthly rent ($150.00) were the commitments of the owners to eliminate the banging noise from the ancient radiators, clean the toilets, and "remove the remnants of the billiard sign" above the entrance. The monthly rent included heat and hot and cold water. Nelson also gained the right to install "audio equipment and other noise-making facilities and guests of the Lessee may sing and otherwise enjoy themselves in any lawful activities." The noise-making and enjoyment about to commence would turn out to be both lawful and otherwise.

In March, Nelson bought three items crucial to the success of a coffee house – a $600 LaCimbali Espresso Machine, a LaCimbali Coffee Grinder, and an agreement from a legal client of his to transfer his dormant liquor license, allowing La Cave to offer beer, wine and spirits.

The infant corporation began life on 23 March with a thousand dollars in stock and a plan that provided for Stanley Heilbrun to become the first paid employee and act as La Cave's manager. He began knocking down a cool $75 a week.

Let the Games Begin

The last week of March, which was the first week of La Cave, went out like a lamb. Nothing much in the way of entertainment – or trade – came its way. No kitchen personnel or wait staff were hired, and the sink wasn't even hooked up yet. No advertising was purchased, and no acts had been booked. Other than that, everything was hunky dory. It became apparent that the shebang was going to be more convoluted than Nelson anticipated. On April Fool's, Nelson signed an agreement with ASCAP[ii] and received his Music Permit from the city, allowing them to host musical performances, with the inhibiting stipulation that "No dancing shall be permitted on the premises."

The first week of April came and went, with Nelson back at his lawyerly tasks and Stanley bravely, if somewhat inexpertly, overseeing the repairs to the club and lending a hand at times. When it came to building renovations, Stanley retained his amateur status.

And then, on the 8th of April, from the depths of whatever chasm these things originate, the *Plain Dealer* broke bombshell news to a groggy Sunday morning readership. In a somewhat tongue-in-cheek article, they claimed that all the Beatniks in town are, "like, gone, man."

What a scoop!

A lesser man than Nelson Karl might have wilted under such a thorough deconstruction of the very clientele that might have supported his fledgling hangout. But Nelson could plant his tongue as firmly into his cheek as any reporter. He fired off a letter of his own to the editor. It read, in part:

"Subject: Beatniks ARE Back, Man, for real

Dear Sir,

I have difficulty reconciling the conflict between your article of April 8 entitled "Where are the Beatniks? Why, Like Gone, of Course," and Glenn C. Pullen's column of March 23 with the headline "New Café, Folk Song, Jazz, Espresso, Opens Tonight."

Exception is hereby taken by all bona fide beatniks, pseudo beatniks, semi beatniks, psycho beatniks and beatnik supporters to remarks of your reporter, Jan Mellow,[iii] who says that beatniks have all gone and all of the coffeehouse are out of business. La Cave de Café, the newest of the beatnik coffee houses, is located at 10615 Euclid Avenue near the campuses of Case Institute and Western Reserve University, near the Institute of Music and the Institute of Art, near Severance Hall and near the art museum. It was built by beatniks for their personal pleasure sand exudes an atmosphere of conviviality and Greenwich Village comfort. The interior of La Cave was decorated by the beatniks themselves. Stereo-Phonic paintings and Avant Garde photography decorate the walls and act as room dividers. One section of the room is furnished with mats and pillows for the benefit of the 'casual' crowd. At any time, beatniks can be found reposing in quiet comfort with their beards tucked neatly away and their leotards supplying comfort and warmth while they suck in the strains of folk music.

The food at La Cave is strictly beatnik cooking and includes such succulent Delicacies as Caffe Espresso, Cappuccino, Rum Espresso, Russian Coffee, Cannoli, Baklava, Farfaletti, Brindza and Fontina cheeses and the finest cheese cake west of Lindy's (complete with manufacturer's warranty).

As for entertainment, it is abundant, varied and highly professional. On Friday and Saturday nights, La Cave offers a folk singing entourage around one of the finest classical guitarists in the mid west. The show lasts for hours and covers the complete range of music from authentic early American folk ballads to fine music that will tickle the palettes of the concert going crowd. Wednesday is hootenanny night for those who cannot restrain themselves from performing and includes the great and the near great. On Mondays, the beatniks hold open discussions and on Tuesday, they offer a folk singing and a guitar clinic. But on Sunday nights, the jazz hounds move in with modern and progressive jazz concerts for listeners.

All in all, man, La Cave is open seven nights a week, so retract that story. The beatniks have not retreated. They are out in force. Although they disdain common, ordinary people, they are cordial and warm to their friends. They have asked me to invite one and all to visit them at La Cave as their personal guests in order to refute the uninformed, inaccurate and obviously biased account that appeared on these pages. In particular, the beatniks offer this one word of advice to reporter Jan Mellow – 'Check your facts, man.' 'Say you the beatniks have gone? Come to La Cave and find out.'

Very truly yours,

Nelson G. Karl"

Madison Avenue could not have written a better advertisement. Nelson's letter had the beneficial effect of informing the student body of Case and Western Reserve of a new hangout, and almost immediately the club began seeing a trickle of commerce. That trickle would improve considerably but not quite cover the monthly nut.

A flurry of activity ensued. Nelson inked ad contracts with both Cleveland dailies, *The Plain Dealer* and the *Press.* At the same time, he hired the Joe Alexander Quartet for an Easter afternoon jazz concert on the 22nd of April and placed ads to that effect. The ads also mentioned folk music every Friday and Saturday nights. Landing Joe Alexander's outfit, which was a temporarily truncated version of his quintet due to having lost Art Blakey's pianist Bobby Timmons to his next two favorite pastimes of liquor and heroin, was something of a minor coup. And though losing a musician of Bobby's talents would be a blow to any ensemble, in this case it really was a moot point. La Cave had no piano.

The die was cast. Nelson had also signed the internationally acclaimed Modern Jazz Quartet for a Sunday in June.

La Cave had been open less than four weeks and fledgling manager Stanley Heilbrun needed a quick refresher course on actually receiving the admission price from a majority of the attendees. Stanley had a beatnik's attitude toward all things mercantile; he was in it for the glory. Needless to say, this cavalier attitude made him a marked man in Nelson's estimation.

In other words, La Cave needed to make some money, and quickly. The discovery of the average beatnik's ability to hide for hours behind a 35-cent cup of espresso, all the while holding a copy of James Joyce and feigning understanding, spurred some creative entrepreneurial thought. The solution appeared with the force of a Sunday morning hangover:

We'll sell beer!

And thus began the Battle of Doan's Corners.

The Battle of Doan's Corners

If Nelson's daytime hustle as Downtown Lawyer taught him anything, it was that good luck is the result of good planning. In a deal that skirted the bartering law, Nelson drew up a contract for La Cave to purchase Nick Lanese's liquor permits.

The 8-block commercial neighborhood centered at East 105th Street and Euclid Avenue, still called Doan's Corners by old-timers, contained 29 establishments that purveyed booze in one fashion or another. It was also home to Cathedral Latin High School, the Fourth Church of Christ Scientist, and a short perp walk from the Cleveland Police 3rd District headquarters. All of these establishments had their own reasons to challenge the approval of a new liquor license in the neighborhood. These interests were contacted for their thoughts on La Cave's application.

Meanwhile, receipts, which were never healthy enough to be self-sustaining, plummeted even further when, in May, the students at the nearby colleges abandoned campus for their homes and took their purchasing power with them. This, coupled with Stanley Heilbrun's creative attitude toward collecting cover charges at the door and the dearth of high-quality affordable entertainment, created something just south of panic in Nelson. He had already decided to cut Stanley Heilbrun loose. Stanley's next adventure as manager of the first "head shop" in Cleveland, would indirectly lead to the series of events that doomed La Cave.

The Big Apple

Nelson could afford a hole in his hired help. He had a hotshot kid who had been stopping by all spring, telling anyone who would listen about his big ideas to put La Cave on the entertainment map. It seems that Stan Kain had taken his new bride to New York City to catch a Broadway show or two on a long weekend that spring. Stephen Sondheim's A Funny Thing Happened on the Way to the Forum opened at the Majestic Theatre on Broadway on 11 May. And while Stan's memory of that show faded, it was the other shows he took in on that weekend in The City that caused his heart to skip several beats, and then pound away with barely controllable excitement.

Never too shy to ask inappropriate questions to the wrong people, Stan and his wife took in "a half a dozen or more shows down in the [Greenwich] Village," which was reimagining itself no longer as a hub of beatnik poetry gatherings, but of the more popular folk music that had captured the imagination and spare change of a considerable slice of the citizenry. At every opportunity, Stan would buttonhole the club manager with questions about the pay scales and availability of the various crooners.

Soon, he met the man who, as much as anyone, would contribute to animating 10615 Euclid Avenue into becoming the premier Midwestern folk music club and midway pit stop between his clubs and gigs in NYC and his many trips to his home away from home, Chicago north side's famed folk music club Gate of Horn - 12-string phenom Bob Gibson. Bob was a mere five years older than Stan.

When Stan returned to Cleveland, he wasted no time in maneuvering his Sunbeam Alpine down Euclid Avenue to the drug store parking lot adjacent to La Cave. He had just turned 26 and knew exactly what he wanted to do with his life, which was to make musical sound and fury happen for adoring throngs of young Clevelanders.

Stan's sense of timing was superb, as was his mother's choice of names for her baby boy. The other Stanley was on his way out, which left La Cave exactly one Stan short of a full complement.

The Hole in the Wall Gang

Meanwhile, up the hill in The Heights, Jack and Danny 31, conveniently billed as the Dalton Boys, were brothers and folk singers, and they found a place to showcase their traditional folk songs: the Rising Moon club on South Taylor Rd. Since January of 1961, the Rising Moon, billing itself as "Cleveland's Folk Club," had been hosting the New Wine Singers, a nebulous aggregation of various singers and instrumentalists who had developed an intensely loyal local following. Six nights a week for months on end the Winers played the small room, located beside Faragher's Lounge Bar in Cleveland Heights, "up the hill" from University Circle.

In 1961 the New Wine Singers were comprised of banjoist and songwriter Bill Malloy, who wrote, among other immortal tunes, "The Hellfire Stare of Bishop Sheen." Sharing the stage with him was Bob Connelly, author of "My Love is a Catholic" and "My Love is a Protestant," Don and Sarah Hale, Don's brother Brad, and "Negro folk singer" Tedd Browne, who was about to hit the big time, musically speaking, and also was about to make tragic headlines in Cleveland that had nothing at all to do with folk music. Another member was Gusti Hervey, she of the Irish operatic voice.

The entire ensemble moved to Chicago and landed at a small club on Pearson Street called, coincidentally, the Rising Moon, but quickly, moved both the name and the band to a larger location, beginning a year-long residency to packed houses. Gusti's residency at the club allowed her to rub elbows with many of the up-and-comers of the folk music genre, and immerse herself in the folk music philosophy of the day, which was one of brotherhood and mutual support. As she puts it, "We were all doing what we loved and enjoying it. We all supported and helped each other… everywhere was the joy of singing. Everyone was really nice…there was none of that "I know this and you don't" crap or secretive things. If you wanted to learn something, there was always someone there to help you – some of them quite well known."

It wasn't unusual for performers like the Kingston Trio, The Clancy Brothers with Tommy Makem, Josh White and just about everybody who was anybody, a Who's Who from the legendary Chicago clubs The Gate of Horn, Second City, and elsewhere, to join in at the Moon to sing together after they'd finished their own paid gigs elsewhere. There was a deep and abiding camaraderie among those traveling troubadours in the folk music community.

The quest for authenticity drove the still young, still naïve, but quickly getting world-wise folkies who were just beginning to glimpse a future of peace, cooperation, and unity among men and women of all stripes. On the national stage, Camelot was beginning to play out. Hope abounded. Our President encouraged us to ask what we could do for our country, for each other. As Bob Gibson joked wistfully years later, "We thought that if we'd written the songs just right, sung them just the right way, even the leaders of the world would stop and say, "Oh, that's the way it should be done."

This generosity of spirit was the engine that powered La Cave through seven years of financial hardship, personnel changes, legal woes, drug busts, FBI investigations, police harassment, and even one of the most violent race riots of that volatile time now known as the Civil Rights era.

The Rising Moon

Jack and Danny Dalton may have been folksingers, but they were no fools. They knew an opportunity when they saw one, and they saw that the Rising Moon, "Cleveland's Folk Club" and home to their nightly crooning, wasn't doing very well and could use an infusion of semi-professional booking talent. Besides, in January 1962 they had lost their nightly gig at the Moon (where they had previously replaced the New Wine Singers) to singer Tedd Browne, and wanted back in on the action. Their folk music stylings had led them to open or close for other acts, among them two brothers, aged 22 and 24, named Tom and Dick, who had recently released their debut album *The Smothers Brothers at the*

Purple Onion and were touring the country with their act, which satirized folk music. These other, Smothers, brothers were still a full three years away from their first national TV program.

The Rising Moon wasn't very big. With axle grease and shoe horns one might have wedged in a hundred folk music fans - if those fans didn't mind being crushed sometime before the encores ended. It was a storefront measuring barely 600 square feet, maybe twice the size of an average suburban rumpus room. Undeterred, the boys forged ahead in their bookings. Unwittingly, however, they were planting the seeds of their own failure and La Cave's success.

Bob Gibson was no stranger to Cleveland. Between 1953 and 1962 the folk singing legend from upstate New York had visited many times from his new home base in Chicago. During many of those visits he had performed in various clubs and living rooms. Well-known to the Daltons, they hired him for an extended residency in late July 1962, to commence immediately. At the same time, they hired a 21-year-old college dropout and local resident named Phil Ochs, who had recently learned to play the guitar, somewhat, and was beginning to write satirical folk songs about the news of the day. Rumor had it he also knew at least three chords.

Bob Gibson claimed to have begun his professional career on the friendly shores of Lake Erie. As he tells it, he was a young man in need of work and, while employed as a free-lance snow shoveler in the Heights area he was approached to sing at a function by a ladies' group in Shaker Heights, one suburb to the east of Cleveland Heights. For his efforts he was paid fifty dollars and when interviewed on the subject, proclaimed, "When I got their check I decided never to work again. And I never have, unless you think of singing as work."

Even traveling folk singers have to eat almost daily and live somewhere while not on the road sleeping on admirers' couches, or oftentimes beside them in their beds. Bob was no exception, and the twenty bucks he was getting for his nightly crooning at the Dalton joint just wasn't cutting it for the Elektra Records recording star with eight long players already to his credit, including the recently released and critically-acclaimed LP *Bob Gibson and Bob Camp at The Gate of Horn*. Bob had a wife and three kids back home to support.

On their sundry nights off, the mainstays of La Cave – Nelson Karl, Stanley Heilbrun and Lee Weiss – as well as the newcomer, young Stan Kain - spent many of their off-hours at The Rising Moon/Dalton Boys Saloon taking in what little ambience it had and immersing themselves in the songs and the singing taking place mere inches from their responsive ears. This was heaven. To enter this dark and thrilling world that held all the promises that fueled young peoples' fantasies, well, it was almost too much to bear. For those who could survive the self-induced ordeal, it was transcendent. As folksinger Gusti Hervey reminisced about those heady days of youthful naivete and energy, "It was a different time, with different attitudes. It wasn't just playing music. It was what the songs were about, what the people in the songs were like. Is folk music a living, or do you do it because the songs move you in some way? Do you feel honest about what you do, and is it important whether you are?"

For Bob Gibson, folk singing was a living, but much more than that. It was to be his ticket out of the bush leagues, but it meant finding a way to earn more money than he could as an itinerant folk singer and sometimes recording artist. When he met Stan Kain in the audience of the Dalton Boys Saloon one evening, the stars in his eyes came into alignment. In Stan, he sensed his meal ticket. Bob fell in love. His ever-active mind rummaged through the possibilities that his new acquaintance Stan Kain presented.

Shitting Bricks – or – All That Jazz

The summer of 1962 was a struggle for La Cave, just "down the hill" from the Dalton's club. Bookings were difficult since not only did nobody in command have the foggiest idea how to go about booking, but funds were scarce to nonexistent. Nelson Karl was, in the words of Stan Kain, "shitting bricks." La Cave was a ton of fun in the evenings, but foundered in the harsh light of day. Then, in May, the school year ended and most college students, the mainstay of La Cave's bottom line, loaded up their VW microbuses or daddy's Buick and bugged out to various suburban enclaves far distant from Euclid and East 107th Street. And along with their clothing and Kingston Trio albums went their walking around money. Receipts hadn't been anything to brag about before they left, so this was an extra blow. Would it be fatal?

Since the end of March, local folkies, including one guy who "knew only a D chord," graced the 8" platform generously known as the "stage" at La Cave. In fact, by summer La Cave had been more a jazz-oriented stop than a folk music paradise. After the Easter Sunday artistic smash/financial burn of the Joe Alexander Quartet, Nelson had followed up on a lead Joe had given him and signed the Modern Jazz Quartet with Norman Davis on saxophone to perform Friday, 22 June, and again on Sundays 8 July and the 15th, sandwiched around the Fred Sharp Group (and Vibes!)'s appearance on Sunday the 1st of July. Wednesdays continued to be Hootenanny Night, where, evidently, knowing a D chord got you onstage, and Fridays and Saturdays remained reserved for "folk singers." There were the odd performances by such standouts as Paul Salisbury, who lasted a couple of weekends in April before returning to the oblivion from which he sprang, as well as folkies important enough to actually sign contracts: Michael Hoffman, Gail Forbes, and Chuck Langmack. But mostly, late spring and early summer saw Nelson and his cohorts nervously sipping espressos and watching the stairs for possible patrons as the D chords rang out. Even as Astronaut Scott Carpenter became only the second American to orbit the Earth in his Aurora 7 space capsule on May 24th, La Cave remained as distant as the moon to Cleveland's music-loving citizens.

After Easter, Nelson had committed $150 to pay the Fred Sharp Group. Fred was something of a legend in Cleveland. Having just turned 40, and although fame and fortune had thus far eluded him, he was a virtuoso guitarist of such repute that he made recordings in Paris with Django Reinhardt's son "Babik," and the younger Reinhardt gifted Fred a guitar his father Django had used during his 1946 American tour with fellow jazz icon Duke Ellington. Fred and his combo played all the clubs up and down Mayfield Rd., the same clubs that vaulted a Steubenville, Ohio native by the name of Dino Paul Crocetti[iv] to international superstardom, alcoholism, three marriages and a similar number of divorces. In between all that, he taught us what amore was.

Paying Fred Sharpe's outfit was one thing, being able to afford the nationally known Modern Jazz Quartet (MJQ) was quite another. The MJQ was formed in 1952 by former members of Dizzy Gillespie's rhythm section. The most popular and enduring lineup comprised John Lewis on piano, Milt Jackson on vibes, Percy Heath on standup bass and the immortal Connie Kay in the drummer's chair. The quartet had released fourteen long players by 1962 and had established themselves as worldwide talents. They weren't going to play for coffee beans.

One night during his residency at the Dalton Saloon in late July, after a long night of folk music, Bob Gibson sat talking with an attentive Stan Kain next door at Faragher's bar behind two tall glasses of Irish ale. Both glasses were for Bob, as Stan never touched the stuff, while Bob's drinking reputation was prodigious. Bob was a big man with bigger appetites. He was in the middle of a two-, three-, or four-week residency at the Dalton Boys Saloon, these things being entirely dependent on whether Bob had traveling money with him at the end of any particular week. Oftentimes he didn't, and so he stayed on another week. Or two.

On this occasion, Bob had an ulterior motive. It was well-known that he was one of the most open, generous folkies who'd give you the shirt off his back. It just might not always be his shirt to give, however. Those after-party all-nighters always ended up in a smoky haze. All around, the winds of change were swirling. Bob Dylan had released his debut album in March to hushed silence from the record album buying contingent, and although at the moment he was better known around the Columbia Records water fountains as "Hammond's Folly," due to that fact, he was hard at work on what would become his breakout record, *The Freewheelin' Bob Dylan*.

On the national front that summer, members of the Students for a Democratic Society (SDS) completed their political manifesto The Port Huron Statement on June 15th, one part a document of idealism, a philosophical template for a more egalitarian society, and one part a call to non-violent civil disobedience. It would come to represent an attitude far more sinister before the turbulent '60s, and our collective innocence, ended. And sadly, many of our collective youthful fantasies also ended on August 5th, when Marilyn Monroe passed at age 36.

Bob Gibson's sights were focused intently on the object of *his* passion sitting serenely beside him. "Stan," he said, "You need me. And what's more, I need you." The ever-present twinkle in Stan's eye grew perceptively brighter. And just like that, more or less, The Dalton Boys Saloon was doomed and La Cave would live to thrill thousands through the Swingin' Sixties.

Chapter 3:

The Great Folk Music Robbery

Bob read the writing on the diminutive walls of the Dalton Boys Saloon. The place would never make a profit because of its tiny footprint. His performing there wouldn't net him getaway money. Stan Kain, the object of Bob's affection, could provide much for the world-wise traveling folk song salesman that Bob had become.

Gibson saw that while La Cave could provide him with a regular gig in front of larger crowds, and therefore larger paydays; he quickly realized that his show business contacts and savvy could also be of big benefit to La Cave. He could provide access to his agent's Rolodex to fill out La Cave's scant schedule. All he needed to do was to get Stan on the inside.

The stage was set. Nelson Karl and Lee Weiss were concerned that Stanley Heilbrun's absence was creating a vacuum of leadership. The plummeting gross receipts, which were never lofty to begin with, were the stuff of nightmares on those few nights when sleep actually occurred. Waiting for the beer permit was excruciating. So was the heightening stack of unpaid invoices. Add to that the insult of being called "amateur" in the newspaper and the situation was perfect for rolling the dice one last time. As it turned out, Stan Kain made the decision an easy one. But he needed Bob's whispered advice, and he got it.

Bob knew, from Stan, that there was a leadership crisis at La Cave. No-show Stanley Heilbrun was out. And Bob knew that he had an eager acolyte in now 26-year-old Stan Kain. Bob set the wheels of change in motion.

Bob Gibson was managed by Leonard "Len" Rosenfeld from Len's office on East 92nd in New York City. Len's stable of folk artists was impressive. Odetta, Josh White, and many other prominent folkies were represented by his office. After his conversations with Stan Kain, Bob had contacted Len with a plan. This plan included Bob playing a residency at La Cave as well as his formal involvement in booking the club through Stan Kain.

A day or two later Nelson met with Stan Kain at Stan's request. Stan described that meeting in a later interview: "I was scared. I never wanted to do something as much as I wanted to be a part of La Cave. I had agreed with Bob to keep his involvement in the background, so I stressed my past experience running sound and lights at Cain Park, my experiences as their stage manager, and the fact that I had already spent several seasons as an independent booking agent for various shows there. My wife had been keeping a scrapbook so I was able to bring a whole bunch of newspaper clippings with my name in them. I said I went to New York to the folk clubs now and then and could find and sign good acts that fit into La Cave's style. I also mentioned that my dad could help me design and wire a sound board which would really make a big difference in the sound quality in that basement. And lights. I also said I was willing to take up Stanley Heilbrun's nightly job managing the club."

Nelson was impressed and relieved in equal parts. He was well aware that the Dalton's had booked Josh White Sr., one of the most popular folk acts in the country, for a week's residency to commence August 6th. This booking would drain further shekels from the nightly take at La Cave. This new association with Stan Kain seemed to check all the boxes necessary to transition La Cave into a club offering more professional entertainment.

Another consideration was this: what did he have to lose? Nelson drew up the papers.

On the 30 July, Nelson invited Stan downtown to his office to review and sign the necessary paperwork. Nelson had, ready for Stan's autograph, an employment agreement, an option to purchase Heilbrun's 25 shares of stock, a cognovit note, and a proxy to act as Heilbrun's agent until the stock transfer was completed. Stan signed immediately. His first day on the job consisted of tearing out the makeshift wiring that had served as La Cave's sound hookups and creating a shopping list of items needed for the upgrades he had in mind. He also called his dad to let him know of his new employment and asked for his help. His dad, a classical music devotee, agreed as fast as Stan had asked.

Momentarily relieved, Nelson dashed off a letter to Russ Kane, the columnist who had landed on Nelson's shit list due to his once referring to his cellar club on Euclid Avenue as amateurish. In two short paragraphs, Nelson mentions several "highly professional" upcoming acts at La Cave: the folk groups The Highlanders and The Travellers, and "one of the finest folk singers in the country," John Winn. In the '50s, while serving in the US Army at Fort Carson, Colorado, John had heard the teenaged Judy Collins, recently graduated from Denver's East High School, at the Exodus folk club in Denver, and later she accompanied him to New York City to try her hand, and voice, at folk singing. John, meanwhile, played in various Greenwich Village coffeehouses with the likes of other folkies Bob Dylan, Dave Van Ronk, and Peter, Paul and Mary. He'd even appeared at Carnegie Hall as part of a folk revival.

Nelson's letter revealed his state of mind as he concluded, "I am very hopeful that you, or someone in your department, can review both The Highlanders and John Winn. I am still smarting over the reference to our entertainment as amateurish and am hopeful of an opportunity to disprove you. Very truly yours, Nelson G. Karl"

La Cave was about to get professional very quickly.

On 6 August, the same day Josh White opened at the Dalton Boys Saloon, Stan borrowed five hundred bucks from Nelson and bought out Stanley Heilbrun's shares in La Cave. Later that night, they tried to get into Dalton's but were turned away due to the crowds that were congregated outside with the same goal. What Nelson didn't know, but Stan did, was that this was a setup. Bob had hooked up the Dalton boys with Josh White as soon as he had come to a meeting of the minds with Stan Kain regarding their nascent silent partnership. As soon as Stan had inked his agreement with Nelson, Bob contacted Josh, his deal with the Daltons' was agreed to, and the Daltons' began advertising the upcoming week-long residency of White. The great folk music robbery was underway.

The following morning's news made Nelson even more giddy than he had been from finding out Stan could get national acts into La Cave. He got word that the State of Ohio was about to approve the liquor license transfer that was crucial to La Cave's success. He sprang into action and fired off two more letters, one to Jim Garrett at *The Cleveland Press* and one to Milton Widder at the same newspaper.

His enthusiastically penned missive to Widder, "in celebration of the occasion [of receiving beer permits from the State of Ohio]" included the following all-capitalized ditty:

> "FROM THE IVY OF RESERVE
> AND THE LABS OF DEAR OLD CASE,
> FROM CARROLL'S HALLOWED CHAMBER,
> B. W. AND OBERLIN KEEPING UP THE PACE,
>
> THE VOICES ARE ALL RINGING OUT

THE MESSAGE, SHARP AND CLEAR,
THEY JOIN TOGETHER IN ONE YELL
"IT'S HERE, IT'S HERE – LA CAVE HAS BEER."

On 8 August, Nelson bought a beer dispenser.

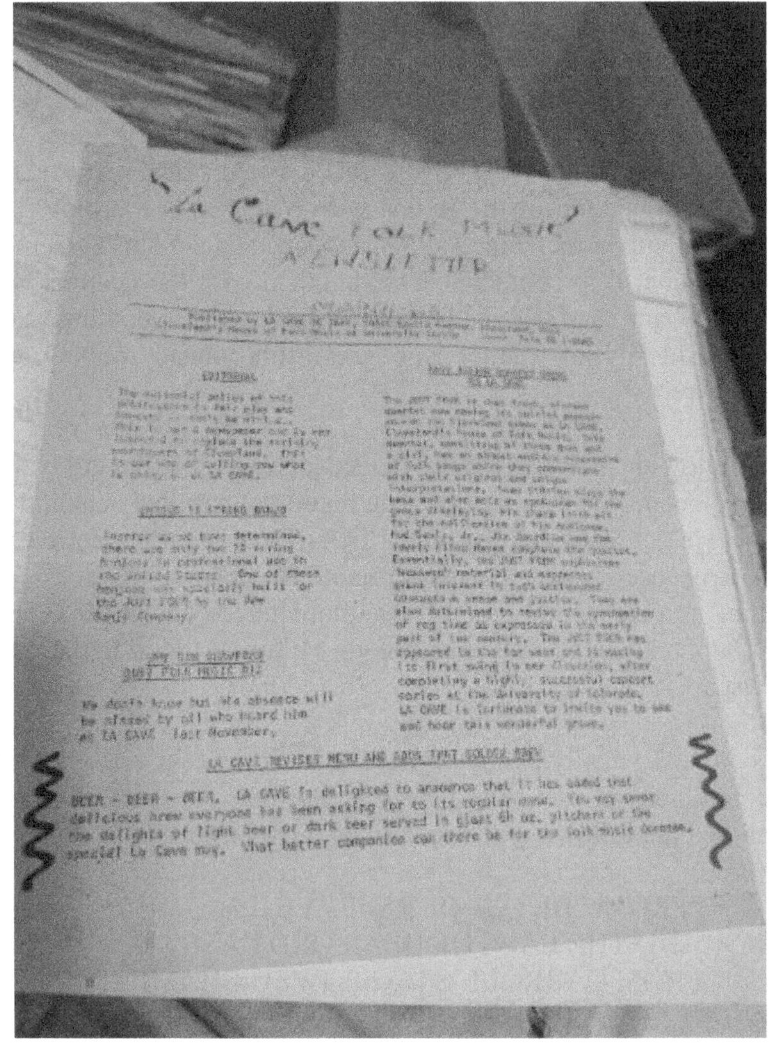

La Cave's first newsletter

Following the Highlanders' turn at La Cave in early August, John Winn played to sparse crowds from mid-month on, highly professional or not. August was a hot, dry month in Cleveland and La Cave was both clammy and muggy. The needle touched 91 on the 4th and came back to it throughout the month. Having held on through summer, in large part due to Nelson loaning the club another grand and also taking a turn managing the evening hours, Nelson knew that the colleges were resuming classes in a matter of weeks. God forbid he start the school year bereft of suds!

As students straggled back to the nearby colleges, things seemed to be looking up for the crew at La Cave. Word spread amongst the undergrads that La Cave did indeed have beer. While Gibson and White were knocking them dead at the Dalton Boys, hootenanny night was taking off for Nelson's crew. Guitar slingers were beginning to discover that it was a place who welcomed even those to whom a D chord was the height of strumming prowess. And if you knew three chords, you were probably going to be asked to open for one of the contracted acts.

Nelson put an ad for a waitress in the classifieds.

Along with the Travellers and the Highlanders beginning to get popular, Nelson brought back Chuck Langmack for a week in August, and then picked up young folksinger Tom Pasle, who used his matinee-idol looks and three-octave voice "to great effect," Bill Moss, another local folkie with a small but rowdy following, and The East Jazz Trio for the jazz crowd that had loyally lingered since springtime for a Sunday in early September. It would be the first of many appearances by Tom and the last by the jazz trio.

And then, on 7 September, a mild and partly sunny late-summer day in the mid-70s, the shit again hit the fan when a certified letter made its way from Columbus to Cleveland. After all the legalese, it concluded:

> "...the Department finds that the transfer of class C-2, D-1 and D-2 permits would result in a substantial prejudice to public decency, sobriety and good order; hence... Application #43365 is hereby refused and rejected."[v]

By day's end Nelson had written his appeal, and the following day a registered letter containing his notice of appeal was on its way to the State Capitol. Even as Nelson saw this as a setback, and it was, it further opened the door to the solution that Stan and Bob were now ready to put into action.

Howdy, Partner

Bob Gibson's run at the Dalton Boys Saloon, which had begun in mid-August, finally ended as the month ran its course. Josh White's sold-out run there had also ended. Prompted by Bob, Stan had no problem convincing Nelson to book Bob for a two-week's residency at La Cave beginning September 25th. And here is where the conspirators got creative. Bob was aware that Nelson was cash-poor and that La Cave was printing their handbills with red ink. He agreed to a weekly performance fee of $500[vi] against an even split in the net profits, if any. The first week's fee would be paid in stock in the corporation amounting to 1/6th of the total outstanding shares. He further negotiated to act as booking agent and to "make every effort to obtain the best available entertainment within the general classification of folk music, at the best possible prices." Nelson retained the right of final approval of Bob's potential bookings. He also retained the notion that it was Stan Kain who had instigated and nurtured this potential solution to La Cave's cash crunch.

Bob had the entire stable of artists from his agent's Rolodex; he also commanded the attention of almost every traveling folk singer of the day due to his high profile as one of the better selling artists in the folk idiom. Even more important was the effect he was having on the younger up-and-coming folkies who followed him from club to club in the Village, or in Chicago.

When the final form of the agreement was revealed, Bob Gibson had a three-week performance contract worth $1,000 in stock options, $500 in the form of a cognovit note payable within 12 months including interest, and a weekly salary of $75, said salary also to be deferred until such time as all past-due salaries became current. Suddenly, Bob and Stan owned 1/3 of La Cave de Café, Inc. and controlled the bookings. La Cave was about to enter the 1962 folk club-version of the big leagues.

It was taken for granted that on performance nights Bob would be provided with a sufficient quantity of Irish ale to insure a spirited stage show.

The Only Bomb Shelter with Entertainment

October, 1962. The Doomsday Clock stood at 7 minutes to midnight. The events that spawned such movies as *The Missiles of October* and *Thirteen Days* and books like *One Minute to Midnight* were unfolding. For the very first time, international political crises were being delivered to Americans at suppertime in front of TV trays holding their Swanson frozen dinners. The nation was collectively transfixed. And scared. As President Kennedy met with the Joint Chiefs of Staff over worries about Soviet nuclear missiles 90 miles off the Florida coast and the specter of international obliteration, Stan Kahn had important worries of his own. But his worries didn't stop him from posting a hand-made sign above the stairs that descended into the darkened cavern that was La Cave with the inviting words "The only bomb shelter with entertainment."

Several months earlier Stan had made a decision that would alter, not only for him, but for many thousands of fellow Americans, the future arc of their lives, the future of American popular music, and the place that Cleveland, Ohio would occupy in that history. He had decided to go all in for the role of Resident Wizard of La Cave. It would become the defining characteristic of his life.

At this time, however, Stan's decision only concerned whether or not to spend the sum of $400 of Nelson Karl's money for a one-night performance. While $400 doesn't seem like a windfall now, in today's dollars, it translates to over $3,400[vii]. The average annual American wage at the time was $6,000[viii], so by today's standards that Sunday performance fee equaled over six months of a middle-class salary!

Stan wanted to spend it on what he called a one-day "Folk Music Festival." Nelson Karl, the man who signed the checks, was horrified. "We'll lose our shirts, for God's sake!" he protested in the strongest language he ever used. "Four hundred dollars! That's more than double our monthly rent!" Stan was unperturbed. For, like all people of vision, he saw a bigger picture. Karl, who at his core was a conservative-minded downtown Cleveland attorney, was rightfully concerned. "Look, Stan, we can't even swing the monthly rent. How are we going to make more than double that on a Sunday? Who do you intend to book for the festival?"

Stan: "Josh White."

Nelson alternately loved and hated the idea. He knew that Josh had sold out every night at the Dalton's club. But he also knew that could be a two-edged blade. Did he wear out his welcome in Cleveland? Should they look for another headliner? And while Josh had sold out the 80 or so seat back room to Faragher's Bar, filling a room four times as big might be problematic. Nelson, for once, threw caution to the wind. This was his chance to propel La Cave from amateurish entertainment to national stage status, paving the way to sign more national artists. And allowing Nelson a few more bragging rights with the local papers.

But there was still the problem of filling the club, particularly since the advertising budget was, to be charitable, miniscule. Nelson had misgivings, but he had hired Stan, and he had hired Bob, and he had decided in for a penny, in for a pound. Let's do it! And it had better work, or we're done for.

"All right, Stan. We need to begin promoting the show right away." "I've already got flyers printed and we'll be peppering the campuses every day till showtime." Nelson's next call was to *The Plain Dealer* to set up advertisements. He already had Bob Gibson signed to play without receiving his fee up front. He had the Knob Lick Upper 10,000, a bluegrass band from Oberlin College, ready to open the festivities. They were led by recent graduate and banjoist Erik Jacobsen, who later found fame producing such artists as Tim Hardin, the Lovin' Spoonful, the Charlatans and others, and starting in 1965 produced seven straight Top 10 songs for the Spoonful. The Lickers were among the first bluegrass bands to play Carnegie Hall, in 1962.

In normal times, Nelson was a peaceful, even a serene, man with head planted firmly on shoulders and feet on ground. These times were not normal, nor would any degree of normalcy be achieved for the rest of the decade. About all he could do was wait out the week or so until Stan's planned "Folk Festival" starring Josh White, Sr. and supported by Bob Gibson and the irrepressible Knob Lick Upper 10,000 played out on the tiny La Cave stage that was about to – unknown at the moment to anyone – reach critical mass, with the resulting fireball of folk talent engulfing not only the University Circle environs of eastern Cleveland, but radiating over the whole of Northeast Ohio and places as far away as New York City, Coconut Grove, Florida, San Francisco and Los Angeles.

Stan Kain was about to hit his first of many home runs in the booking biz. Between homers, there'd be many foul balls and strikeouts. Such is the nature of both baseball and booking.

1962 La Cave poster

Josh White

Sunday the 7th of October arrived, cool and calm, unlike the racing hearts of the La Cave brain trust. The warmth of the morning sun promised a mild autumn day, the soft and easy kind of day that makes Cleveland's springs and autumns the stuff of Chamber of Commerce pamphlets. This could be very bad. A sunny fall day could drive the buying public out of doors to enjoy one of the few remaining Sundays before chilly Lake Erie breezes and lake effect snow effectively shut down the outdoor activities of this bustling metropolis of almost a million. La Cave had not yet reached that sophisticated stage of business development that included selling tickets in advance. There simply was no effective medium for doing so. The average college student didn't have a Diners Club or American Express charge-a-plate, and Visa, then known as BankAmerica, had to wait four more years before being available nationally.

And even if the students had been lucky enough to have Dad's charge-a-plate, La Cave had no way to accept it as payment. So they fretted.

Stan need not have worried. When he showed up just before noon – he actually had managed a couple of hours of blessed sleep – a line of humanity was queued up all the way to 107th and all the way down that street to the elementary school lot two blocks north on Chester Avenue.

Everything was going to be alright.

The Second Battle of Doan's Corners

Once again, Nelson's legal skills had saved La Cave to entertain another day. His quick filing of the appeal to the Board of Liquor Control's decision to keep La Cave dry kept the preliminary license approval intact. Until the appeal could be heard, La Cave could sell beer. In fact, scheduling the Sunday "Folk Festival" at 2pm was a strategic decision designed to circumvent the Blue Laws (laws prohibiting certain activities on Sundays) in Ohio that, at the time, prevented liquor sales of any kind before 1pm, the time that most church services ended. A 2 o'clock kickoff would maximize beer sales, which was the highest profit item La Cave had to offer. And even more important than immediate sales was the club's reputation as a burgeoning college hangout that, without alcohol, would have taken a direct hit amidships.

Stan's memory is vague, but he recalls, "I think we sold out [of beer] in a couple hours. Somebody grabbed some cash and headed out to find some more."

As soon as Nelson had filed his appeal of the Liquor Control Board on the 7th of September he had begun prepping for the process. He woke early and made the three-hour trek the Board of Liquor Control in Columbus. Present that morning on South High Street to adjudicate the matter were Judge Creed Jopling Lester and three members of the Board of Liquor Control. Somewhat amazingly, considering the relatively trivial nature of the proceedings, both Attorney General Mark McElroy and Assistant AG Leo Stark attended on behalf of the state. Also present for the hearing were Frank DiCiccio, representing the Cleveland Police Department, and Raymond Placek from the Fourth Church of Christ Scientist. On the way in were Vincent Bonomo and Father James McKay, representing the police and Cathedral Latin High School, respectively.

Nelson testified that La Cave didn't serve neighborhood patrons. Because of its unique position as the only club in the area that was primarily a "theater," as opposed to a tavern or package store, the clientele was comprised mainly of college students from the nearby schools. He also noted that a cover charge was in effect, which acted as a deterrent to any casual drinkers in search of a place to imbibe. He also testified by producing maps, pictures and a geographical survey. These documents showed that, while both the school and the church were indeed within the legal distance of 500 feet, they were only that close "as the crow flies." When walking the shortest distance from La Cave's door to the other buildings, the evidence showed that the distance was much further, more than twice the legal distance.

The state threw a large monkey wrench into Nelson's gears. Assistant AG Stark testified that the Department had another objection, namely that Nick Lanese, the owner and transferor of the liquor permits, had pled guilty to violating the Liquor Control Act in 1959 by selling some hooch to a minor. The objection exposed what was perhaps the only, but certainly the biggest, mistake Nelson had made. When making the deal for the license transfer, Nelson had insisted that payment would be withheld until the transfer was completed. In turn, Lanese insisted on collateral, which Nelson provided in the form of La Cave stock. So, technically, he was transferring the license to himself. And even that wouldn't have been a problem except for his prior conviction. That was a big problem.

Sensing defeat, but not defeated, Nelson proposed a counter offer. Nelson made it known to the state officials that he would willingly give up claims on the C-2 and D-2 licenses since the only spiritous product he was interested in purveying was "3.2 beer," a holdover from Prohibition days. In Ohio, while the legal drinking age was twenty-one, eighteen-year-olds could drink "low-powered" 3.2 beer.

Nelson was setting up the conditions for further appeal, and it's a good thing he did. By a three to one vote, the state found the objections reasonable and dismissed La Cave's appeal. It was back from the Liquor Board to the drawing board. Two days after the highly successful Josh White, Sr. Folk Festival, he filed an application for a D-1 permit only and a motion to reconsider this most recent decision. Nelson offered some compelling, if not outright hilarious, arguments in favor of getting a D-1 liquor permit. Among these arguments were the following:[ix]

1. There are no homes nearby, only other businesses.
2. La Cave is a theater, not a saloon
3. No one notices La Cave's entrance.
4. La Cave is, specifically, a folk music club.

5. The entertainers are "the finest masters of their craft."
6. Besides college students, doctors, symphony members and "the concertgoing crowd" attend these shows.
7. No dance floor means no dancing.
8. It is "not possible to dance to folk music" anyway.
9. Folk music refers to narrative stories about the "settling of our nation, [its] wars and people."
10. Folk music is not lewd, suggestive or off-color and "does not appeal to man's more base motives."
11. The audiences are "well-dressed persons who conduct themselves with propriety and dignity."

In conclusion, Nelson opined that "Too much has been said and too little proved." Once again, his entreaties were denied. Once again, Nelson dictated a brief in opposition to the decision. This one took a full fifteen pages to contain. Finally, on 19 February, 1963, Judge Dana Reynolds of the Franklin County Court of Common Pleas signed the terms of surrender as he overturned every objection raised by the state and motioned them to issue a D-1 permit to La Cave backdated to 7 November 1962. Finally, the cave-dwelling folk music aficionados, also known as college students, could enhance their subterranean experience with a pitcher or two of "non-intoxicating"[x] 3.2 beer. The war was over.

There would be more battles in the months and years to come.

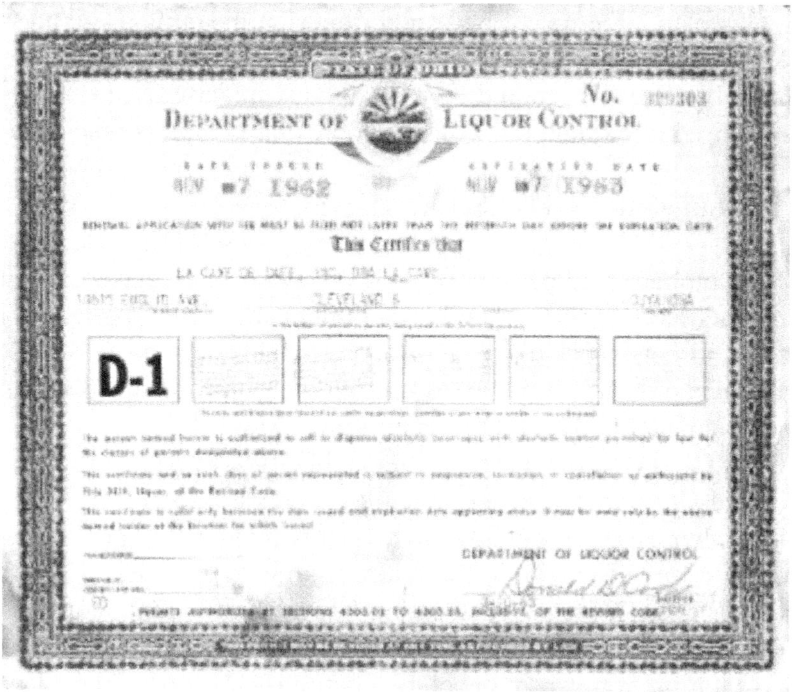
Department of Liquor Control

No.

Date Issued
NOV 7 1962

Expiration Date
NOV 7 1963

This Certifies that

D-1

DEPARTMENT OF LIQUOR CONTROL

La Cave's first liquor license

Movin' On Up

As October 1962 faded into the rearview mirror of life, both President Kennedy and the leaders of La Cave breathed sighs of relief. Their respective troubles had shrunk to a fraction of their former size. And while analogies to nuclear Armageddon might be overstated, the very survival of both the United States and La Cave had been very much in doubt when the month began. But by November both the national and local scene had changed for the better. School kids still practiced duck-and-cover, and college students still drank 3.2 beer, but neither academic group was as concerned about their near future survival prospects as they were a month previously.

In Cleveland, the date 4 November took on meaning as being the closing date of the Dalton Boys Saloon. The dagger applied to their backs by Bob Gibson and Stan Kain back in summer, as they sat conspiring at Faragher's Bar next door, finally had its fatal affect.

The Stan Kain Era Takes Off

Mid-October of 1962 saw Stan Kain make one of what would become many long-weekend trips to that shrine of American folk music, Greenwich Village. This one proved fruitful as he returned to Cleveland with acts booked through the end of the year, and more contacts made. Don Crawford, Mike Settle, Greco & Willard, Don Paulin, Terry Callier and Buffy Ste. Marie all signed contracts to perform in the upcoming weeks. Around the first of November Tom Pasle agreed to a weekly residency "for a while." A while turned out to be the entire month, with time off for the Wednesday Hootenannies. Back home, Stan's dad continued designing the sound and lighting systems that would enhance the presentation of music at the club. Unamplified acoustic music was fine when the patrons were sparse, but in a club where drinks and snacks were served to patrons sitting at tables or in former church pews in the back of the club, as opposed to a venue with theater seating, there was enough background noise to disturb the more thoughtful and attentive patrons.

LACAVE

Cleveland's House of Folkmusic

Dec. 18-23

DON PAULIN

Dec. 18-Jan. 1

TERRY CALLIER

Dec. 25-Jan. 13

BUFFY ST. MARIE

106515 EUCLID

Phone 231-9405

La Cave poster, 1962-1963

Each of Stan's signings in late '62 fit the mold that would become the hallmark of Stan's bookings in the years to come. All of them were near the beginning of their careers, all were unknown on a national level, and all of them later found degrees of fame, if not necessarily fortune. Don Crawford's[xi] appearance at the end of October was groundbreaking in a city that was a few short years from exploding race riots. Don was an African-American sometimes bluesman, sometimes actor who released four unnoticed albums and two singles, first on Verve Folkways and later on Roulette Records, but was best-known as an actor, playing a black militant in the avant-garde movie "The Cube" in 1968. The significance of hiring an African-American entertainer at this place and time cannot be overstated. La Cave was situated at the southeastern corner of the large inner-city area east of downtown that was overwhelmingly black and was referred to by non-residents as "the ghetto." Further east was the University Circle area of schools and museums, and an increasingly white population.

Stan Kain was both color- and gender-blind. He saw talent and never considered the package containing it. Besides black performers, Stan was willing to hire female artists when few women plied the folk music trade. Buffy Ste. Marie was two years removed from recording her first of seventeen albums and becoming an international spokesperson for the rights of indigenous people of the United States and Canada, her country of origin. Among the many highlights of her 50-year career was an Academy Award for co-writing "Up Where We Belong." She was the recipient of a dozen honorary degrees and is an inductee in the Canadian Music Hall of Fame and recipient of the Office of the Order of Canada, the second-highest Canadian civilian award.

But in 1962 she was a 21-year-old unknown folkie dividing her time between clubs in Toronto, New York and First Nation reservations. Stan hired her to a three-week residency beginning Christmas Day. It lasted over a month.

Stan Kain saw what others would come to see.

Greco & Willard were an up-and-coming comedy duo out of the Greenwich Village nightclubs such as the Village Vanguard, the Bitter End and the Café Wha? Before they ended their run, they had enjoyed residencies at various Playboy clubs and numerous television appearances on Ed Sullivan's show, The Smothers Brothers Comedy Hour, Johnny Carson's Tonight Show, and others.

In later years Vic Greco would reclaim his birth name Gus Mocerino and find more success as a songwriter, newspaper columnist, teacher and solo performer, winning several awards for his songwriting. The other half of the duo was Fred Willard, a native Clevelander who achieved sustained international comedic success starting with the Second City comedy troupe and continuing through movies like *This Is Spinal Tap, Waiting for Guffman, A Mighty Wind, Best in Show* and *Anchorman: The Legend of Ron Burgundy.* He appeared on Johnny Carson's show over 50 times. But in 1962 Vic and Fred were unknowns. Stan offered the duo six hundred dollars for a two-week stint. It was, to them, a windfall.

Terry Callier was a seventeen-year-old guitar phenom at the very beginning of his long career, which ultimately saw the release of fifteen long players and twenty singles in a career spanning almost half a century. Terry opened each evening's festivities from 18 December through New Year's.

Once again, Stan saw in these "nobodies" what others would eventually see. Stan's superpower would become the driving force behind La Cave's success through the decade, and its enduring place in the hearts of countless cave dwellers. Word of these early successes quickly spread to Greenwich Village, the epicenter of folk music, primarily through the efforts of Bob Gibson, and were to lead to more success when, early in 1963, Bob brought Stan to the offices of his manager, Leonard Rosenfeld. Leonard, like Bob, knew how to recognize an opportunity when one happened along.

Chapter 4:

1963 - No Good Deed Goes Unpunished

New Year's Day, 1963, dawned bitter cold on the southern shore of Lake Erie. Clevelanders slowly regained consciousness from last night's revelry. One amazing aspect of the first morning of the new year was merely that we were all still here, the Doomsday Clock notwithstanding. The new year would find a slight ratcheting down of international tension with the August signing of the Partial Test Ban Treaty between the US, UK and USSR.

On 2 January, news filtered in that five American helicopters had been shot down and thirty Americans killed in a place with a strange name, the Mekong Delta, by a group of insurgents with an even stranger name, the Viet Cong, in a place that few Americans could find on a globe: the former French Protectorate of Vietnam.

Locally, the big news was that there was no news. The Newspaper Guild struck the two big daily newspapers, *The Plain Dealer* and *The Press,* during the holiday season, and by January had set back the local economy "as badly as a tornado would have." It became the longest newspaper strike in local history, not ending until 8 April of '63. The strike occurred so suddenly that nobody, either in management or staff, was prepared for it. Having happened just as the Christmas advertising season was set to start, it was devastating to businesses that depended on advertising in an era when there were no other affordable ad platforms. TV ads were out of reach, financially, for most local businesses and the strike spotlighted the many different kinds of businesses that depended on newspapers to keep afloat.

Local radio tried in vain to take up the slack.

La Cave, having just begun to get on its financial feet, was hit hard. Even Stan's attempts to paper the campuses with handouts met with difficulty, as the toughest winter in forty years had moved in by 5 December and kept the ground snow-covered until mid-March. There were five or six stretches when the thermometer dipped below zero for days in a row, and on 19 January, it set a record low for Cleveland (only tied once): nineteen degrees below zero. The picket lines were a sea of signs, masks, high snow boots, ski garb, and fur gloves.

No one could not find houses to rent or buy, report lost property, find out how to buy or sell used cars, find out which movies were showing where, could not keep track of plays, concerts, or TV programs. Florists could not learn of weddings, engagements, or deaths. Employment agencies could not advertise job openings. Undertakers and pastors could not notify friends of the times of funerals. When schools closed, there was no way of notifying parents. No stock market reports, no sports. People died, and many of their friends did not know of it until days later. The Associated Press (AP) and United Press International (UPI) teleprinters continued to tap out yards and yards of news from all over the world, but it went directly into wastebaskets, thrown there by bored editors.

Few people ventured out during those first three months of the new year, and fewer still found their way to La Cave, which simply closed up for parts of January and February. The bills, however, never went on strike.

Stan Kain was untroubled. He spent a hectic but enjoyable long weekend in Greenwich Village in mid-December. The enjoyable portion was the time spent in various folk clubs seeing performances by mostly up-and-comers, with a couple household names thrown in. The hectic part was fitting in meetings with Len

Rosenfeld, concerning Len's stable of folkies, their cost and availability. Len offered to hook Stan up with Jesse Fuller, the 67-year-old one-man band, for later on in the spring in exchange for hiring an "experimental act" he had just put together. Jesse had written and performed songs his entire life, but until the late 1950s never was a working musician. But television appearances on the west coast highlighted his talents and his popularity on the circuit quickly grew. As an example of his influence, he had played Denver's Exodus Gallery Bar in the summer of 1959, a summer that saw a teenage Bob Dylan spend a few weeks in Denver. Bob quickly picked up Jesse's technique of playing the harmonica mounted in a brace around his neck. When Jesse played La Cave in spring of '63, reviews noted that the "Lone Cat" played a 50-year-old 12-string guitar, a kazoo, harmonica and his own weird invention called a "fotdella," which combined a bass fiddle, a washboard, and six piano strings that produced strange sounds.

But about this experimental act – Len represented folksinger Tim Rose and in late 1962 hooked him up with another folkie, John Brown, and a young, powerful voice belonging to an unknown sometimes-cloakroom attendant at The Showplace in The Village named Ellen Naomi Cohen, who was already going by her nom de chanson Cass Elliot. They were only together for a few months, working under the name The Triumvirate, before John was replaced by James Hendricks and the group's name changed to The Big 3. But during the short time they were together, they cooperated with Len's strategy of playing outside the Big Apple to hone their chops, and "Mama" Cass became the first of many Rock and Roll Hall of Famers to grace the stage at La Cave before hitting their strides as household names. The trio held a two-week residency in the cave from 5 February through the 17th. The trio earned the princely sum of $275 per week[xii] – in cash per contract – and Stan graciously put them up in his new crash pad off of Murray Hill Boulevard for the duration.

The Triumvirate, featuring Cass Elliot, at La Cave

During Josh White's two-week residency at La Cave to start the New Year, his longtime manager Doug Yeager relates the following story, as told by his friend "Bobby" Fries. Bobby was a folk singer in The Village before becoming a filmmaker who produced, among other films, documentaries for a couple of Johns: "John Lennon Live in New York City" and "Ten for Two: The John Sinclair Freedom Rally."

Remembering that January of 1963 in Cleveland was a series of snowstorms punctuated by stretches of sub-zero days and nights, Doug relates: "Before becoming a film maker Bobby was a folk singer, and worked several times at La Cave as an opening act for Josh White and Ian & Sylvia, among others. He vividly remembers opening for Josh at the time of Cleveland's greatest snowstorm in years. Stan gave them the option of being paid and closing up for the night or being paid and giving the concert. Josh responded, "If there's one person out there who pays to see me then I have to sing for them."

Bobby had the joy of spending the afternoon and evening with Josh, and being one of three people in the audience that night to see Josh White in concert!"[xiii]

1120

U.S. CORPORATION INCOME TAX RETURN—1962

La Cave de Cafe, Inc.

10615 Euclid Avenue

Cleveland 6, Ohio

Cuyahoga

IMPORTANT

GROSS INCOME

DEDUCTIONS

TAX

181.35 (carry forward)

Secretary

La Cave's 1962 IRS tax return showing
$8,000 operating loss for the year

The lack of advertising was a giant stone in the road. In a February letter to Len, Nelson outlined the club's ongoing financial woes. Nelson wrote, in part:

> "As you so well know, the Cave has been running in the red and its liabilities are heavy...We plan to borrow $6,000...it is necessary for us to personally guarantee the loan. Obviously, repayment from the Cave is predicated on a profitable picture in the future but we have enough confidence in the venture to guarantee the additional investment."

To close out the letter, Nelson proposed that

> "...we would be satisfied if Bob [Gibson] were to give us an additional two weeks of entertainment on the following basis: ...the $1,000 value of Bob's services will go on the books as an account payable and when the above-described loan is reduced to $3,000, then we will make a payment to Bob...that will equalize the liabilities to the 4 of us."[xiv]

Meanwhile, the newspaper strike showed no sign being resolved.

Nelson dispatched Stan to New York to meet with Len and see some shows, with the hopes of inking more quality acts at wholesale prices. Stan had a remarkable eye for talent, but when it came to the fine point of negotiating with an experienced New York artist manager of Len Rosenfeld's stature, he was at a decided disadvantage.

Stan did see some exciting new performers, among them José Feliciano and Ed McCurdy. Each of them was to make memorable performances at La Cave.

On the flip side, his meeting with Len created more than a little misunderstanding.

A Young Man's Fancy

Springtime in Cleveland arrived delightfully in 1963. One of the longest, coldest, snowiest winters on record had finally given up its assault on its citizens. With the lengthening days and milder evenings, students and other concert-going types flooded the city's clubs. Cabin fever has its upside. Attendance at La Cave swelled. Tom Pasle sold out half of his twelve dates in late April, and the relatively unknown Berkeley Squares did almost as well in early May. Lydia Wood, opening for Jesse Fuller later in May, was a surprise hit with the cave dwellers, her strong contralto voice booming off the back wall. And Jesse Fuller himself, playing for only $175 per week, hit a home run for Nelson's crew, netting the club over $2,400 and allowing Nelson to breathe normally for the first time in months. And while the club's financial woes were far from over, the light at the end of the tunnel no longer resembled an onrushing locomotive. Even as colleges sent their students packing for the summer, door receipts didn't register a drop off.

Josh White signed on for later that summer, followed by the unknown José Feliciano, the known Bob Gibson, and the elusive Ed McCurdy. Nelson also inked a deal with radio station WCUY-FM to tape for rebroadcast several Hootenanny Nights for their late-night programming.

That $2,400 windfall couldn't have come at a more opportune time. Local entrepreneur Winston Willis had been operating the Jazz Temple at the corner of Euclid Avenue and Mayfield Road across the way from the Commodore Hotel, in the heart of the Case Tech and Western Reserve Academy campuses. But Winston was a black man whose club brought black patrons into a white neighborhood. In 1963, this was verboten. Not so strangely, one night the club caught fire.

Winston gave up the ghost, declaring the Jazz Temple bankrupt. The news traveled through the local music community and landed in Nelson's lap in the form of a listing of club-related gizmos the bankruptcy court was offering for auction. Included in the booty, which Nelson obtained for $525, were items that would electrify the performers at La Cave and, hopefully, the audience as well. Along with the tables, chairs, cash box, stove and refrigerator, deep fryer and such were a Harmon-Kardon PA system complete with speakers and 35-watt amplifier, and 4 Shure microphones with stands.

The first performer to use the mics and PA was Saline Fjeld, who had already played La Cave on various hoot nights and was gaining a reputation as a quality opening act by Stan. As she mounted the stage, a quick look of confusion clouded her brow. Then she found her footing: "Why are all these mics up here?"

FILED

IN THE DISTRICT COURT OF THE UNITED STATES
FOR THE NORTHERN DISTRICT OF OHIO
EASTERN DIVISION
NO. B63-2000

In the Matter of:)
WINSTON WILLIS, AKA WINSTON E.) ORDER CONFIRMING SALE
WILLIS, AKA W. E. WILLIS, DBA) OF PERSONAL PROPERTY
JAZZ TEMPLE,)
Bankrupt.)

At Cleveland, in said District, this cause came on to be heard on the 7th day of June, 1963, upon the Trustee's Report of Sale of the following assets, to-wit:

60 wooden tables; 42 theater chairs; 3 upholstered five-place seats; 1 large painting; 1 Emerson Combination Radio and Record Player; 1 desk; 1 two-drawer card file cabinet-metal; 1 metal cash box drawer; 1 large file cabinet-metal; 1 stove; 1 General Electric refrigerator; 1 deep fat fryer; 1 hot chocolate machine; 47 small serving baskets; 13 packs of hamburger buns; 19 full cases of pop; 19 empty cases of pop; 5 seat cushions; 2 University Column speakers; 2 University Horn speakers; 4 Shure microphone stands; 1 Harmon-Kardon 35 watt PA Amplifier; miscellaneous cups; saucers; glasses; flatware, salt, pepper and sugar holders.

and upon oral statements of the Trustee and his counsel and the evidence; and the Court having been fully apprised in the premises,

THE COURT FINDS

That the Trustee, being advised that a public sale of said assets was not warranted by the amount thereof, did offer at private sale through Rosen & Company, all of the above assets, free and clear of the claims of:

Winston Willis, aka Winston E. Willis, aka W. E. Willis
Charlene Preston
Joseph Crosswhite
American Automatic Vending
Sound & Audio Electronics Laboratories, Inc.

as set forth in the Order of sale.

The Court further finds that the highest and best bid obtainable for the above chattels was made by Nelson G. Karl in the sum of $525.00, free of the claims as set forth herein.

Nelson Karl's purchases

Beginning with the improving mid-March Cleveland weather, Ginni Clemens and Don Crawford each signed up for two-week residencies in March, while Gene Farmer's and Tom Pasle's acts ran from 2 April to the first week of May, at which point the folk duo Berkeley Squares camped out for their own two-week stay in the Cave.

"Calypso Gene" Farmer made it onto, and just as quickly off of, the La Cave stage and later the national scene with his 1972 tongue-in-cheek composition "The Ballad of George McGovern." More importantly for La Cave, the devastating newspaper strike that had set back not only La Cave but hundreds of other small Cleveland businesses, concluded 8 April with the Newspaper Guild agreeing to settle for the originally offered raise of ten dollars a week. The first post-strike edition of *The Plain Dealer* was 80% advertising. Most of the remainder was 129 days' worth of death notices.

Tom Pasle, he of the devastatingly good looks and a three-octave voice, had appeared once at La Cave in 1962, earning a slick thirty-five bucks for his 26 August concert. Beginning in spring of 1963, he would soon become a popular mainstay of the La Cave stage, appearing a half dozen times or more over the next three years. In '61 he had begun the long grind of the traveling troubadour, playing in clubs from coast to coast and never failing to appear at La Cave every time his travels took him through the Midwest. Tom's only appearance on vinyl consisted of a single song included on the 1962 anthology "Folk Festival."[xv]

The Berkeley Squares took the stage in early May and shared an unlikely connection to the Beatles. Each group labored at the Top Ten Club in Hamburg under the grueling conditions of playing up to eight 45-minute sets per day. Unlike the Beatles, they made absolutely no impact on the world at large, and after 1967 or so vanished with nary a trace

---

Nelson redoubled his marketing efforts, running off a few hundred flyers and placing ads in both Cleveland dailies for Jesse Fuller, Tom Pasle, Bob Gibson and newcomer Lydia Wood. He also inked a deal with FM radio station WCLV-FM[xvi] to carry a taped broadcast of one of Bob Gibson's sets that Stan recorded on his recently purchased, massive Ampex two-track tape recorder that he mounted on a pad on the front of the stage. On 17 May he dashed off another missive to Len Rosenfeld and quickly got to the point: addressing a disagreement that had arisen "between New York and Cleveland," a euphemistic way of saying he was pissed off at Len.

It seems that Len Rosenfeld had taken it upon himself to negotiate and conclude several contracts between his unknowns and La Cave, with the tacit approval of erstwhile La Cave business partner Bob Gibson, who profited from these bookings. To Nelson, this arrangement was a clear conflict of interest. Not to mention unaffordable, considering La Cave's constantly precarious financial health. It really irked him.

Reluctantly, Len withdrew the contract for native Clevelander/New York transplant Fred Neil, who would go on to become one of the most iconic influences in the folk and burgeoning folk-rock genres, with dozens of major stars covering many of his compositions.

Just a Couple of Cleveland Boys

Phil Ochs and Jim Glover met Stan Kain while hanging out at Faragher's. It was unavoidable. Stan was sitting next to Bob Gibson as Bob held court. While Bob regaled the young college students with tales of New York City and folk music fame, Stan presented the boys an offer they were in no position to refuse: their own "headlining" act at La Cave. When the evening of their appearance came, Phil was a no-show and Jim was forced to handle the set alone, which turned into one of those better-forgotten performances. But the die was cast. The two would find a measure of fame, if not fortune, separately, Phil on his own and Jim as part of another duo, Jim and Jean, with his future wife Jean Ray. After dropping out of college during his final quarter at Ohio State, Phil followed Jim's bus route to New York.

Regardless of the false start at La Cave by their duo The Sundowners, both Jim and Phil would each make many a triumphant return to La Cave, separately and together. Stan embraced the duo as they began making waves in the larger world of folk and protest music in New York and points east.

Phil Ochs poster 1968

José, Can You See?

School was never a priority for José Feliciano; music was. He dropped out of school at age 17 and began busking in various Greenwich Village "basket houses," rubbing elbows with the likes of Dylan, Fred Neil, John Sebastian and the other folkies playing the same clubs.

José's first paying gig was in Detroit at The Retort coffeehouse in the cellar of the Mount Royal Hotel. He recalled making two or three hundred bucks, "a fortune to a guy who didn't even have a hit record." On the way back from Michigan, he and his wife Janna stopped in Cleveland, signed a two-week contract with La Cave on 29 July to start the very next day! His fee was $200 per week, plus lodging.[xvii] He was two songs into his first set when he decided to work on his Dylan impression. He sang an impromptu commercial for La Cave to the tune of The Times They are a-Changin', to thunderous applause.

José would make many triumphant returns to La Cave, playing there at least once a year (for at least one week each time) from 1963 through 1967, when he reached international superstardom.

CONTRACT BLANK

AMERICAN FEDERATION OF MUSICIANS

OF THE UNITED STATES AND CANADA

LOCAL NUMBER______

ADDITIONAL TERMS AND CONDITIONS

Form B-2a

José Feliciano contract

Everyone Knows It's Gusti

Gusti could sing. Let me rephrase that: Gusti could SING! Long before Prince and Madonna, Gusti was unique enough not to need another name. She sang solo, in duos, and in a group named The New Wine Singers, which later morphed into Spanky & Our Gang when band members Elaine “Spanky” McFarlane and Malcolm Hale broke away.

Gusti was raised in a very musical family, her grandfather being a multi-instrumentalist and her father seeing to it that Gusti became a classically trained vocalist. And of course, being Irish was no impediment to singing lusty traditional hard-fighting, hard-drinking and hard-loving songs.

Her husband Don Hervey, whom she married at age 20 in 1958, was knocking down a cool $200 a week by late 1961, and she was making a solid $25, but their rent alone was ninety bucks, so when the New Wine Singers offered her $75 a week, the decision to work in Chicago was an easy one, two little kids by this time notwithstanding. And there she remained through 1962 and into the wee months of ’63.

For most of 1963 Gusti’s husband Don was the nominal day manager of La Cave, although it was Gusti herself, her two ginger-topped toddlers in tow, who usually hopped the bus down the hill to La Cave to open up, clean the kitchen and otherwise prepare the club for the evening’s festivities and, most importantly, to meet and pay the beer deliveryman. And, more so as the year unfolded, she took the kids back home and returned as the opening act for more and more headliners.

Buffy Ste. Marie, whose two-week residency turned into a six-week stationary tour of La Cave, was one of those headliners. The two women instantly hit it off and, after just two nights in the Versailles Motor Inn, Buffy hauled her one suitcase over to Gusti’s apartment for some rent-free accommodations in the true folk spirit. Of course, this allowed the two interpreters of song to exchange vocal techniques, guitar licks, and stories of the road. One of Gusti’s more dear memories is how Stan Kain went out of his way to hire women folksingers in an era when many more men than women ascended stages and women, if at all, were often accompanists at best and adornments at worst.

Buffy Ste. Marie at La Cave c. 1963

Katie Lee fit in perfectly with the La Cave crowd, which is to say that she really didn't fit in very well in gentle society. Simply put, she was a badass, albeit a pleasant one. Much older than the typical itinerant folkie at age 43, by late '62 she had already released four albums to little, if any acclaim, including her most recent effort, a live album titled *The Best of Katie Lee: Live at the Troubadour*. Katie was a real sucker for the turn of a phrase, so much so that, while being treated to lunch with Carl Sandburg at The Dill Pickle Club in Chicago, she made use of a trip to the ladies' room by copying down, verbatim, the words on the stall wall that became the lyrics for her madrigal "My Chastity."

And while Katie and the Cave's paths never again crossed, Katie's career took an amazing upswing when she began a 50-year career in environmental activism, beginning with 1964's *Folk Songs of the Colorado River* on Folkways, and culminating with seven more albums and the authorship of five books, including the legendary *Ten Thousand Goddam Cattle: A History of the American Cowboy in Song, Story & Verse* in 1976, and culminating in 2014's *The Ghosts of Dandy Crossing,* published when she was 95 years old!

Katie Lee wasn't the only one venturing outside the folk music realm to make waves in society at large as a social activist. In 1963, Nelson Karl began what would also become a lifelong passion when he went to work, pro bono, on a number of legal cases on behalf of the American Civil Liberties Union (ACLU). His first case representing the ACLU became a landmark case in the ongoing controversy regarding the respect, or lack thereof, due the American flag.

The first decision regarding treatment of the flag occurred in 1907 when the Supreme Court affirmed in Halter v. Nebraska that states did indeed have the authority to ban flag desecration. The case at hand involved the now-innocent printing of the flag on a beer bottle. For decades afterwards and through two world wars the American flag made iconic news, particularly when its being raised on Mount Suribachi on a faraway place called Iwo Jima in March of 1945 came to symbolize the ascendancy of the American century.

Then came the 1960s. The intense patriotism of the war in the 1940s and the so-called Red Scare in the decade following had faded, as former servicemen and women were now much more preoccupied with family and career, and younger citizens – a generation removed from the hyper-patriotism of those times – became increasingly more concerned with personal expression through music, clothing and even anti-government activism.

The year 1963 brought Nelson, the ACLU, northeastern Ohio, and a high school teacher named Arlie McCartt, a 39-year-old resident of Kent, Ohio, to national prominence for their requisite fifteen minutes of fame. The outcome of their foray into First Amendment rights would reverberate for decades to come. Arlie taught American Government to seniors at Kenston High School, a rural community 25 miles east of Cleveland. According to sworn testimony, on 19 February Arlie threw the flag on the floor, stepped on it, and left it there for two or three minutes. In his testimony in court, Arlie averred that many of the students were not paying attention, and he wanted to make a point about the ills of extreme nationalism, saying that in the past, he would be taken out and shot.

Nelson's arguments in favor of acquittal were persuasive. It took the seven women and five men less than half an hour to acquit McCartt, noting that the law required a guilty intent. Geauga County Common Pleas Court Judge Robert Ford warned Arlie never to do it again. Later, Judge Ford noted that the case had set national precedent. The decision became an integral building block in the Supreme Court decisions *Street v. New York* from 1969, and 1974's *Spence v. Washington,* both of which upheld the rights of citizens to express unpopular, even disgusting, displays of political speech. And just like Clarence Darrow did during the infamous Scopes "Monkey Trial" a generation prior, Nelson forever altered the mighty flow of the American jurisprudence stream.

Last Night I Had the Strangest Dream

Born the same year as Katie Lee, 1919, and possessed with a deep, arresting baritone voice, good looks, and a talent for stage performance, coupled with over two decades of experience in several fields of entertainment, by the late 1950s Ed McCurdy was wildly popular with the college set. Not because of his carefully honed professionalism, but rather because he knew how to tell a dirty joke, actually many dirty jokes, and still manage to evade the censor. In this respect, he was the antithesis of Lenny Bruce. His mastery of language and his familiarity with risqué Elizabethan ballads, as well as his ability to deliver the many double entendres in those songs with attendant sighs, winks, smiles and shrugs made his performances devastatingly popular, as rapt youthful audiences waited with barely restrained libidos for the next reference to body parts and their impolite uses. It became a mark of sophistication to be among the first listeners to "get" the lascivious meaning of Ed's most recent obscure word choice.

Ed had a secret weapon that kept him near the forefront of these daring interlopers. He had written a song of his own, and it was a dandy. It also fit the times perfectly. As the Vietnam War began to heat up and college-age kids who were subject to the military draft began to realize that the cannons were increasingly pointed at them, Ed's 1950 antiwar classic "Last Night I Had the Strangest Dream" made an appearance in the playlists of the day.[xviii]

Ed graced the La Cave stage during the last week of August and the Labor Day weekend, grossing the club a little over $5,500, and Stan re-upped Ed for a reprise performance in December. Of course, circumstances were going to change dramatically before then.

A Rose by Any Other Name

Biff was weird. No other way to say it. He had both weird and talent in somewhat equal amounts. Another one-name wonder, Biff, whose full name was Biff Rose, released seven albums of comedy, music and musical comedy between 1968 and 1979, after which he quickly faded back into the obscurity from which he had recently climbed.

At La Cave, Biff wandered through the crowd performing his off-color and borderline misogynistic and racist material, singing the occasional song to break up the patter, and engaging the audience in a battle of puns. He would single out individuals for, in many cases, unwanted attention. People didn't know how to take Biff, and often a song or comedy bit would end to complete silence. At times, as the meaning sunk in, scattered applause would occur, while other times it seemed as if silence was Biff's desired reaction to his oddly risqué and often incomprehensible word salad.

Biff's two-week run at the Cave ended 17 November, 1963, less than a week before everything changed again, forever.

The Tarriers were one of those groups that drove Nelson up the wall. On the one hand, they were wildly popular. That's good. On the other, they were ridiculously expensive. That wasn't so good. They demanded, and got, the equivalent of over $13,000 for their week-long residency beginning 19 November.

The Tarriers hit town on Tuesday, 19 November, and for three nights played to exceptionally large weekday crowds, so large that the bonus clause of their contract was activated, earning the band an extra $205. Was La Cave finally turning a financial corner? While the answer might have been a qualified "yes" after their

Thursday performance on the 21st, it took fewer than twenty-four hours to recalculate the answer.

Johnny, We Hardly Knew Ye

Friday, 22 November, dawned sunny, breezy and cool in Cleveland. The temperature would eventually hit 64 degrees around 5pm, but by then the weather was of no concern to anyone. Nor was opening La Cave for the weekend. As chronicled extensively elsewhere, President John Fitzgerald Kennedy died at an assassin's hand in Dallas, and Walter Cronkite, America's "most trusted newsman," breaking into an episode of As the World Turns at 1:40 pm EST on ABC-TV, informed Cleveland and all of America. After various updates, at 2:38 pm EST, Walter looked over a new bulletin for a moment, removed his glasses, composed himself, and made the official announcement: "From Dallas, Texas, the flash, apparently official: President Kennedy died at 1 p.m. Central Standard Time, 2 o'clock Eastern Standard Time, some 38 minutes ago."

Nobody was going to enjoy live musical performances for a while.

Ian Tyson was a cowboy. A Canadian cowboy, although his nation of birth probably never mattered to the cows. He grew up to be a rodeo rider on Vancouver Island in British Columbia, but soon found out that singing and playing guitar was much more conducive to his physical health than busting broncs and bones. Besides, he had the best voice in his school and, as it turned out later, became one of the most heralded songwriters in Canadian and folk music history. His "Four Strong Winds" was voted the greatest Canadian song of all time by CBC radio listeners and has been covered countless times, and his "Someday Soon" was honored by the Western Writers of America as one of the "Top 100 Western Songs" of all time.

After graduating from the Vancouver School of Art, he moved to Toronto to work as a commercial artist. Around the same time, Sylvia Fricker left Chatham, Ontario, her birthplace, also for the bright lights of Toronto. Regardless of her parents' wishes otherwise, she had decided early on to be a singer. Her voice was angelic and, like Ian, it just so happened out that she was no slouch at penning ballads. Her song "You Were on My Mind" shot to number three on the Billboard Hot 100 when the We Five covered it in 1965.

One day in 1959 a friend of Ian's heard Sylvia sing at a party and told Ian to check her out, which he promptly did. By 1961 they were a full-time folk duo and a couple years later became a full-time married couple. Ultimately, the duo was inducted into The Canadian Music Hall of Fame and inducted into the Canadian Songwriters Hall of Fame individually. The same level of proficiency can't be said about their marriage, which ended in 1975.

What happened at La Cave the week of Ian & Sylvia's residency was nothing short of completely unexpected – and spectacular. Four of the six nights sold out, ticket sales for the week topped eighteen hundred dollars, beer sales were through the roof – at least two extra beer runs were needed – and when the final note from Ian's big Martin D-28 stopped ringing, without knowing it, a small cadre of performers, waitresses, club managers, music lovers, beat cops and a couple dozen underaged sneak-ins had begun, in their small way, the healing process from the previous week's trauma. Intimate local clubs had found an important raison d'etre. In times of tragedy, gatherings like those at La Cave took on added meaning and importance, and the folk songs of the day told and retold the stories that have long since become part of the canon of American music. Folk music has always been the music of the oppressed, the disenfranchised, and all people who suffer indignities due to circumstance.

Protest music was about to become very popular.

The year ended on a surprising, upbeat, note, notwithstanding the Corporation Financial Valuation Statement that Nelson filed with the state on 10 October, averring that La Cave de Café, Inc.'s assets were $4,560.25 and its liabilities were $21,343.35. These totals included a mortgage amount of $6,500.00, unpaid salaries totaling $2,475.00 and accounts payable of $1,943.35. Fortunately for all concerned, beer purchases were on a strictly cash basis.

WCLV-FM, Cleveland

Earlier in the year WCLV had re-broadcast a couple Bob Gibson concerts and begun airing Hootenanny Night on a somewhat regular basis during their late-hour programming. Now the time had come for some more professionally produced prime-time radio spots. The cost was a staggering eight dollars a minute. The frugal Nelson Karl knew that to make money, it takes money. So he made the eight-dollar plunge and booked three commercials to run late nights on Martin Perlich's show on "Cleveland's Fine Arts" radio station WCLV at 99.5 FM. In 1963 it was a rare household that had an FM receiver, and even fewer automobiles were equipped with what was still a pricey option.

The first La Cave commercial, which aired on 11 November, featured the Tarriers, Ian & Sylvia, and Jo Mapes. And don't forget, Tuesday is Hootenanny Night! Bring a borrowed guitar and claim your very own fifteen minutes of infamy! By the way, parking is no problem at La Cave (other than the high percentage of auto thefts in the Cleveland Police Third District). We are right next to the Fenway Motor Hotel! A subsequent commercial aired on 27 November, featuring Ian & Sylvia again, and one more aired the week of 3 December, once more mentioning Jo Mapes and the irrepressibly bawdy Ed McCurdy, the "folk singer's folk singer, back by popular demand!" By now, word of La Cave was being spread not only by word of mouth, but by ads in the *Plain Dealer*, *The Press*, *The Cleveland News*, and *The Akron Beacon Journal*, as well as by radio.

There was one important bit of business to settle before year's end – who would perform at the planned New Year's Eve bash that was already being talked about in the beginning of December. Bob Gibson, through agent Len Rosenfeld, had been lobbying Nelson heavily on his own behalf, but both Nelson and Stan were well past the honeymoon period when it came to leaning on Bob and his agent to feed them talent – especially when they felt they were being taken advantage of. On a recent foray into the belly of the folk music beast, Greenwich Village, Stan, never shy to strike up and hold lengthy conversations with total strangers, had discovered that a number of performers played the iconic Village clubs for basket tips and didn't receive any compensation from the club itself. He went in search of other agents.

Nelson felt pressure to wrap up the year-end booking, get the ads and commercials in the works, set up his wait staff, plan for a gala, and hopefully profitable, New Year's Eve, and set aside a little time to think about the Florida family vacation he was contemplating. He set about lighting a fire under Len Rosenfeld's office chair. It was still mid-November when he dashed off a 4-cent letter to Len's East 92nd Street headquarters. He cancelled Bob Gibson's New Year's Eve contract.

Bob solved the Len Rosenfeld part of the problem by firing him and hiring his brother Jim as his new agent. He also agreed to having folkie John Winn as his opening act. In return, he got the New Year's Eve gig reinstated, extending his stay through 4 January of 1964, and 55% of the net proceeds. He also got the ticket price raised to an astronomical two dollars and twenty-five cents.

Several flyers placed in various locations crowed that, on New Year's Eve at La Cave, "$4.50 gets you everything but beer!" Two hundred and twenty-five folk music (and beer) lovers paid their way in, more to ring out the bad old year 1963 than to contemplate what the new one might hold in store. As it turned out, as eventful as 1963 was, the new year would be every bit as historic.

Chapter 5: When It's '64'

The new year's resolution of many was to forget the past and forge on, slightly older and hopefully much wiser. The tragic ending to 1963, while never to be forgotten, was something that the country – perhaps unconsciously – was determined to move on from. And to varying degrees, the commitment worked. The new year was destined to be one of innovation, entertainment, and advancement. Camelot was gone; it was time to be more realistic. To help achieve that goal, entertainment was to be a key factor in forgetting the pains of the past. La Cave was well-positioned to provide that panacea.

On the tube during the just-ended Christmas week, the TV show Hootenanny featured The Modern Folk Quartet, The Chad Mitchell Trio, Josh White, Carolyn Hester and the Serendipity Singers while being broadcast from the University of Maryland. The popularity of the show portended good things for La Cave and other folky caves.

On 15 January, The Whisky a Go Go opened its doors to patrons on the Sunset Strip between Clark and Hilldale Roads, beginning the west coast rock-n-roll era and ultimately gaining international recognition for introducing many acts that gained fame and, sometimes, fortune.

In January, the San Francisco Giants made Willie Mays the highest paid athlete in America. It will take more than decade to take Major

League Baseball to end the indentured servitude of the reserve clause in players' contracts.

The most powerful earthquake in North American continental history occurred in Alaska on 27 March at a magnitude of 9.2, inflicting massive damage to the city of Anchorage. Less than seven weeks earlier, though, the largest non-geological earthquake in recording history took place when, on 9 February, two out of every five American eyes (still the largest percentage of Americans doing the same thing at the same time) and ears were stunned by the British re-taking the Colonies in North America without firing a shot. The Beatles' appearance on The Ed Sullivan Show was perhaps the only time in Mr. Sullivan's long TV career that he lost control of the audience, the performers, and almost himself. When the final chord from George Harrison's 1963 Gretsch Country Gentleman faded away, everything had changed forever. Everything. The next day, Hofner, Rickenbacker and Gretsch guitar companies, Vox amplifiers and the Ludwig drum company were furiously figuring how to increase production and distribution capabilities to meet the unprecedented demand for their products.

The garage band was invented.

On the local scene, Frank Sinatra and Dean Martin rang in the new year with Anita Ekberg and Ursula Andress in the forgettable big-screen flick "4 For Texas" at the Allen Theater, Paul Newman and Elke Sommer thrilled audiences at Loew's State Theater with their starring roles in "The Prize," while Jimmy Stewart and Sandra Dee co-starred in "Take Her, She's Mine" at The University Theatre.

Critics of the City of Cleveland's massive urban renewal project for downtown, the 125-acre Erieview Project, complained loudly about the number of businesses displaced by the project. The Chamber of Commerce brushed off those critics, claiming that the project was the largest urban renewal plan in history and predicting that it would not only revitalize the city, but would be the model for years to come for other cities to emulate. Sadly, time proved the critics right. By 1973, architectural critic Ada Louise Huxtable described "a huge, bleak, near empty plaza with a complete set of non-working fountains and drained pools," and lamented that the plaza was flanked by "vast, open parking lots." She further derided Erieview as a "monument to everything that was wrong with urban renewal thinking in America in the 1960s."

Cleveland was entering a long, dark tunnel of bad decisions, poorly-planned solutions and other important governmental miscalculations that would ultimately cause a 65% drop in population, fuel the "white flight" of the '60s and '70s, and earn the city the pejorative nickname "Mistake on the Lake," while fueling standup comedians with decades' worth of material.

Gusti Redux

Gusti and husband Don, the de facto managers of La Cave, had welcomed their third child into the world in mid-December and were raring to go with new material in their repertoire as well as in a crib back home.

And the bombardment of letters from agents and managers touting their clients' prodigious talents, solicited by Stan during his NYC forays, which flowed in during the waning months of 1963 had their effect. Maxine Sellers from the APA agency contracted for two weeks commencing 7 January, as soon as Bob Gibson had skedaddled. Gil Turner, repped by Folksong Artists Unlimited, was picked up for February. Soon to be contacted and signed were, from APA: The Outsiders, Mike Settle (late of the New Christy Minstrels) and Carolyn Hester. ITA would bring in José Feliciano, Lynn Gold, Judy Henske, the Modern Folk Quartet, Dick Glass, The Just 4, The Travellers and Glenn Yarbrough. Stan Kain, on behalf of La Cave, turned down unknown comedians Woody Allen and Jon Byner, perhaps because his superpowers did not extend to evaluating funny guys. Bob Carey, late of The Tarriers and repped by Willard Alexander, Inc., and Lordly & Dame, Inc.'s Ramblers Three and Dayle Stanley agreed to residencies in late spring and summer.

Bob Gibson, who, notwithstanding the internecine booking warfare playing out over New Year's, stayed another full week into January, drawing consistently large audiences[xix] and was rebooked for the first two weeks of spring, 26 March through 5 April.

Alix

Perhaps the most surprising and satisfying success of Stan's signings in late winter was a Leonard Rosenfeld-backed unknown 22-year-old folkie from the City, Alix Dobkin. If her name isn't instantly recognizable, that's understandable. But the deep irony surrounding her career beginnings is the kind of story that cannot be made up, so it has to be true. And her mark on her community is indelible.

Alix Dobkin's message to La Cave, 1963

Alix was the kind of young woman that everyone noticed. She had arrestingly good looks, a strong, clear voice and was no shrinking violet. She had auditioned in New York along with an equally unknown 24-year-old comedian. And here's where the irony of that unintentional pairing needs to be noticed. In 1968, after her marriage to Gaslight manager Sam Hood ended, Alix came out as lesbian, a quite uncommon event in that time. She went on in her career to become the first openly lesbian performer to tour Europe and became an outspoken voice for feminism and gay rights. She released seven albums, wrote three books, and was called, according to her online entry, a "women's music legend" by Spin Magazine, "pithy" by The Village Voice, "Biting...inventive...

imaginative" by New Age Journal, "uncompromising" in the New York Times Magazine, and "a troublemaker" by the FBI.

But at the time in late 1962 she was just another aspiring folksinger, and the 24-year-old would-be comedian who auditioned with her? His name was Bill Cosby, who went on first to fame and then to infamy, taking a life direction as different from Alix's path as one could imagine.

Alix's La Cave debut was a big hit, garnering well over 200 paid patrons on both her opening and closing nights. At least a couple of those patrons recall being "mesmerized" even before she sang a note. And the notes she sang did nothing to diminish that first impression.

In what serves as a kind of epilogue to Alix's career is the fact that *Curve Magazine*, a website for LGBTQ folks," in their 2013 list of the top twenty "Great Lesbian Love Songs," slotted Alix's "A Woman's Love" in the number three spot, all time.

Those Cleveland Boys Again

Sometime after Jim Glover left Cleveland and began busking in the Village while meeting soprano Jean Ray, the two, now Mr. and Mrs. Glover, hit it big.

Stan signed Jim & Jean to a two-week stay in late April/early May and contracted Phil Ochs for early June. On 26 April, 1964, *The Pee Dee's* entertainment guru Glenn C. Pullen devoted an effusive amount of column inches to the exploding career of Jim & Jean. Stan had connived to have the newspaperman stop by the club, all expenses paid, to see the talented couple for himself and perhaps write up a complimentary blurb. He got much more than he had hoped for. Glenn countered with an offer to have the handsome couple visit his offices at East 18th and Superior in Cleveland's downtown business district.

Jim & Jean at La Cave

The conversation began briskly. Glenn knew his stuff and began asking about specific songs in their repertoire. When he mentioned the Phil Och's penned "The Ballad of Billy Sol Estes," a topical ditty about a man the New York Times once described as "a fast-talking Texas swindler who made millions, went to prison and captivated America for years with mind-boggling agricultural scams, payoffs to politicians and bizarre tales of covered-up killings and White House conspiracies," Jim and Jean broke into song. When the song ended, the entire staff broke into applause. After several more spontaneous musical interludes, the *Plain Dealer* staff wished the young merry-makers a fond "good luck" and Glenn waxed enthusiastic in his column.

The Lineup

Stan Kain, with Nelson Karl's blessing, visited New York City at least twice during the spring and early summer of '64 and made a flurry of signings, based at least in part on the growing reputation of La Cave and the rising revenues that the increased attendance provided. And while the word "throng" did not quite yet apply, there was a good reason for the combined exhale of breath held by the brain trust since the Beatles upended the music world.

In short order Stan inked Josh White, Leon Bibb, Bob Gibson, Phil Ochs, Tom Pasle, Buffy Ste. Marie, The Inn-Mates, Bud & Travis, Carolyn Hester, Bob Gibson and Josh White again, local boy Tom Shipley (not yet the latter half of Brewer and Shipley), the Just 4, and Buzzy Linhart. He supplemented these headliners with second-act talent including Gail Aldritch, Sean & Gusti, Don and Gusti, Gusti solo, Jim Carder, Dick Glass, Gene Farmer, Lydia Wood, Mike Hoffman, Pinky & Jim and a newcomer to the scene: Candy Forest.

Candy remembers, "When I first set foot in La Cave, the late great Cleveland coffeehouse that became my musical home base, it was Bob Gibson and his 12-string guitar that I heard on my way down the steps. He was sharing a bill with Josh White on a Sunday afternoon and I took a Greyhound bus to get there from my hometown of Painesville, 30 miles east. The club was located at the corner of 105th St. and Euclid Avenue, at the time considered the most dangerous corner in the entire city! My parents were out of town that day and I decided to sneak out on this adventure because I knew about Josh White and wanted to hear him live. I was 17 at the time. Bob Gibson was not familiar to me, but I fell in love with his voice and his big beautiful 12-string guitar in an instant. His signature song was "Foghorn," something he had been inspired to write because he lived in Chicago where there is plenty of fog. That song hit me with a force that moved me to borrow a guitar from a friend and learn to play (that guitar was a $17 plywood box from Sears loaned to me by a friend)."

"As soon as I had learned the 3 songs required to appear at a La Cave Hootenanny, I was onstage with my sister Gayle singing harmony. We were The Mordush Sisters and I'm sure were quite an amusement to the other participants who included Tom Shipley, Gusti & Don Hervey and soon after, Buzz Linhart among others."

Candy Forest at La Cave

"I began saving money to buy my own guitar and by the time I graduated from high school, I had enough to go to Pfabes Music to see if they had a 12-string guitar for sale. I knew that's what I wanted, not just because Bob Gibson played one but because by then, I had heard Tom Shipley play his on a pretty regular basis and I loved the sound. Edsel Pfabes (pronounced "fabeez") knew us of course, because Gayle had once worked there and also his sons took piano lessons from our teacher, Ferne Pearcie. I remember looking up on the wall at a long line of guitars. I told him I wanted a 12-string and he handed me a brand-new Gibson that was huge and beautiful. I fell in love instantly and bought it for $250. Gayle had not intended to buy a guitar but Edsel handed her an antique Martin D-28 which I think she bought for $175! It's probably worth many thousands now and sadly she gave it away a long time ago to one of her undeserving boyfriends!"

"So, there we were, The Mordush Sisters, walking into La Cave for the Hootenanny with these two amazing instruments. The boys backstage just couldn't believe it and of course, they all wanted to play them. It was a wonderful night, and for me marked the beginning of my life as a career "Folksinger." About a month later in mid-July, Stan Kain called me around 5 in the evening on a Wednesday. I guess the person they had booked to open for Tom Shipley that night couldn't make it. I didn't drive or have a car so Stan said he would come out to Painesville and pick me up. The pay would be $8 and I would do 2 sets. I remember the look on my dad's face when I told him. He did not approve of any of this business but I was of legal age at last, and I guess by this time he knew that there wasn't any use trying to stop me. It was my first paying gig and I was beyond excited. I put together my set lists, taped them to my guitar and off I went."[xx]

Summertime

La Cave's summer lineup was shaping up: Josh White, Leon Bibb, Phil Ochs with Lydia Wood opening, the Just IV Singers, Oscar Brand, Buffy Ste. Marie, Tom Pasle, The Outsiders, Bud & Travis, Carolyn Hester, Ian & Sylvia, Bob Gibson and Josh White, Jr.

Nelson remarked to a reporter that "the salary budget for these headliners will total about $14,000." The hottest act in the world at the time, The Beatles, earned less than $3,500 for their historic appearance on Ed Sullivan in February of 1964. That figures to about $875 per Beatle. Bob Gibson and Josh White were each earning $1,500 at La Cave for their weekend residencies that same summer.[xxi] Public Hall, the Beatles' venue, held almost 11,000. La Cave, a few hundred. Even a beer-swilling undergrad could see the impossibility of sustaining such costs. But for now, that fact was obscured.

Summer in Cleveland in '64 was hot. Not as hot as when the urban riots visited town in a couple of years, but June *averaged* 80 degrees, well above its historical average. And it didn't rain much. Then, July roasted the city. Complaints about the steamy, stuffy, damp and dank atmosphere in the basement with no access to fresh air were piling up like last night's beer mugs. Nelson sent Stan on a mission: find an air conditioning unit we can afford, and preferably one that works. Stan was up to the task, and on 27 June borrowed a pickup truck and hauled a slightly scratched-and-dented 5-ton Chrysler Air Temp unit, complete with enough ductwork to vent it, and with his father's help installed it in a matter of days. It set Nelson and Stan back a cool three hundred bucks. And it worked! Somewhat. Finally, the cave was sort of cool.

In celebration, perhaps, Nelson let Stan sign the brilliant Carolyn Hester, she who had "discovered" Bob Dylan just two years previous.

Carolyn Hester

Carolyn tells the story best: "It's a funny thing. A lot of this I didn't find out until much later. I knew Bob from Gerde's Folk City and around [Greenwich Village], but what I didn't know was that he had been trying like mad to get some paying gigs, you know, and he found out I was playing up in Boston at Club 47. So when I get up there, there he is sitting outside the club on a step. So I kinda felt sorry for him and brought him into the club with me, and now they're letting him open for me, I mean, I had no idea he had followed me there. Well, when I got back to New York I was gonna record my album for Columbia, it would be my third album, and when Bob found out that I was [going to record], he asked if he could play on the album. He said it was slow going and people were trying to help him out."

"Well, I already had this terrific guitar player, Bruce Langhorne,[xxii] and a terrific bassist, Bill Lee,[xxiii] so that's all covered and I really didn't need him. But then…I decided to play "I'll Fly Away" and I wanted to have harmonica on it and a few other songs. So I asked [Bob] if he would mind playing harmonica, and he just said "Oh my God" or something like that. I told him there was going to be rehearsals and that he wasn't going to get rich or anything. So he said, "Here's my phone number. I'll be there."

"So when I got down to Columbia, this was in September, now, [1961], and John Hammond was there and I told him I had a wonderful guitarist he might have heard of, Bruce [Langhorne], and this great bassist, too, and he said, 'Oh, I know Billy [Lee], he's a jazz type of bassist.' I said, 'Oh great, OK and I said, well now I've met a young fella in the village named Bob Dylan and I want him to play harmonica, he's really excellent' and so Hammond said, 'Well,' he said, 'you know, I know what you are but I haven't heard your band, so if you're playing down in the Village I'd like to come see [your band].'"

"So he did. "He came and that was the first time he had seen Bob, and he couldn't take his eyes off him. Columbia was looking for folk singers at the time, so they snapped up Bob and I believe his album came out a month or two after mine."

"The really funny thing is that, at the time, Bob didn't even know he was "Bob Dylan" yet!"

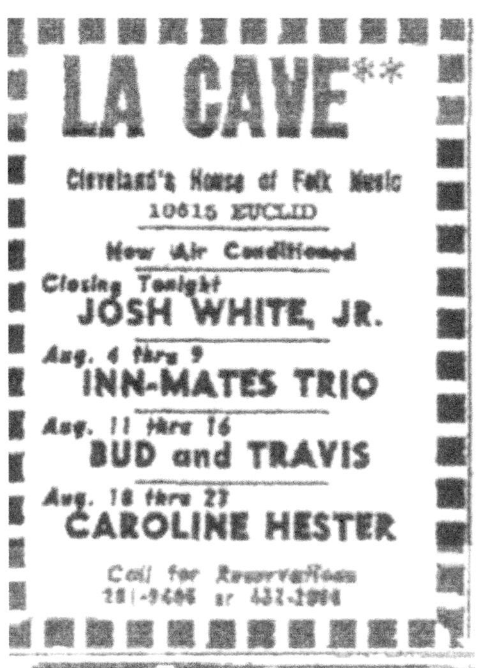

Newspaper ad, Summer 1964

By 1964, Carolyn had established herself as a popular, if not wildly successful, folkie with five albums under her belt. Her week-long gig at La Cave beginning Tuesday, 18 August, and lasting a week, was held over for another week as students began straggling back to classes. The newly-installed air conditioning was a mixed blessing. Stan loved it, as did the paying patrons, not to mention the freeloaders. Nelson thought that it dampened beer sales. Chances are good that both were true.

The summer of '64 continued unabated. It was good times. The pain of last year's national tragedy, like the dirty slush that clogged the winter alleyways of Cleveland, had been melted away by the heat the Beatles generated with their upbeat message of teenage hijinks and their cockeyed sense of humor.

President Johnson, running for office again, took a trip to Ohio and made his first reference to his plan for a "Great Society" on 7 May at Ohio University. Folksingers were having a field day as the nascent genre of the protest song gained traction – and detractors. Phil Ochs explained, "A protest song is a song that's so specific that you cannot mistake it for bullshit." Phil knew what he was talking about. He had just released his first album, "All the News That's Fit to Sing," giving rise to the description "the singing journalist" and ushering in the era of '60s protest music.

Phil, once a headliner on Nelson's shit list, almost blew it again. Visiting friends in Cleveland Heights, he strolled down the stairs to the inner sanctum of youthful indiscretions a good hour late on his first summer date at La Cave, the ninth of June. Nobody in the crowd seemed to mind. After all, these were all mostly people to whom promptness was an alien concept. Besides, Lydia Wood was on stage, regaling the rowdy crowd. It seems that many of them had begun their personal parties in the parking lot around some cupped hands, a pack of matches, and a little vegetable matter. Mellowness was rampant.

That's when the cops on patrol stopped by. This was an era, after all, when LSD was legal but possession of a couple joints of pot could put you in the custody of the state for months or years. Lydia noticed that she had momentarily lost the audience's attention, and looked in the direction their eyes had wandered to. "Good evening, officers," she offered. And giggled at their obvious disapproval. "Uh oh. Shouldn't have said that." Seconds ticked by in silence. Anyone who had been chatting a moment before, wasn't. And anyone who had glanced door ward, which was everyone, suddenly found their beer mug the most interesting detail on the planet. Lydia suddenly remembered that it was she onstage, and was the only person within a hundred yards of a working microphone. "Oh, well." And she regained her momentum by launching into her rollicking version of "Shimmy Like My Sister Kate." Evidently this either pleased or pissed off the patrolmen, but either way, they left without so much as a surly snarl. Everyone knew they'd be back.

The rest of the summer was a triumph of sorts, in that the club remained solvent and launched a successful flanking maneuver on the invading British horde. But the more prescient in the music business felt the earth tremble beneath their feet. Folk music, recently ascendant as the dominant pop music genre, was going to quickly evolve into a more electric, band-based medium. Young adults still wanted their message-laden lyrics, but they also wanted them delivered to a rollicking beat. For small venues, this would be problematic. It's one thing to pay a solo acoustic performer and an entirely different affair to find the stage space and equipment for a band, not to mention the need to pay them.

Buffy Ste. Marie

In a landmark event, on 2 July the Civil Rights Act of 1964 that outlawed discrimination based on race, color, religion, sex, national origin was passed into law.[xxiv] For La Cavites, there was particular irony and triumph in the timing of this groundbreaking legislation since simultaneous to its passage, Indigenous folk singer Buffy Ste. Marie was back in town for an extended stint in the cave, beginning Tuesday, 30 June and staying through Sunday, 19 July.

Buffy had recently released her first album, "It's My Way," in late April and while the album didn't even make the charts, and in the year that the invading Beatles outflanked and rolled up their competition sales-wise, it was Buffy who was named Best New Artist by Billboard Magazine!

Buffy's stay at La Cave in July, originally slated to end on the 12th, continued for a full week, having attracted some of the largest door draws in the 2+ years of the club. Buffy, in the span of a few days, became La Cave's reigning attendance royalty. Her good looks certainly helped pull people through the door, but it was her sparkling personality, her willingness to engage the crowd, often by name as she played requests, and her striking voice that kept 'em coming back. One fan fave was a song sung in French, with which she asked, with a wink, the audience to sing along. She explained that the words were a seduction scene, which piqued everyone's interest. The impossibility of singing along in a foreign language often propelled her new fans into paroxysms of laughter as they strayed farther and farther from the actual song and began to shout out competing lyrics. The punchline, delivered after the raucous gang had settled down, was her deadpan announcement that the seduction had, in the final verse, failed.

Stan and Nelson met during the last week in July to map out bookings for the remainder of the year. While both brought ideas to the chat, each man's recommendations reflected his style: Nelson, the conservative spender who wrote the checks, and Stan, the dreamer with the eye for talent. For the most part, Stan prevailed. On the 31st they inked Bob Gibson for the last week of August, guaranteeing him $1,500[xxv] against 60% of the gross, reflecting Bob's bargaining power. Stan offered Josh White a four-day engagement in November, also for a lofty $1,500 performance fee. In both cases the performers insisted on a minimum ticket price of two dollars and fifty cents. These performers weren't going to pay themselves!

In somewhat of a coup, Nelson succeeded at landing Canadian folk singing sensation Oscar Brand for four days in December. Oscar was a Renaissance man by any yardstick. He wrote and performed hundreds of songs ranging from novelty tunes to serious political commentary. In the early 1960s, Oscar hosted the popular Canadian TV program *Let's Sing Out,* introducing fellow countrymen Joanie Anderson (later, Joni Mitchell) and Gordon Lightfoot to wider audiences. Both would quickly burst into superstardom, not to mention signing agreements to play at La Cave in 1965.

On stage at La Cave, Oscar reached into his extensive back catalog to pull out a few chestnuts. With six volumes in his "Bawdy Songs & Backroom Ballads" series among twenty LPs in total, plus enough sea shanties and drinking songs to make a slightly tipsy crowd lose control, the evening turned into one of the few nights in La Cave history when the basement stopped being a listening room and became a scene where strangers became instant friends and did their best to out sing one another. From the stage, Oscar smiled with delight.

Zahariah Malmoli

The person who made the biggest impression on both Stan and Nelson in the latter half of 1964 was completely unknown outside of Greenwich Village, and not very well-known there, either. A striking young girl with sensuous Middle Eastern looks, the kind that conjure up images of the biblical Dance of the Seven Veils, held court with her acoustic guitar and sultry voice that sent listeners to places better left undescribed, at a hole-in-the-wall basket house called the Four Winds Café. Ed Simon, who owned and managed the Gaslight, also owned the Four Winds and used it as a kind of farm system for his larger, more popular venue. If you could garner attention, and tips, at the Four Winds, you might have a chance to move up the folk singing food chain. And if not, Ed had nothing invested in you.

At the Four Winds, Stan Kain fell in love with the lovely and somewhat talented Zahariah. Instantly he knew two things: one is that she would "wow" the gang back home in the cave, and the other was that he could get her cheap. But like all things this good, it might be *too* good, and it was. The first problem was that Zahariah was only 16 years old. The second was that she already had an agent-in-waiting, Jacob R. Solomon. He was waiting for her to make her first dollar. When Jacob saw Stan, *he* fell in love. And while this love affair would be brief, for a moment it was intense. As they gazed into each other's eyes after one of Zahariah's sets, Jacob blinked. For once, Stan knew he held the better hand, so he called Jacob's bet and landed the teenager for a hundred bucks a week, agreeing on a three-weekend residency in late October/early November. Stan agreed that he would give Zahariah "sole star billing." He also graciously threw in room and board for her and her mom at the rented house he had taken a half mile away.

That house, known to the cognoscenti as "Stan's Pad," had yet to acquire the kind of reputation that made the Sixties "swingin'."

Stan knew all he needed to do was get Zahariah's picture into the newspaper and attendance would take care of itself. It worked. Her photogenic good looks graced the ad he placed prior to her first show, calling her a "specialist in traditional blues and jazz tunes." For most of the people who saw her picture, a further description wasn't necessary.

Stan wasn't worried, and his confidence was rewarded. She was a smash. Not only did she earn her fee a couple times over, word spread to the ubiquitous *Plain Dealer* music critic Glenn C. Pullen, who attended Saturday's show on 24 October and filed his review for publication on the following Friday. His complimentary words glowed with a light of their own.

Rounding Out the Year

Tom Shipley was a tall, skinny, clean-cut undergrad at a local school, Baldwin-Wallace College, and he had the home field advantage of living in suburban Bedford, a half an hour from Cleveland. He also came from a musical family, his parents holding down spots in the church choir and teaching campfire singalongs to Tom and his sister Mary Jo. These family song sessions with his dad, "WW" (for Woodrow Wilson), his mom Josephine and his sister imbued Tom with a lifelong love of music and a longing to perform. Tom later remembered, "That really got me into harmony singing. I still prefer that to [singing] lead."

Tom Shipley, 1959

Born in 1941, Tom was the right age to embrace rock & roll. Cleveland radio was part of the vanguard of disc jockeys playing this hot new music form just as Tom reached teen status. Alan Freed, the DJ who popularized the term "rock and roll," held court nightly on WJW radio with his show "Moondog House" and featured the r&b songs that quickly morphed into r&r. When Freed hosted the first major rock & roll concert, "The Moondog Coronation Ball," at the old Cleveland Arena at East 38th and Euclid, Tom was there. A few years later, as a college freshman, he got to see Pete Seeger play at Baldwin-Wallace, one of the few places in the country that would challenge the Senator Joe McCarthy-inspired blacklist on Communist entertainers, and that got Tom into playing banjo. He got himself a long neck Vega Pete Seeger banjo, his best friend found a guitar in his attic, and "before I knew it, we had a trio called the Green Valley Singers with my sister."

Within a year, Tom graduated to guitar and around '60 or '61 began hanging out at Faragher's Back Room on Mondays, open mic night. Tom got up to sing one night and was hooked. He began to play regularly there and at the open mic night at the Commodore Hotel lounge – they were still called hootenannies at the time – and thus began something that nobody could imagine at the time: a lifelong career as an acclaimed singer-songwriter. By the time La Cave opened in the spring of '62 he was already a seasoned veteran at age 21.

By late '64 Tom had played La Cave as an often, but not always, unpaid opening act, earning a small step up the performing ladder when on 26 September, he saw for the first time his name in a newspaper ad. He would close the show that night and the night after, with Tom Pasle also on the bill. It would take a couple years and many miles, but Tom would eventually meet up with another solo performer from La Cave, a hep cat from Oklahoma City named Michael Brewer. They met at The Blind Pig, a small club in Kent, Ohio, not unlike Cleveland's cave. In short order they became the infamous Brewer and Shipley and found their way onto then-President Nixon's so-called "enemies list." But that's a story for another time.

The La Cave stage next hosted Candy Forest, Buzzy Linhart, Saline Fjeld, the Stoneman Family, Bud & Travis, the Whites: Josh and Josh Jr., separately, Bob Gibson with Pinky (Clementi) & Jim (Jenkins) opening, and a number of local opening acts whose names and performances are now too dim to be recalled. But the think tank that guided La Cave's destiny had one more delight for the growing number of folk music devotees: they brought back Ian & Sylvia for a gala year-end stay. The duo hit the stage on Tuesday, 29 December. By the end of their six-day run they had earned almost $3,500 in door fees alone, covering their $2,500 guarantee with a grand left over in profits. Almost doubling that figure were the beer sales, bringing a measure of delight to the always taciturn Nelson Karl. One of the reasons that the duo, very popular on their own, packed the house at year's end was that they had asked Stan permission to bring their own opening act with them and Stan, vividly remembering their popular previous visits to this underground lair, quickly assented. It was one of those small seemingly random decisions that would pay huge returns. The couple brought their friend, a 26-year-old stalwart of the Toronto coffeehouse scene who was widely unknown south of the Canadian border. His name was Gordon Lightfoot.

The afterparty at Stan's pad began while that first concert was still echoing down Euclid, and by all hazy accounts didn't end until sometime in the harsh morning light of Monday morning, 4 January, a week later. To borrow a song title from the Chairman of the Board, 1964 was a very good year. 1965 brought high hopes for Nelson, Stan and the others manning the cave.

Chapter 6:

1965

1965 was the year that La Cave hit its stride. The year began bitterly cold on the windy streets outside the relative warmth of the club. The thermometer hit 2 degrees or below on fully half of the short, slushy January days. Newly-minted President Johnson, sworn into office on 20 January, would soon move away from his predecessor's aversion to escalating the southeast Asia conflict. The Gulf of Tonkin incident of August 1964 became the pretext for initiating full involvement in the armed conflict. News of the incident, in which North Vietnamese patrol boats allegedly attacked the destroyer USS Maddox while patrolling the gulf was distorted and used as a false-flag opportunity to begin sending combat troops to replace the "military advisers" already there as a nominal peacekeeping force. On 7 January the President declared "I've had enough of this," referring to Viet Cong raids in South Vietnam.[xxvi]

On 2 March he initiated the 8-week bombing campaign known as Rolling Thunder, which ultimately lasted over 3 years, dropped 4 times the tonnage of bombs dropped in all of WWII, and ended up being completely counter-productive to efforts to pacify the country. The year would see the first large-scale antiwar demonstrations, huge increases in the number of draftees, wholesale military actions and, significantly, daily televised news reports of the war during the average Americans' meal times, giving rise to song lyrics like "Breakfast where the news is read/television: children fed."[xxvii] By year's end, American troop levels in Vietnam reached 184,000.[xxviii]

In Cleveland, racial tensions were front page news on New Year's Day. But many Clevelanders remained unconcerned, instead choosing to bask in the joy of their NFL team, the Browns, shutting out the heavily-favored Baltimore Colts 27 to 0 to earn the league championship the previous week. In entertainment news, local favorites Dave C and the Sharptones invited people to "twist tonite" at the Columbia Ballroom.

During an early January meeting of the board of La Cave's directors, a number of observations and decisions were advanced and agreed to by Lee Weiss, Stan and Nelson.

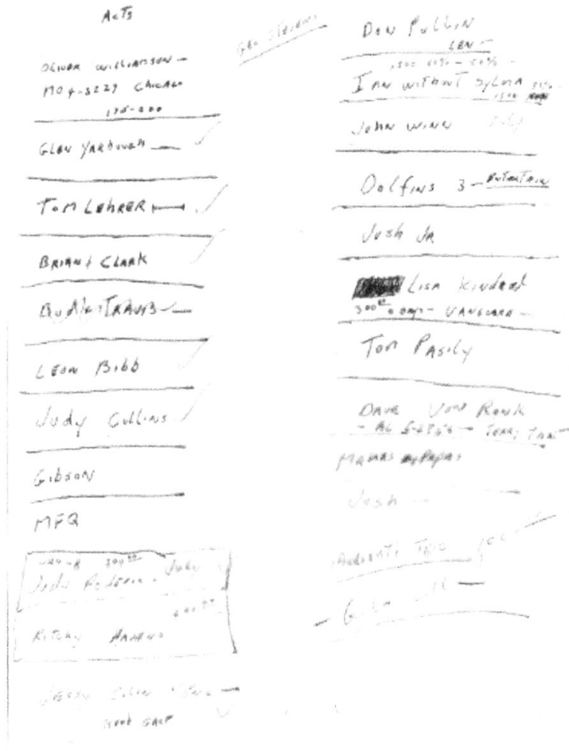

Stan Kain's 1965 wish list

Nelson shared good news with his partners: the past due tax liability had been reduced $2,000 to $512 and the mortgage owed to the Teamsters Credit Union had been halved to $3,376. Stan reported that entertainment was operating at a reasonable profit and that beer was "operating at an excellent profit." It was agreed to continue operating the club; however, the club would close Mondays to cut costs and Hootenanny Night would move to Tuesday or Wednesday.

La Cave Grows Up

1965 began four-year string of musical triumphs for La Cave that easily eclipsed past successes. By now, a lot of kids – and older types, too – would go to the club regardless of the artist on stage. In fact, those youngsters without too much spare change would avoid the costlier acts clocking in at two bucks or more. The place was increasingly perceived as a cool venue for meeting friends, hanging out, maybe scoring some weed or acid, and drinking cheap beer. You stood an excellent chance of making new friends, too, in these days of sudden '60s freedom. New friends meant new opportunities to experience the trinity of youthful life: sex, drugs and rock & roll. To many youngsters, La Cave was dangerously exciting.

The ultimate in coolness happened if you were invited to one of the almost nightly afterparties routinely held at Stan's pad, or at a nearby bar like the Regent. That's where the real action was. And although there was a rotating cast of characters, sometimes with household names and more often without any specific name at all, almost everyone joined in the strumming, singing, smoking, drinking and screwing that defined the capital-s Sixties. Invitations to these shindigs became a holy grail of growing up.

This phenomenon pretty much insured the viability of La Cave. A couple years prior, nightly receipts approaching a hundred bucks were coveted and rare; now, that amount was reached by 9 o'clock or earlier, covering the expenses and leaving hours for profit. Leaving early meant no chance at an afterparty invite, so the gang at 1 a.m. was often larger than the one there for the beginning of the show.

1965 was also the year that both La Cave and some of the acts they brought to town began to receive some serious ink. On Sunday, 31 January, the *Plain Dealer* published a fluff piece on Jim & Jean, Phil Och's erstwhile partner Jim Glover and his wife Jean Ray, now touring the country and preparing to release their debut album "Side by Side"[xxix] on the Philips label.

Hearts, Minds and Wallets

Winter warmed into spring and spring staggered toward summer. Cleveland's rarely-plowed streets were slowly cleared by the incessant rains of late March and April that drenched Cleveland in near-record amounts. And then May's weather was blazing hot, with half the days hitting 80 degrees or higher, coinciding with the end of college classes for thousands of youngsters. On local radio, a broadcasting skirmish that had been simmering just beneath the surface for months exploded into open warfare when, as Billboard Magazine's 3 April issue gave front page news status to it, the competition for ratings in the all-important teen and young adult categories reached bloodletting stage.

Hey, Mister DJ

The influence of radio on youthful listening preferences in the 1960s cannot be overstated. The major record labels played gatekeepers to what songs the radio played, and radio stations were the final filter to determine what consumers heard. This made for a two-headed monster, namely the overly-powerful labels and the overly-unregulated disc jockeys. *Everyone* listened to the radio, with portable transistor models for the bus or the beach, swanky consoles for modern suburban living and car radios becoming the number one Detroit option for commuters and Sunday drivers alike. What songs the DJ played, and with increasing importance what the DJ *said* about the songs he played made all the difference between revered Dion & the Belmonts and unknown bands like Bop and the Beltones.

What's more, the DJ was the guy everyone invited into their houses. He ate meals with you, talked to you about cool things like songs, singers and acne cures while you did homework or chores, invited you to call in a special request for this week's crush, or maybe call in to cast your vote to name the station's pet alligator.[xxx] They even talked about talking to the stars!

There simply was no other way for passionate young music lovers to hear the music they craved. The DJ held all the cards. All the fervor and excitement for the music they incited needed another outlet. A shiny plastic box on the shelf sporting a volume knob, bouncing a tinny Diana Ross off the bedroom wall wasn't cutting it. An outlet was needed that was more visceral, more hormonal, more social. And, on reflection, one that had beer.

Live music took off in Cleveland in 1965, with radio shaping the kind of sounds young people liked, and the clubs that adapted the most quickly standing the best chance of prospering. Up to this point Stan's and Nelson's instincts had pulled La Cave's fat from the fire and it seemed a good time to begin cashing in on all the goodwill and trust they had banked.

Both men were well-prepared for summer and beyond. Between them they had made four treks to New York City, taking in shows, talking to fans, agents, managers, club owners and musicians, and signing a number of acts soon to attain A-list status.

The first summer concert of note, opening on 11 June, was the duo Brian and Clark, not yet known by their surnames Maffitt and Davies, the order of which they soon reversed for reasons unknown. Perhaps Brian lost a bet. Whether he did or not, Brian was already experienced as half of a folk duo, having played in the Missing Otis Trio, and was a veteran of La Cave, having played both solo and in the two-man "trio." Their shows were heavy on humorous songs, witty banter and virtuoso guitar playing. A typical set would open with the boys doing their best Smothers Brothers imitation, to the delight of the fans, Brian's straight-man "Dickie" setting up Clark's "Tommy."

Clark: "Welcome to our show at the gay and exciting La Cave, Cleveland's largest and finest folk room. Awfully glad you came. Woulda been lonesome if you hadn't." Polite chuckles. "My name is Clark Maffitt, and this is Brian Davies, and together we compose the team of Clark Maffitt and Brian Davies. We were talking earlier, but of course you weren't here, about childhood. And someone once said childhood is a very beautiful, wonderful thing."

Brian: "*I* said it."

Clark: "Brian once said that childhood is a very beautiful, wonderful thing." Scattered laughs.

Brian: "I didn't say that, Sam Levinson said that." More laughs.

Ignoring him, Clark continued: "Except that it comes much too early in life. If it came along a little bit later, when you're old enough to appreciate, it would really be neat."

In apparent retaliation after their next song, Brian says, "Out of a false sense of profound modesty, Clark never wants to say that he did write that song." Looking over at his partner, he goes, "I'm sorry, Clark, I didn't mean to embarrass you. It's just that it is so seldom that you do anything worthwhile, that I thought…" as laughter erupts.

Clark feigns his lack of concern at his partner's barbs: "As of late the last few months there has been a movement taking place in the United States that I don't know if you are familiar with or not. It's one of utter terror and panic on the part of a great percentage of American folk singers. It's the age of folk-rock, ladies and gentlemen. This is Mr. Brian Davies' contribution."

Brian commences to play a droning, two-note figure he repeats over and over, simulating a rock beat. More laughter.

As an antidote to the simple repetition of rock & roll, Clark says, "We'd like to do an instrumental for you. It comes from the days of vaudeville. However, we defy any of you to recognize it in its present condition. It's now called Buck Dancer's Choice and we found it to be the choice of most of the buck dancers around the country. Brian is re-tuning his complete guitar. There is a good reason for this and that is that…now do I have to go through all this?"

Brian: "No, we don't have to go through any of this if you don't want to. We could just leave."

Clark: "OK, let's don't." The audience is amused as he reconsiders. And continued, talking as quickly as he can: "Originally the song was written in neither a major nor minor key but was written instead in one of a combination of the Greek modes which simply means that there is no third in the chordal structure and is based largely upon a whole tone pentatonic scale with certain positions being raised in the ascending scale while certain other positions are lowered in the descending scale. (huge intake of breath) Since there is no third in the chordal structure this means the chord is composed entirely of tonics in fifths and since the 5th is a fifth above the tonic the tonic automatically becomes the 4th of the 5th. This gives an illusion of double tonality." (another huge breath)

As the audience looks about, amused but confused, Brian launches into the exact same two-note drone he had just played to mock the concept of folk-rock. In a moment, the audience gets the joke and the guys get the biggest laugh so far as they launch directly into a beautiful weaving of delicate guitar interplay punctuated by several virtuosic solos. They end with a flourish to extended applause.

"We'll be back in about five minutes to do that again." More laughter and applause.

More José

A couple of days after Maffitt & Clark left La Cave for other venues, José Feliciano returned for another triumphant residency. True to his comedic roots, he opened one evening' crooning with a humorous take on a popular deodorant, to the tune of the Beatles' "Do You Want to Know a Secret:"

"Listen, doo wah doo/do you want some Ice Blue Secret/Doo wah doo/Do you promise not to smell? Whoa- o-o."

And so on.

José displayed the guitar chops and personality that made him a fan fave in Cleveland and would, in three years, propel him into the stratosphere of international performers. He was on the verge of issuing his flamenco-flavored debut LP *The Voice and Guitar of José Feliciano* to little acclaim. But in a sign of his growing popularity, his fee to play for Nelson and Stan's patrons had risen from $200 per week when he first played here at age eighteen to $1,300 in a little over a year. Not too shabby for a kid born blind into an impoverished family of thirteen in Lares, Puerto Rico.

The cave crew couldn't have been happier. Costs had been cut as they learned to streamline the business, eliminating unproductive nights and dropping superfluous advertising. And when José attracted almost two thousand paying folks to his eight-day stint, the check writers were so thrilled that they extended his stay another week. They were well-prepared for their next star attraction, Odetta. At $3,000 for her six-day stay, she was easily the most expensive performer to ascend the eight-inch stage in the basement on Euclid.[xxxi]

Odetta

Odetta was folk music royalty – literally. In 1961 Martin Luther King crowned her "The Queen of American Folk Music." She sang a memorable version of the song "Oh, Freedom" at the 1963 March on Washington next to the operatically trained Marian Anderson, of whom conductor Arturo Toscanini once said had a voice "heard once in a hundred years." The same statement was made more than once about Odetta. Carly Simon remembers "going weak in the knees" upon hearing her. Joan Baez and Bob Dylan had also sung alongside her at The March.

Odetta at La Cave

At the time of her appearance at La Cave in July '64 she had recently released her fourteenth album, "Odetta Sings Dylan," the first major artist to cover Bob's songs. In fact, in his first full-length interview, for Playboy Magazine, Bob admitted it was Odetta who had turned him on to folk singing. He heard her "Odetta Sings Ballads and Blues" in a record store, and next thing you know, he went out and traded his electric guitar and amplifier for an acoustic guitar, a flat-top Gibson, and learned everything she sang.

Odetta was much more far-ranging than just civil rights and protest music. She sang love songs, gospel standards, jazz tunes, the blues and show tunes. Like Josh White three years previously, the lines outside La Cave's door wound around the block, not once or twice, but every night. Twice during her stay the Fire Department stopped by to count heads, aware that the legal limit for the room was 325 persons. And while no show was stopped for overcrowding, many accounts place several of the crowds closer to 400.

As phenomenal as Odetta was, the biggest payoff from the drawing power of her personality was an unknown Canadian by the name of Gordon Lightfoot.

Welcome to the States, Mr. Lightfoot

When Ian and Sylvia asked Stan if they could bring their own opening act to La Cave the previous New Year's weekend, they might have known Gordon would be a smash. By the end of their stay, Gordon was at least as popular as the handsome couple who recommended him, and they were very popular. Stan promised Gordon a headlining spot, but then had a better idea. He'd bring Gordon back to open for another very popular headliner. Putting him in front of a large roomful of people was going to further everybody's ambitions. As fate and the schedule would have it, the first best opportunity was opening for Odetta. And by opening, it often meant closing, or doing the last set of the night while the star is off to his or her next pursuit.

Not everyone stuck around to see Gordon, having been more than satiated from Odetta's stirring sets. But more than enough souls did hang out, convincing Stan to hold Gordon over a week longer after Odetta's week. He wanted to see if Gordon had the chops to be a headliner.

"He was staying at my house and writing songs the whole time," Stan remembered about Gordon's first time at La Cave last New Year's. "He was writing this one song that he said he might play that night. When he got to it, he asked me to turn off the tape recorder. He hadn't copyrighted the song yet. As soon as he started singing, I knew he was going to be big. I turned off the tape recorder. [The song was] *Canadian Railroad Trilogy.*

In fact, years later In 1971, long after Gordon had attained stardom, he related the story in front of a rapt audience at Cleveland's Public Hall.

Gordon responded to Stan's headlining challenge by playing his ass off. Normal club sets usually lasted thirty to forty minutes, with anywhere from 5 minutes to a half an hour between sets, more time if the club is emptied for a new crowd. But typically, if there was room, early show goers were able to stick around for the later shows. Gordon had a lot to say, and sing, and rarely finished a set in under an hour. He introduced "Peaceful Waters" by telling everyone he usually only sings a couple verses of the long folk song, and then performed a 12-minute version of the song.

Near the end of his run, he took a moment to connect with his new fans: "This was the longest set of my life! This has been my first [headlining] club engagement in the States. We actually were all jammed up all last week. Of course, Odetta was here so the crowds were very big. I've gotten the privilege of singing to a lot of people in Cleveland in the last couple weeks. It has been a privilege for me to sing for you all. When we got here tonight, they were lined up to get out (chuckling) – as you can see! (audience laughs) But I'm glad to see you made it and I hope the set hasn't been too long."

Judy Henske

The stars were slowly aligning for La Cave. The future was not as big a question mark as in years previous. As the popularity of "pure" folk music began its slow decline among this next wave of music consumers, the cave's reputation as a good employer allowed them to begin stretching out in terms of their music offerings. Two signings in August of 1965 spoke to this. The first was Judy Henske who, while having begun as a solo folk singer, had made the revolutionary step of recording her 1964 album *High Flyin' Bird* with, of all things, a drummer. And not just any drummer, but one of the mainstays of the New Orleans session players soon to find uncharacteristic fame as part of Los Angeles's Wrecking Crew, Earl Palmer.

When Judy sang, people got riled up. One attendee remembers the party spilling out of the doorways, following her outside on a cigarette break, where the singin' continued for an extended period of time. It may have been a passing patrol car that cooled the temperature below boiling and got the aroused crowd safely back into the basement where the damage could be contained.

Judy's stay at La Cave, and the club's first real foray into what was quickly becoming the musical style fans were being driven to, soon to be known as folk-rock, ended on the 8th of August, but the afterparty continued for several days more. And even after the last roach grew cold and the final drop of Mogen David had been drunk, it was abundantly clear in what direction the offerings at La Cave should take. Hard on the heels of Judy Henske came another Judy, sandwiched around a six-day stay by a group that represented the more traditional sounds of the New Folk Revival acoustic presentations.

Erik Darling and the Rooftop Singers

The Rooftop Singers were another in a growing line of successful club engagements at La Cave. Comprised of 12-string guitarists Erik Darling and Bill Svanoe, they also boasted the vocal talents of jazz-oriented Lynne Taylor. Their swinging attitude had listeners stomping their feet and screaming for more, as they invited people to "Walk right in/Sit right down." On their last night in Cleveland, the band played four encores. But it was what happened next that blew the doors off of everybody's expectations.

Bob Stops By

No, not *that* Bob – although to this day people fondly, even excitedly, remember the artist formerly known as Zimmerman from Hibbing, Minnesota's memorable appearance at La Cave. Except that it never happened. He *did* play to a sold-out crowd at Cleveland's Music Hall on Friday, 12 November, prompting a sarcastic review in the local daily by Mr. Glenn C. Pullen, which in turn prompted outraged rebuttals in the form of a letters to the editor the following week from high school students.

The "Bob" that arrived a little worse for wear was the "Bad Boy of Folk," Bob Gibson. The years of constant touring and performing nightly, complete with the requisite all-nighters that followed, and the constant attention of fans had been taking a toll that began to be too heavy a burden on him. But his involvement at La Cave included an agreement that he would appear when holes in the schedule demanded. And a hole opened in September when Josh White cancelled and rescheduled for November. Bob inked a two-week stay starting 7 September – on the 7th!

Evidently Bob could not pass up the chance to make a guaranteed $1,500 per week. His income for those two weeks would translate to over $26,000 in today's buying power. His addictions were expensive in addition to being extensive.

Bob Gibson (upper right) with some cave dwellers

Bob's days as a Cavite were about to come to a conclusion. When he appeared back in June, he missed one show on the 18th and was late for two other shows, the final two days of his residency. Brian and Clark filled in, playing both opener and headliner. And now, in September, things were worse. Stan took time off from his day job to babysit Bob with disastrous results. By his own account, he was not the moderating influence he needed to be. Bob struggled through his sets. The fans in attendance were patient and supportive, but Bob was burning bridges at breakneck speed. And finally, Nelson had enough. Stan remembers, "I don't remember ever seeing [Nelson] so pissed off. I thought he was going to strangle [Bob]. He definitely wasn't going to pay him and told him so." That sobering thought gave Bob pause. "After he calmed down, we figured a way to mollify each other. We had signed Judy Collins for two days only, and so we 'asked' Bob, more of a demand really, if he would stick around after his two-week stint concluded, to introduce Judy to the audience and duet on a few numbers with her. It was the kind of chance Bob would jump at." As it turned out, Bob gave La Cave his best, sticking around a full week to packed rooms each night. Judy Collins was for the moment the antidote to what ailed Bob.

Judy, Judy, Judy

Judy Collins, like Joan Baez, had a crystal-clear voice that stopped listeners in their tracks. The clarity of her sound brought tears to the eyes of many listeners. And, she was gorgeous. After graduating from high school in Denver, she married and began performing at Michael's Pub for a hundred bucks a week and all the pizza and beer she could consume. After her husband got a teaching job at the University of Connecticut she began playing at clubs along the east coast. It didn't take long after moving to Greenwich Village that Jac Holzman signed her to his Elektra label when she was only 21, and Elektra released her debut album *Maid of Constant Sorrow* in 1961.

By 1965 Judy had released five albums, but she was still a full two years from attaining the superstar status that came with the release of her single "Both Sides Now," which earned Judy her first Grammy Award and catapulted her onto the A-list.

The opportunity to book Judy came to La Cave, not the other way around. Her manager, New York impresario Harold Leventhal, was much more famous than Judy, and was arguably one of the most highly respected managers of folk artists at the time. Harold had done business with the boys at La Cave: Erik Darling and the Rooftop Singers were clients of his. Harold had been impressed with the professionalism and vigor by which the Singers' appearance had been promoted and realized that Cleveland's growing reputation as a vital stop on the Boston-NYC-Philly-Detroit-Chicago pipeline meant profits for all concerned.

Harold had another motive: he wanted to road test the new folk-rock arrangements. He hired a bassist to accompany Judy and when Bob Gibson agreed to play 12-string guitar accompaniment, the pieces were in place. He had his office fire off several versions of press releases, something he was very good at, trumpeting Judy's "special appearances" on Wednesday the 22nd and the following evening. He made it known, much to Bob's delight, that it was Mr. Gibson who had arranged for Judy's audition for Elektra, even if it wasn't exactly true. After all, what is folk music but a dramatic retelling of historical events?

It was an early-arriving crowd on Judy's first night, and the din was as thick as the tobacco smoke that always hung suspended like some ghostly presence in the poorly-ventilated basement. While the records indicate that 247 tickets were paid for the first night and 256 the second night, by all accounts well over 300 fans packed the club each night. A lot of people near the back ended up standing on chairs or the two former church pews that adorned the back wall. That's when Bob Gibson strode out from behind the curtain stage left, approached the mic, and smiled. It took a couple of minutes of Bob standing there, mute, hands at his sides, to quiet the gang. People in front caught on and began shushing those behind them, until a tsunami of quiet engulfed the paying customers.

Bob's smile got bigger and invaded his eyes, which twinkled in the dimness. He cleared his throat for effect. He had always had an impeccable sense of timing. At the exact right moment, he began, pausing at all the right places: "This spring in April…Billboard Magazine, one of the major trade magazines, published the results of their annual Disc Jockey poll. And in the section for girl folk singers, they recognized something that I think probably we've all known for several years now…but this year…in the number one spot…the number one folk singer…girl singer…number one artist…female gender in this country…they recognized that it was Judy Collins."

"Here she is."

Judy approached the stage from the same hiding place Bob sprang from. A few whistles of appreciation spoiled the air. Dirty looks were exchanged. Quiet again descended. Everyone knew they were going to witness something special, something they could boast about to the unlucky few who stayed home. And they did.

Judy began with a smile and a nod. "Thank you very much. This is the first time that I've worked in a club for a long, long, long while. And there's something very special about it because Bob Gibson and I used to sing together, sometimes at the Gate of Horn in Chicago, in the good old days and it's a very lovely place. This is the closest thing I've seen to it. La Cave. Even the telephone operators know what you mean when you ask for La Cave. It's really funny. They have their finger on the pulse of the world, those people."

Then she launched into her first song. Evidently not wanting to spook the rapt listeners with her new-fangled sound right off the bat, she sang the 19th century whaling ballad "Bonnie Ship the Diamond" and then her version of Lydia Wood's "Anathea," the first song from her album *Judy Collins 3.* Having properly warmed up the audience, she waited for the applause to die down, and announced, "Well, it's really, uh, a storm that's raging around Bob Dylan nowadays. There was a time some years ago when a lot of people felt that topical songs were a travesty to the folk tradition and the song couldn't be written and couldn't even be sung unless it was sung with the dulcimer or possibly unaccompanied. Those rules were broken forthwith. A lot of other ones are being broken. One of my favorite songs of Dylan's is an old song that he wrote quite a while ago. Quite a bit less controversial."

Beginning with Bob's "Endless Highway," she finished the set with more modern tunes set to a fuller accompaniment than she had previously used. The folk-rock revolution was under way.

1965 was well on its way to being the most successful year in La Cave's short run, and the men in charge weren't finished impressing the growing clientele with their musical offerings. During the leadup to the holiday season, Stan brought in a double bill featuring folksinger/humorist Paul Phillips and Candy Forest, two local favorites of the basement brigade. Both had risen through the ranks of hootenanny crooners to opening acts to headliners on their own. Evidence of this climb was manifested in their pay rate. Where Candy had begun performing at the bargain rate of eight bucks and Paul not much higher, they both eclipsed the three-figure mark, with Candy earning $150 and Paul $125 for their four-day stints in November. The bills continued to be paid on time and the all-important beer deliveries continued unabated.

The stage had barely enough time to cool down from the exciting long weekend when Josh White, Sr., the once and future savior of La Cave's fortunes, happened by for his own four-day weekend run beginning on the 25th, Thanksgiving night. Once again, the line began to form well before the door opened around 5:30 as the festive crowd enjoyed the balmy 50-degree weather and, presumably, each other's company. At $1,500 for his four-night stand, the club needed in the neighborhood of six or seven hundred paying customers. Fully half that number attended Thursday's show, guaranteeing another black ink month for Nelson and staff.

Josh began each night's set by immediately launching into his crowd-favorite tune "One Meatball," the not-very-sad story of an underfunded fellow and an intimidating waiter. It was Josh's biggest hit song. In fact, the song was the first million-selling song sung by an African-American. Another fan fave was his arrangement of "House of the Rising Sun," which he had first recorded on Keynote Records in 1942.

By the time Josh White took the stage each night, the music, the camaraderie, the time of the season and, oh yeah, the beer and the weed had alchemically transformed the usually more sedate cavern creatures into wilder, less inhibited versions of themselves. And then something that rarely, if ever, happened at a folk music concert in a dim dungeon: people began to dance. It started when one tableful hopped up and began to writhe. Seconds later, seemingly half the room was happily gyrating in dance moves that were never learned by at Arthur Murray's. By the time the beer taps ran dry and the music stopped, nobody wanted to leave. Quickly, word spread about the various nearby afterparty opportunities, and when the metaphorical dust had cleared, there sat an ecstatic Stan and Nelson and their merrily exhausted helpers.

It was the kind of night they had dared dream about when visions of folk fests first danced in their heads.

You Got to Have Friends

Hometown hero Buzzy Linhart's La Cave sets were of the high energy, almost manic, variety. If he wasn't singing, he was explaining the song he just sang or the one he was about to sing. Or, he may have wandered into a Buzzy-ish stream of consciousness rap that may or may not have any connection to anything else. It didn't matter much. He always held listeners rapt. It also didn't hurt, and actually helped a great deal, that Buzzy's two accompanists, billed as the Seventh Sons, were the accomplished duo of Steve De Naut and Serge Katzen. But it was Buzzy's unique secret weapon that, above all else, that made his performances memorable to all: he was a concert-level vibraphonist.

Buzzy and Stan were having a lot of fun during Christmas week. Not only were there the concerts, but there were the afterparties at Stan's pad, where Buzzy held court nightly, after the obligatory interim stop at the Regent Bar that always lasted until closing time.

And there were the meals. On Christmas Eve and Christmas Day Stan treated Buzzy and his crew to a couple of "huge spreads" at dinnertime. "It was the first home-cooked family-style meal I'd had in probably two years. I remember it well," said Buzzy.

No sooner had Buzzy moved on than Judy Henske arrived. She had come to Cleveland a couple of days early to visit with friends and caught Buzzy's last night at La Cave on the 26th. Nelson had only placed a single ad trumpeting her six-day residency, including what had become a La Cave tradition, a New Year's Eve buffet, as well as a matinee show on the 1st. He didn't need to do any more. Reservations were so good he had a momentary thought of cutting them off. Then he regained his senses. For the low, low price of $7.50 you got your admission and an all-you-can-eat spread. The crew pulled a couple all-nighters to ready the club and ultimately served 264 dinners. This time, too, the beer cost extra.

Chapter 7:

Get Your Kicks in Sixty-Six

Cleveland ushered in the New Year with balmy weather, highs in the 50s, on the 1st and 2nd of January. But on the 3rd the thermometer plunged to zero and for the rest of the month it was a typically frigid time on the Lake Erie shore.

Out west in San Francisco, author and raconteur Ken Kesey hosted the first of his series of Acid Tests at The Fillmore, which advocated the taking of LSD, a drug which would not become illegal in the United States until 6 October, in other words, not until it changed almost everything about American popular music. From across the pond, the Beatles album *Rubber Soul hit* #1 on 8 January and remained atop the heap for six weeks.

By the end of January almost 200,000 American soldiers were stationed in Vietnam, sparking many demonstrations on American city streets. This number would explode to half a million before the end of the year. LBJ had previously announced that the US would stay until Communist aggression is ended. That didn't work out too well, by the way. Up above, Ohio native and astronaut Neil Armstrong took his first trip into outer space in the Gemini 8 capsule on 8 March, his first venture on his way to 1969's moon landing.

Tom and Jerry

They met at age 11, both growing up in the Queen's neighborhood of Flushing. Art was three weeks Paul's junior. By age 13 they were singing together. While 16-year-old students at Forest Hills High School, they played high school dances and recorded "Hey,

Schoolgirl" as the duo Tom and Jerry and experienced some very minor music success as the song hit number 49 locally. In early 1964 they wangled an audition at Columbia Records with Clive Davis, who signed them to release an album. The record company assigned an up-and-coming but still inexperienced staff producer, Tom Wilson, to oversee production of this mainly acoustic effort. This platter, too, was met with complete indifference, selling fewer than 3,000 copies. Having failed miserably and being washed up at age 22, Simon and Garfunkel disbanded their duo with Paul moving to England to suffer the life of an itinerant couch-surfing troubadour while Art continued his collegiate education at Teachers College, Columbia University.

What a Difference a Year Makes

Nineteen Sixty-Six commenced and with it came a new sound, not yet known as "folk-rock," a hybrid of folk-tinged lyrics backed by a "Beatle beat," as the leader of the Byrds, Jim McGuinn, described it. The Byrds soon came to be known as "the American Beatles." They put Bob Dylan's "Tambourine Man" in front of an arrangement that included lead and rhythm guitars, bass and drums, with some gorgeous harmony singing up front. The title single hit #1 in June. Now, Simon & Garfunkel were the next Big Thing. It was time to go out on tour. First stop, La Cave.

The Big 5 Upbeat Show

Actually, La Cave was the duo's fourth stop in Cleveland on Saturday, 22 January, but their first completely live stage appearance in support of their hot-off-the-presses album. No sooner had they arrived in town than they were spirited off to the WEWS-TV studios at the corner of Euclid Avenue and East 30th Street around noon to tape a "live" show which actually wouldn't air until later that afternoon at 5pm, which was good because the boys hadn't eaten all morning. Stan Kain was there to see the duo sing "Sound of Silence" to a small roomful of shaky mod-clothed dancers and the two large cameras of the Big 5/Upbeat TV show, and then commence chaperone duty for the two 24-year-olds. The New York City boys wanted a real city-style meal, so Stan took them where he took almost everyone, to Sunny Solomon's joint, Solomon's Deli on nearby East 105th Street.

Pleasantly sated, the trio took a quick swing over to Stan's pad to freshen up and relax a bit before their unadvertised gig at La Cave. A small mention in the previous day's *Plain Dealer,* coupled with having a hit record and a TV appearance guaranteed a crowd big enough that some (it turned out to be many) would have to be turned away.

Fans and performers alike descended the same set of stairs into La Cave. No one recalls seeing the duo arrive, guitars in hand, but no one forgets hearing the freshly-pressed album *Sounds of Silence* played in its entirety. The night of the 22 January was perhaps the quietest the sometimes boisterous La Cave crowd ever was. Stan recalls the reverie the two buttoned-down young men commanded from their perch atop La Cave's well-worn stage treads. Even though there was barely room to take a deep breath, the crowd was packed in so tightly, no one recalls the slightest disturbance as the boys plowed through their two half-hour sets. When the house lights came on and the 602 paying fans, not to mention the few dozen freeloaders, dispersed into the wintry Cleveland breezes, the not-yet-existent Rock and Roll Hall of Fame had itself two more future nominees.

The Mayor Drops By

January 1966 also witnessed the first of half a dozen or so appearances in the cave by the so-called Mayor of MacDougal Street, Dave Van Ronk. So-called because, just as the intersection of Bleeker and MacDougal Streets was the epicenter of Greenwich Village, so too was Dave the epicenter of all things folkie in that neighborhood. As Bob Dylan described him, "Van Ronk was king of the street, he reigned supreme." Dave cut an imposing figure just walking down the street. He collected followers like dogs collect fleas, and shed them with equal difficulty. He had a stare that could freeze you solid, and melt you just as quickly as he twinkled his eyes and broke into one of his disarming, almost shy, smiles.

At La Cave, Dave left nothing out of his performances. He ended each night drenched in sweat, his creased face having aged visibly by the conclusion of each set. The two nights he played La Cave were the polar opposite of Simon & Garfunkel's turn. Dave's wasn't the only hoarse voice in the room when the singalongs ebbed into violent, extended and appreciative applause.

The afterparties, both nights, have become legendary, even if the details are hazy. Everything about Dave Van Ronk was larger than life.

It Takes a Village

Sometime in early February Stan traded the snowdrifts of Cleveland for the slush of New York City streets. He was a busy man for four or five days, taking in at least a dozen shows and hanging out afterwards at the various watering holes frequented by itinerant folkies and their meager entourages. At one club he was introduced to Arthur Gorson, who was in the infancy of his almost six decades at the top of the music and film producing heap. Like Stan, had a keen eye for talent. They hit it off.

Stan also met with agent Herb Gart, whose first foray into the folk music universe was helping a young Alix Dobkin get some gigs around the Village before she signed with Len Rosenfeld. At the time of Stan's meeting him, Herb repped Patrick Sky, Jesse Colin Young, Don McLean, and a few others. By the turn of the century Herb's artists would have at least four albums routinely listed on "best record" lists. Stan signed Patrick and Jesse.

The template for a successful year was set: booking premium acts for weekend gigs and filling in weekdays with local artists. The result was lowered operating costs without much of a drop-off in attendance. And while that meant that getting into La Cave on a weeknight only set you back a buck, Stan and Nelson both knew that the profits didn't come from the door as much as from the beer and snack trade. It turned out that no matter the onstage events, the patrons consumed the same number of potables. And truth be told, since pot was also a major influence on folk music aficionados, having a roomful of thirsty, hungry and high youngsters was a tidy recipe for profit.

Freddie and Albert

Stan booked Fred Neil for the first weekend in April. On 27 March, La Cave's *Plain Dealer* ad boasted that Fred would make his first Cleveland appearance. They misspelled his name and his record label. Then, in a cruel twist of fate, the ballyhooed weekend appearance by Freddie downstairs on Euclid became an unfunny April Fool's joke. Fred never showed. Said Stan, "I called everyone in New York I knew. Nelson hit the roof when he saw our long-distance phone bill. Nobody knew where Fred was, but no one seemed surprised. Finally I ran out of phone numbers, so I called Gusti and someone else, I forget who, and they filled in. Luckily for us, only half or so of the people with reservations decided not to pay up and stick around."

Nelson did a little detective work and found out that due to his extracurricular activities, Fred had been in no shape or inclination to drive to Cleveland. Unlike Stan, Nelson had a hardnosed business side. He might have threatened a lawsuit or wielded some other such lever, but whatever the reason, Fred agreed to come to town and play for a full six days instead of two in mid-July, from the 19th through the 24th. That appearance, too, would be preempted by even more disastrous events beyond anyone's imagination or control.

Getting free-jazz proponent Albert Ayler to bring his jazz combo to La Cave would be strategic for reasons that had nothing whatsoever to do with music or cheap beer. And it was all luck. Albert would attract a primarily Black audience, unlike Josh White and other more mainstream African-American folksingers, since folk music was still, primarily, "white" music. And while the thought leaders at La Cave had always been color-blind, preferring green to black or white, patrons and the neighborhood alike were well aware of the racial tensions produced by integrated establishments in the year immediately following passage of the Civil Rights Act. More crucial than the expanded customer base was the reputation that La Cave was truly an equal opportunity establishment. In the fickle world of entertainment, there was no substitute for a stellar reputation.

Stan desperately wanted to make the most of the last month of school and collegiate pocketbooks. And he had another problem. Tom Paxton had cancelled due to illness and been rescheduled for the following week. That left a three-day weekend hole in the schedule, which would be devastating to the bottom line. Having headliners cancel two weeks out of three was bad mojo for any music club. Vicious tongues would wag. Stan again began working the phone. He got a hold of Dick Wedler, who agreed to play. Dick was popular but was no headliner. As the hours ticked away, Stan almost got nervous. He had told Dick that he'd be the opening act if Stan could land a headliner, but the odds against that happening were getting long. And then, just like that, his dilemma disappeared. Albert Ayler walked down the stairs, looking for a place for his jazz combo to rehearse. That allowed Stan to play spider to Albert's fly. The two days Albert's band played were historic, and a story better told in Richard Koloda's book, *Spiritual Unity*.[xxxii]

In addition to the headliners in spring and early summer, opening for the main weekend acts were, in no particular order, David Budin, Toni Dell, Gusti, The South Shore 4, Pinky & Jim, Jim Craig and Reeve Little (as the Double Exposures), Dave Barabach, Sherry Salisbury, Mike Johnson, Diana Joy, Paul Phillips, Rick Curtis, Gusti & Sean, Joanie Kent, Dick Wedler and Chuck Mitchell. Yes, *that* Chuck Mitchell, who had recently married an unknown Canadian folkie named Joanie Anderson. She wouldn't remain unknown much longer.

But there were a handful of bookings for midsummer that would propel La Cave into its future, all being electric bands based more in rock and blues, but with folk music influences. You know, folk-rock acts. The landscape was shifting around the music world, and the clubs and record labels quickest to respond to the subtle changes in listening trends would be the most successful, all other things being equal. Stan signed New York City's Blues Project for a date in late June, Terry Knight & the Pack for July and Jesse Colin Young and the Youngbloods for August. Terry Knight would return in September and the Blues Project in November, sandwiched around an October appearance by the Blues Magoos. And Jesse Colin Young would bring his band back to ring in the new year.

None of this was going to be cheap. Nelson told a reporter that the summer's talent will cost approximately $15,000. Somehow, Nelson was banking on the notion that his favorite folk club would attract in the neighborhood of 7,000 paying customers or more in the dozen-weekend summer stretch. Whether this was hubris or confidence would soon be revealed.

Tom Rush

Tom Rush at La Cave, 1966

Tom Rush's first night at La Cave was rather sparse, under a hundred, so Stan decided to let anyone wishing to stick around to do so. It was usually good business. Often, for obvious reasons, a fuller room meant a more exciting show, which led to higher attendance down the road. La Cave's attendance policy was, to say the least, informal. Later on, when Larry Bruner took on management duties, he proclaimed, "No longer do the words 'I'm a friend of Stan's' get you in the room." Tom's 4 March concert marked one of the last times Stan'd be so lenient. In a testament to the power of the grapevine, between his first and second set, news of a great show being missed traveled from the dank basement to the surrounding environs. Tom's second set was standing room only, and understandably there were upset patrons who came early to the second set, only to find all the up-front tables taken. Tom Rush knew how to get a crowd's attention, however. As the crowd got more boisterous, he walked onto the stage from behind the curtain, stepped to the mic empty-handed, turned to look back from where he had just appeared, and hollered, "Bring out the naked lady!" Instantly, order was restored as youthful imaginations were piqued.

Out from the backstage area appeared an employee holding an Epiphone Texan guitar with an interesting inlay of a shapely woman's silhouette and a snake on the fretboard and handed it to Tom, who thanked him. "Meet the naked lady," Tom smiled as he held up the instrument. For the next 40 minutes or so he had the rapt attention of the room. And the attention was worth it, as Tom would "road test" some of the high-quality songs he was considering for his upcoming album, including rocked-up versions of Bo Diddley's "Who Do You Love?" and Willie Dixon's "You Can't Tell a Book by Its Cover."

When the performance ended, a sizable percentage headed directly for the Regent Bar and other oases like Adele's down the street, ultimately to gather after hours at Stan's pad to relive the night and partake in each other's bonhomie.

Chapter 8: Changes

As spring sprung on the dirty streets of Cleveland and dandelions made their annual appearance in the cracks of sidewalks, March's dirty slush gave way to April's monsoons. The next nine headliners were all solo acoustic acts (except for the acoustic duos Jim & Jean and Gusti & Sean): Tom Paxton, Jim & Jean, Eric Andersen, Patrick Sky, José Feliciano, Phil Ochs, Gusti & Sean, Judy Henske and a rescheduled Fred Neil all plied their trade standing solo, or with sparse accompaniment, onstage. And then, a sea change was poised to take place. As Stan modestly told it, he was no Wizard of Oz behind a curtain and didn't really have a master plan. "I just booked bands I liked," he would often say. This was especially ironic, since he had borne the mantle of "Resident Wizard" since his earliest days at the helm. But it was much more than chance that of the next eleven headliners booked into October, five of them were full bands. What had started as a trickle became a deluge as folkies all around the country followed the electric trail blazed by Dylan, McGuinn, and seemingly everyone else. Acoustic music had had its place near the top of popular taste since the late 50s, when rock & roll "died."[xxxiii] But a few years later, after the Beatles had changed everything and the music world struggled to keep up, rock & roll became "rock" and began to fragment into discreet styles. Soon, the music-consuming public would begin to categorize the songs they liked into all the hyphenated pigeonholes of pop music. A year from now, the emergence of FM radio would further subdivide listeners.

After Tom Rush began spring's lineup in April with his "naked lady" routine, Jim & Jean brought their revamped folk-rock routine to the basement. They had one album on the Phillips label and were about to go into the recording studio for their sophomore effort. They mixed originals in with covers by, at the time, little-known David Blue, Phil Ochs and the next singer to grace La Cave's stage, Eric Andersen. To complement their burgeoning taste from acoustic to electric, they brought a harpsichordist with them, and began their opening night set with Andersen's "Tonight I Need our Lovin'," always a fan fave. After running through a couple of Phil Ochs covers, the couple launched into two harrowing tunes: David Blue's atmospheric "Stranger in a Strange Land" and Phil's nine-minute cinematic retelling of the Kennedy assassination, "Crucifixion." They followed with a couple Glover originals and the Jean Ray-penned "One Sure Thing" before sending everyone home happy with their wonderful harmonies delivering Blue's "About My Love" and Bob Dylan's "Lay Down Your Weary Tune." Not that everyone went directly home.

Eric Andersen

The 20th of May brought another newcomer to the La Cave stage, although Eric Andersen was already making a name for himself elsewhere. His biography reads like a fictional itinerant troubadour's tale except for the tiny detail that it is true.

Eric Andersen at La Cave

His first New York gig, at Gerde's Folk City, was attended by the estimable New York Times music critic Robert Shelton, the same Robert Shelton whose superlative review of Bob Dylan had brought that young man to national attention. He was equally impressed by Eric, peppering his review with similar superlatives.

Soon after Eric took the stage at La Cave on Friday, 20 May, he asked if anyone was planning on attending next month's Newport Folk Festival. The previous year's festival was, of course, notorious for hosting Dylan's electric "conversion." A few hands rose. He mentioned that he had been invited and was saving some new songs for that appearance, eliciting some good-natured hoots before he let himself be talked into playing songs he had always intended on playing anyway. Gusti, who opened for Eric with her partner Sean, recalled with warmth how gracious he was to the crowd and saw what Shelton, Stan and the stalwarts of the cave saw: a raw talent being honed to a razor's edge in front of their eyes. His performances had, by accounts, a seductive quality that swept you up in its grasp and never let you down.

José Redux

José Feliciano was already a crowd pleaser with his virtuoso guitar skills, his wicked and sometimes off-color sense of humor, his gorgeous songs and his playful manner. For a young man who had yet to experience his twenty-first birthday, he had developed into a seasoned stage performer. He was still a full two years from stardom and the international acclaim and Grammy Award that his 1968 release *Feliciano!* would garner. Remembering with delight how well-received José had been during his previous appearances (he had been held over for a full week in 1965), Stan went off his new formula of weekend bookings at nabbed José for eight days in mid-June.

José's between song patter was always almost as much a highlight of his turn onstage as his songs were. Almost. "I'd like to welcome you all to La Cave. It's so great to see such a large crowd on such a rainy night. I'd like to play a tune for the pretty girls…I'll play a song for the other ones later."

"This is a song for a young lady who asked for it. The song, that is." José played a song in Spanish, then another impromptu La Cave commercial, then Ivory Joe Hunter's "Since I Met You, Baby." "C'mon, guitar, talk to me!" In between each song he'd play the Stones' "Satisfaction" guitar lick. Finally he played the entire song, substituting his own words wholesale. "I'm going to play my guitar at Newport wearing gloves, for the folk hipsters." Out of nowhere: "Is it OK if I take my shoes off?" Then, in his best Bob Dylan voice and to the tune of "Don't Think Twice," he crooned "Well, it ain't no use to for you to start to sing, Bob/it doesn't matter anyhow/It ain't no use for you to start to sing, Bob/you sound lousy anyhow." And then he made sure that everyone knew it was all meant in good, clean fun. "You should see Bob imitate me." And then the blind singer clumsily "accidentally" knocked over the mic stand with his guitar, to raucous laughter.

Over 1,300 people attended the six nights for which records exist, so José' averaged over 200 patrons each of his eight nights in the cave, making his run one of La Cave's most successful yet.

Rounding out the lineup heading into the July 4th holiday were mainstays Phil Ochs and, separately, Judy Henske. Phil had just released his third album, *Phil Ochs in Concert*, and Judy had dropped her fourth solo record *The Death Defying Judy Henske*.

Mister, You're a Better Man Than I

Former Flint, Michigan, DJ Terry Knight was a talented, charismatic dynamo, and was happiest when self-promoting. His new band, the Jazz Masters, quickly assented to changing their name to Terry Knight & the Pack in recognition of Terry's leadership qualities and music business contacts. When the Rolling Stones played in front of 17,000 screaming teens at Detroit's Cobo Hall, his Pack was the opener. Same thing when the Yardbirds played Flint's IMA Auditorium – the Pack opened. They also heard the song that would become their first and only regional number one record. That song was "Mister, You're a Better Man Than I."

Stan Kain and Terry Knight at La Cave ca. 1966

How popular was Terry Knight & the Pack in Cleveland? Due in equal parts to Terry's promotional ability and the band's talent, they became semi-regulars on Cleveland TV's nationally syndicated Upbeat Show. They hit #1 in Cleveland with a song the Yardbirds made popular everywhere else. And they played La Cave not once but many times. Guitarist Mark Farner and drummer Don Brewer would go on to become two-thirds of Grand Funk Railroad and experience sustained international fame with Terry as their manager. But in 1966 they were still fissile material in Stan Kain's test tube. The fans ate it up. The gaggle of folk music purists hoping for some sea chanties and murderer ballads, not so much. But they were respectful, as folk audiences are wont to be.

After Judy Henske rang in the 4th of July and Double Exposure filled up the first half of July's bills, Paul Phillips came back for a return engagement from the 12th through the 17th with Joanie Kent opening. But everyone was on the metaphoric edge of their seat awaiting the ballyhooed appearance on the 19th of Freddie Neil, who had no-showed in April.

And Then All Hell Broke Loose

In a decade marked by supersonic change both musically and geopolitically, the effects felt from events in 1966 topped anything the tumultuous decade had yet thrown into the path of history's tornado, and in midsummer Cleveland made the kind of news no city ever wanted to. While the country's past is littered with the refuse of countless race riots, Cleveland had never witnessed anything like what the city endured from 18 to 23 July, when, after a minor racial incident in a local bar, the Hough neighborhood erupted into violence and flames, and La Cave was situated at the southeast corner of the neighborhood. Gunfire claimed four lives. Millions of dollars in damage and hundreds of fires caused by looters reduced large swaths of the neighborhood to rubble. Fortunately, the fact that La Cave had from the start been a gathering place for integrated crowds probably went far in insuring that it wasn't a target of violence.

The effects of the riots, and the complex set of circumstances leading up to them, became a slow-motion dagger to La Cave's heart, which, like many other inner-city businesses, saw a long, slow, permanent decline as flight to the suburbs took on, for many citizens, an imperative. Most of those residents prosperous enough to move further out of the inner city already had done so, further segregating the city. Poverty and racism were rampant, and were the proximate causes of the riots, regardless of the widely-debunked grand jury findings that the affair was a Communist plot.[xxxiv]

Commies or no, the immediate effect was panic. Nelson asked Stan to make sure no one associated with the club went anywhere near it, including Stan, who was only too happy to comply, not that it mattered. No one was going clubbing for a while. Once again, Fred Neil would not appear.

The riot ended on Saturday the 23rd, and torrential rains kept people indoors on Sunday. Slowly, the city pulled itself as upright as it could. Scores of homes and businesses no longer existed. Rubble and refuse lay in piles and swirled up and down the deserted streets. Blame was being liberally tossed about to no great effect. Slowly, as religious and civic leaders called for calm, the city began to cool off. Slightly. "Hough cast a pall of fear and resentment that took years to dissipate, if it ever truly passed", said Michael Roberts, who covered the Hough Riots as a reporter in 1966.[xxxv]

In a rather small miracle, La Cave was untouched except for a kicked-in front door. Nothing had been taken or broken. The band equipment that was always being stored for one outfit or another was intact. Which was a good thing since the next ten weekends had already been booked. Tom Rush was back for what should have been a triumphant return based on the success of his recent residency. No records of attendance or monies collected exist and no one remembered any details of his weekend, but he did cash the $450 check that Stan wrote him on 31 July.

The Shows Must Go On

Go on they did. Fans responded to Tom Rush's "I Don't Want Your Millions, Mister," and Josh White's "One Meatball," songs describing the pain of poverty, Jesse Colin Young's take on Chester Powers' immortal "Get Together," which became the unofficial anthem of the '60s peace movement, Tom Paxton's biting song protesting the escalation or troops in Vietnam "Lyndon Johnson Told the Nation," Dave Van Ronk's ode to those who have passed, "He Was a Friend of Mine," Odetta's plea against racism, "Oh, Freedom," which she sang at Dr. King's March on Washington, Judy Collins' call to revolution "Marat Sade" and Bob Gibson's screeds against militarism "One More Parade" and "Too Many Martyrs,' both co-written with Phil Ochs. Speaking of Phil, his "I Ain't a-Marchin' Anymore," a song detailing the history of American wars and this generation's refusal to participate in them, was sung, like "Get Together," by almost everyone. The times continued to change. Bob Dylan's lyrics were being lived in real time at La Cave and Cleveland, and in clubs and cities coast to coast: "There was music in the cafes at night and revolution in the air."

Captain Trips

In 1966 Congress passed the Drug Abuse Control Amendment, which banned the individual manufacturing or sale of LSD and other hallucinogens. The law only allowed legitimate manufacturing, distribution, and use in research and medical situations. While illegal manufacturing and sale could be prosecuted, the law did not address personal possession of the drug. Personal use of LSD was still not punishable under the law as long as the individual was not making or selling the drug.

Street drugs and alcohol of all types have always been around, but there was an explosion of drug use in the years La Cave existed. La Cave's clientele, not to put too fine a point on it, was young, white, middle-class Americans. This era provided the perfect storm for rampant drug use, the complex set of reasons for which are better explained elsewhere. Whether people brought drugs with them, or got them from friends after arriving, or bought them on the street, is irrelevant. Drug use was rampant. There were societal pressures as well as personal ones. Teenaged boys were reminded through the daily news that their time in the barrel, so to speak, was fast approaching. The military draft took nineteen-year-olds, which gave rise to the lyrics in Eve of Destruction: "You're old enough to kill/But not for votin'." There were escapes from this danger, but many of the cures were scarier than the disease. Fleeing the country, going underground, sudden allergies, asthma attacks and a healthy aversion to violence were debated endlessly. Importantly, the heavyweight boxing world-champion Muhammad Ali was drafted in 1966 and refused induction on the grounds of conscientious objection, saying in part, "Why should they ask me to put on a uniform and go ten thousand miles from home and drop bombs and bullets on brown people in Vietnam while so-called Negro people in Louisville are treated like dogs and denied simple human rights?" Ali gave hope and strength to the anti-draft movement. After all, if a tough guy like Ali could resist the draft, there was less of a stigma on others who followed his lead.

The marriage of music and acid quickly sent bands in search of ways to recreate the sonic experiences they and their fans had while "tripping," and it inspired club owners to look for the kinds of bands that would interest this new demographic: "turned on" kids. The upside was new music, new fans, new profits. There was a downside to attracting the trade of drug-consuming youths, and it was going to either make La Cave stronger or kill it. First it did one, then the other.

The Blues Magoos

Meanwhile, back at La Cave, the Blues Magoos stretched out lead guitarist Mike Esposito's distorted guitar jam for a good twenty-five minutes on their incendiary cover of the John C. Loudermilk classic "Tobacco Road," and just like that, La Cave transformed from its quaint black-and-white period into, as NBC might have put it, full living color. The mural on the back wall exhorting the crowd inside to "Feed Your Head" took on new, mystical meanings, individualized for each patron according to their personal level of psychedelicness. It just so happened that La Cave was one of those places where for an extra dollar that guy in the back would slip you a hit of Orange Sunshine or, if you had five bucks, a nickel bag, complete with a package of Zig Zag rolling papers. No one remembers that Detroit-born acoustic player Chuck Mitchell was the opener for the Magoos' weekend or that his wife, now known as Joni Mitchell, accompanied him to the club, but not onstage.

California, always ahead of the curve, declared LSD illegal to possess on 6 October, 1966. A national law against possession was in the works and would soon follow.

What's in a Name?

Eagle-eyed veterans of the "Business Opportunities" section of the classified ads did not miss the three-week run of an ad in June of 1966 promising free rent for the first month for a 15-foot by 86-foot store front at 2122 South Taylor, "up the hill" in Cleveland Heights. As summer faded into fall, word of mouth let it be known that soon, live music would have another venue on the east side of town. A couple small display ads popped up as well, touting appearances by the Grasshoppers on Friday, 9 September and the Shadows of Knight the following day, with the Tree Stomps (sic) on the 30th and the Rationals, from Detroit, on Saturday, 1 October. The name of the new club caused more than a few double takes. It was… "The Cave."

The décor of The Cave showed artistic originality. It looked like a cave. Nelson Karl was not amused. *He* was the cave man, not these Johnny-come-latelies, trying to make a buck off all the groundwork laid over the previous four and one-half years of risky behavior. He pounced. And the wheels of justice spun a lot more quickly in '66 than they do today. On the following Monday, 10 October, Nelson made a couple of phone calls to The Cave with no apparent reaction, and by the end of business had secured a court date two weeks hence to adjudicate this apparent name theft.

When you awoke on Thursday, the 27th of October, gulped down your coffee and slugged it out with the morning newspaper, you found out that La Cave's popularity and success had not gone unnoticed. The courts had found in short order that the only true cave was La Cave. Had the proprietors on South Taylor been paying closer attention, they would have realized that it was the quality of the music, not the ambience of the venue, that kept 'em coming back in ever-growing numbers. The Cave (not to be confused with La Cave) tried to soldier on, but after changing their name to The Cavern and hosting local bands Tree Stumps, Kicks Inc., Richie & the Fortunes and, finally, Muther's Oats on 18 November, they quietly folded their tent and faded into obscurity.

Koop

Stan Kain sat attentively, sipping his orange soda pop while his new acquaintance Al Kooper regaled him with rock-n-roll stories after a Greenwich Village show in late fall 1966. After the stranger-than-fiction events of the summer of '65, the stories he spun were probably mostly true. Stan had just taken in a gig by the Blues Project, Al Kooper's latest band, at the Café Au Go Go. Their concerts were selling out night after night and their style encompassed a lot of influences besides folk and rock. There was blues, r&b, and an original blend of styles. While on the west coast promoting their first album, the Blues Project had played to a large, enthusiastic crowd at the Fillmore Auditorium, including members of the Grateful Dead, who were thoroughly entertained. Now that their second long player was in the can, it was time to hit the road once again, leaving the friendly confines of the Village to ply their trade in the hinterlands. Stan wanted to make certain that La Cave was on the band's itinerary.

Don't Count Us Out Just Yet

On the other hand, Nelson and Stan had no thought of biting it by forsaking the folkies who sustained La Cave throughout its growing pains. Folkies got them where they were, and solo acoustic players were still the most affordable acts around. Consequently, the remainder of 1966 offered mostly these soloists, everyone a battle-tested draw in the cozy confines that was La Cave. The week before the Blues Project camped out at La Cave, Jim & Jean popped in for a brief, well-attended two-day appearance. The roomful of listeners thoroughly enjoyed their sets, which included covers of a number of Phil Ochs' songs, including duetting on the beautiful "Changes," which began the set. Then, Jean took the lead on Phil's "Flower Lady" and David Blue's "About My Love," and then they both shared Blue's ethereally spooky "Strangers in a Strange Land" before their always-popular 12-minute closing tune, the Ochs-penned "Crucifixion."

The weeks following Al Kooper's gang saw Eric Andersen, Phil Ochs, Terry Knight & the Pack, Eric Andersen again, Ramblin' Jack Elliott, Tom Paxton, and Jim & Jean once more, over Christmas, before Jesse Colin Young and his band the Youngbloods sang out the old and rang in the new. This New Year's Eve shindig included an all you can eat buffet for the low, low price of $7.50 and, once again, the watery but ever-popular three-two beer was available at an extra charge. Stalwarts Gusti and Sean performed yeoman duty by serving as the de facto house opening act for fully half of these shows.

Chapter 9:

1967 - Brave New World

In Cleveland, the new year began with a series of weather extremes that played havoc with scheduling shows. The January thermometer dipped to zero or below on seven days, but contrariwise, the mercury topped fifty on seven other days. Clevelanders affectionately call these mid-winter temperature swings "flu season." At local clubs, James Brown and the Famous Flames dropped by the Cleveland Arena on New Year's Day, it was a Go Go Tonite at the Columbia Ballroom featuring the Baskerville Hounds, and the Temptin' Temptations announced a six-day residency at Leo's Casino beginning 12 January, supported by Gladys Knight and every last one of her Pips.

Acknowledging the changing musical landscape was foremost on Nelson's and Stan's minds as the met to discuss the year's lineup. Although they were heartened by the fact that 1966 had been their best year, based on attendance, receipts and feedback, both were still apprehensive about their ability to afford to pay full bands and support them technically. After all, although most of their bills were paid, neither one of them had taken their meager salary since the beginning, with a few exceptions. Both Stan and Nelson were still making $75 a week nominally, but the total owed to them increased weekly by that same amount. Thankfully, both men had day jobs to support their volunteer efforts at what amounted to a hobby, albeit an exciting and important one.

A number of acts had already been booked for early '67. Canadian folkie and sometimes-Shakespearean actor Cedric Smith was booked for the first weekend of January and then the Blues Project came back for a week. Then Dave Van Ronk, Terry Knight & the

Pack, John Hammond & His Screaming Night Hawks, Michigan's Southbound Freeway, Tom Rush, David Blue & the American Patrol, the Reverend Gary Davis, Spider John Koerner, the Baskerville Hounds, and teenager Arlo Guthrie rounded out the first three months of the year. Six of these acts had feet, and amplifiers, firmly planted in the rock or folk-rock camp. Gusti & Sean, Candy Forest and Dick Wedler opened for a number of these acts and also performed on weekdays. And although the main acts still played to sparse crowds on Sundays, the fortunes of La Cave continued to look up. Attendance for the winter shows averaged over a hundred and fifty, with two-thirds or more of that total getting raked in on Friday and Saturdays. On the rest of the days of the week Nelson and Stan took turns biting their fingernails to the nub.

Flexing those same fingers on the fancy Selectric typewriter in his office, Nelson used up several pages in vain attempts at a clever opening for the year's first newsletter. His conservative nature won out over several more smart-alecky openings:

To all Folk Music Fans:[xxxvi]

In keeping with our tradition of the finest in folk entertainment, La

Cave is very proud to present its early 1967 schedule. We are featuring the "blues" as performed by some of the oldest and youngest spokesmen and also the new electric groups. Reservations can be made by calling 231-9405.

In fifty elegant words, Nelson used the same impressive communication skills he had hoped to a razor's edge in front of juries during closing arguments. He covered every single important point without exaggeration or humility. La Cave had become much more than a "folk" club. Like Dylan "going electric," not every patron was pleased. The purists always have found something to complain about, but the lineup had plenty of acoustic, folky acts to appeal to them, too.

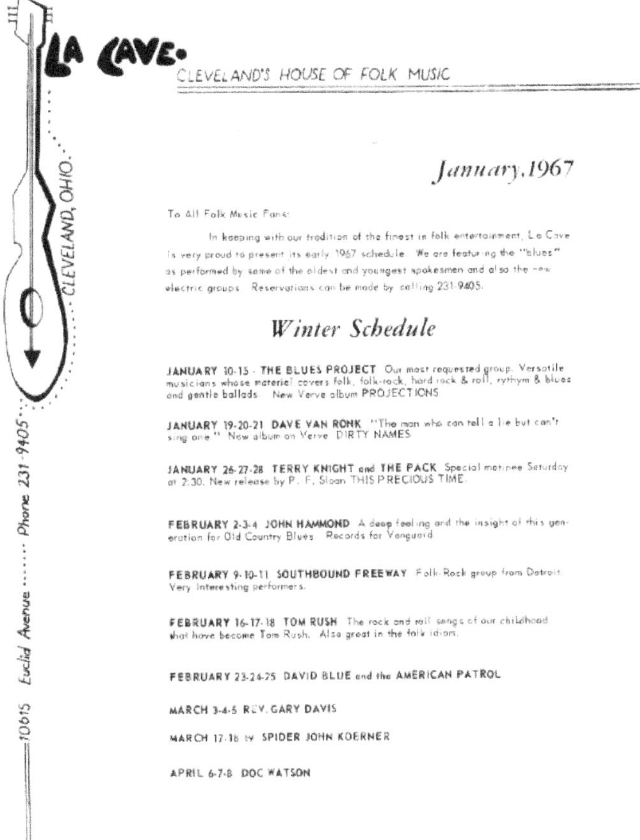

LA CAVE
CLEVELAND'S HOUSE OF FOLK MUSIC

10615 Euclid Avenue .... Phone 231-9405 .... CLEVELAND, OHIO.

January, 1967

To All Folk Music Fans:

In keeping with our tradition of the finest in folk entertainment, La Cave is very proud to present its early 1967 schedule. We are featuring the "blues" as performed by some of the oldest and youngest spokesmen and also the new electric groups. Reservations can be made by calling 231-9405.

Winter Schedule

JANUARY 10-15 - THE BLUES PROJECT Our most requested group. Versatile musicians whose material covers folk, folk-rock, hard rock & roll, rythym & blues and gentle ballads. New Verve album PROJECTIONS

JANUARY 19-20-21 DAVE VAN RONK "The man who can tell a lie but can't sing one." New album on Verve DIRTY NAMES

JANUARY 26-27-28 TERRY KNIGHT and THE PACK Special matinee Saturday at 2:30. New release by P. F. Sloan THIS PRECIOUS TIME.

FEBRUARY 2-3-4 JOHN HAMMOND A deep feeling and the insight of this generation for Old Country Blues. Records for Vanguard

FEBRUARY 9-10-11 SOUTHBOUND FREEWAY Folk-Rock group from Detroit. Very Interesting performers.

FEBRUARY 16-17-18 TOM RUSH The rock and roll songs of our childhood that have become Tom Rush. Also great in the folk idiom.

FEBRUARY 23-24-25 DAVID BLUE and the AMERICAN PATROL

MARCH 3-4-5 REV. GARY DAVIS

MARCH 17-18 ty SPIDER JOHN KOERNER

APRIL 6-7-8 DOC WATSON

La Cave Newsletter, January 1967

C'mon, People, Smile on Your Brother

After his New Year's Day show, Jesse Colin Young left town and abandoned over nine hundred paying patrons from his stint over the long New Year's weekend, plus three more days leading up Saturday, New Year's Eve, perfect timing for the big shindig. Two hundred and thirty-five aficionados of the "new" folk-rock sound paid $7.50 on New Year's Eve alone, enjoying a fine buffet feast from Alesci's Italian market on Kinsman Road, including fried chicken, potato salad, baked beans, coleslaw and a relish tray, plus two deep vats of sausage and meatballs smothered in marinara sauce and Alesci's famed crusty Italian bread rolls. Topping things off for those still unsatiated types were custard puffs and assorted pastry delights.

The band kicked things off with a rockin' version of the former folk song "Get Together." They also closed each show with a folkier version. "Get Together" has as interesting a backstory as any song could boast. Written in 1964 by a cat named Chester Powers, better known in the years to come as Dino Valenti, it languished off the charts until 1969, when it was used in a radio public service announcement as a call for brotherhood by the National Conference of Christians and Jews. The exposure from the commercial caused the Youngbloods to re-release the single, and it shot up to #5 on the national parts, and has forever since been known as the '60s anthem of peace and brotherhood.

But the song's story has a modern twist to it as well. In the wake of the 9/11 attack, Clear Channel Communications, the media conglomerate, listed it on its list of "lyrically questionable" songs for its over 1,200 radio stations. Because, obviously, smiling on your brother and loving one another have always been subversive activities.

The Winter of Love

Stan showed the love to Danny Kalb and his merry men the Blues Project, signing them for a six-day stint beginning 10 January, for $2,500, or just under $21,000 in today's buying power.[xxxvii] This pay rate signified several interconnected facts and conjectures going forward. One was that electric acts were here to stay. Another was that La Cave was becoming a money-maker. It also illustrated the fact that a larger venue could make more money on fewer days. Yet another fact exposed was that Stan was, indeed, a soft touch, something not lost on Nelson, who sat down with Stan sometime in January to discuss the cost of entertainment in this brave new world of full bands. Stan remembers how concerned Nelson was when he confronted Stan with the figure that January's entertainment alone was costing him about six grand!

The *Plain Dealer* heralded the change in direction that La Cave's entertainment when they informed their readership not to expect to hear anything folksy at La Cave for a while, since it has turned its stage over to Terry Knight and his pack of rock-n-rollers.

Terry Knight, for his part, brought his Pack for three days beginning the 26th of the month. Stamping the snow off their boots along with Terry came bassist Herman Jackson, drummer Donny Brewer, guitarist Curt Johnson and organist Bobby Jean Caldwell. Mark Farner, who had temporarily replaced Herman on bass the previous year, had yet to officially join the band. In what certainly was unintentional irony as far as La Cave was concerned, the band opened their sets with a song they had released in '66 as a single, "A Change on the Way," a slow-paced psychedelic ballad with lyrics that reflected the battle between the adults of the country and their kids: "Is it true what the people say/About the way things are going today?" Without skipping a beat, they wailed directly into their next song, a speeded-up, full rock & roll treatment of the Stones' "Satisfaction," another anthem to youthful discontent. As the first eight notes of what is now considered the single most memorable rock guitar lick ever rang out from Curt Johnson's fuzzed-out guitar, heads began to explode. By the time the song ended, it was close to bedlam. Two hundred and twenty-five rowdy patrons sounded like three times that many during an extended applause after the show openers. Forty minutes later a sweat-drenched and nearly exhausted band hightailed it to the green room for some much-needed liquid libation. By the end of their long weekend, they had performed in front of over seven hundred paying customers, and probably another fifty or so "friends of the band." Over a thousand bucks had been grossed on beer and chips alone. The fact that the band was almost a regular on WEWS-TV 5's Upbeat Show, which aired Saturdays at 5pm, plus the high energy level of their performances pretty much guaranteed full houses, or close to it.

Midwinter in Cleveland shivered along. In smooth succession as frigid January thawed into merely chilly February came a handful of celebrated folkies – the ones the *Pee Dee* thought had been forsaken - down those stairs and onto the stage, all of who sprang from the New York connections Stan had massaged. Dave Van Ronk, "Johnny" Hammond, Tom Rush and David Blue blew through town in quick succession.

At the time of his signing a contract to perform at La Cave, the younger Hammond was going by "Johnny" and he wasn't without accomplishments of his own. Known around the Village as "the white Robert Johnson," he had already recorded four albums on his way to thirty-four long player releases and a Grammy Award. He had already done something significant and unique, although at the time it was barely noticed. While knocking around New York in the summer of '66, Johnny was approached by a young left-handed blues guitar slinger who, between gigs, had asked

Johnny if he could help him out. Johnny put together an ad hoc band he named the Screaming Night Hawks and installed Jimi Hendrix in the lead guitar slot for their 3-day stay at the Cafe Au Go Go, where Chas Chandler, the erstwhile Animals' bassist and neophyte band manager, saw him play, was blown away, and took Jimi with him to England in a counterattack to the British Invasion. When Jimi returned to the States, he looked up Johnny and sat in with him again, this time at the Gaslight Café. Sitting in with Johnny already was another guitarist, an Englishman named Eric Clapton, who had the week off after arriving in America with his band Cream. For five days, Eric Clapton and Jimi Hendrix exchanged licks as bandmates in the Screaming Night Hawks in a club half the size of La Cave.

The Screaming Night Hawks that played La Cave in February of '67 was a hot trio, even without guys named Jimi and Eric wailing away on their axes.

Blue and More Blues

No, David Blue did not write "Blowin' in the Wind," but he did strum the chords he was told to while Bob Dylan scratched out the words. Tall, ruggedly handsome, well-dressed and literate, with a pleasant, easygoing voice, no one could quite understand why this guy, who had been in the Village scene from the very start, hadn't achieved superstardom. His first album, released in 1966 on Elektra, *David Blue,* went nowhere. Sometimes David was ahead of his time, sometimes behind. He had begun his inauspicious career modestly, as a part-time dishwasher at the Gaslight Café, where he met and was accepted, even liked, by the folk crowd before he sang a note. When he did finally sing, he decided to forgo acoustic performing in favor of the electric sound.

Forsaking "folk," David had hired a four-piece he called the American Patrol, and played loudly – too loudly at times. David would find only artistic success and evade the fortune part of fame and fortune to become another casualty of the Sixties, succumbing to a heart attack in 1982 at age 41. In an elegy for him, Leonard Cohen said, "The death of such a man unifies us, and recalls to us how precious we are to one another." But his band's weekend at La Cave rocked, for what that's worth.

As February melted into March and the slush in Cleveland's streets turned from filthy gray to coal black, storefront owners swept and shoveled away the worst of winter's wonders. It was rumored that a snowplow had traversed Euclid Avenue, but proof was difficult to come by.

March witnessed a succession of popular shows. With local faves Gusti & Sean providing most of the show opening duties, the Reverend Gary Davis filled the club the first weekend and Spider John Koerner the second. These two performers, along with Doc Watson, who would grace the La Cave stage in April, had come to Stan Kain's attention through Josh White. Josh had hooked Stan up with his good friend Manny Greenhill, whose company Folklore Productions represented Gary, John and Doc (and Doc's son Merle). Manny had been around the New Folk Revival from the beginning, booking the Weavers and becoming a teenaged Joan Baez's manager/booking agent. In a heady flurry of signings, Stan and Manny resolved all the details of the three performances in one "ten-dollar long distance call," according to Stan. Stan also recalled that Manny was the easiest-going east coast agent he had had the pleasure to deal with. So bam, just like that, Stan had booked a month's worth of shows in little more time than it took to sing three verses and a chorus.

Unlike many up-and-comers, the Reverend Gary Davis was already legendary, not measured by album sales, but rather by his outsized influence on his peers and protégés. Seventy years old when he came to town, he had been playing guitar, harmonica and banjo since the 1920s, and was a founding father of the Piedmont Blues scene, which favored a syncopated rhythm style of playing, often described as ragtime-influenced blues. Playing a mix of gospel and secular blues, he had a considerable portion of the audience singing and clapping along to his fast-paced delivery. Peter, Paul and Mary had recorded his song "Samson and Delilah," renamed "If I Had My Way," on their eponymous debut album and, rediscovered, he was invited to play the 1965 Newport Folk Festival, sparking renewed interest in his style and music. Davis often said that the money he earned from their version provided what he called "The House That Peter, Paul and Mary Built" for his mother.

Spider John Koerner brought a similar style with him, stompin' acoustic bluesy material, although he was a full twenty years younger than Davis. While at the University of Minnesota in the late 50s, he teamed up with fellow Minnesotans Dave Ray and Tony Glover, recording as Koerner, Ray & Glover, although Dave Ray noted that all three also recorded in various combinations of each other and should be referred to as ""Koerner and/or Ray and/or Glover."[xxxviii] They appeared as a trio at the 1964 Newport Folk Festival, where they were recorded and filmed for the 1967 documentary *Festival*. It is rumored that they jammed with a fellow U of M student by the name of Robert Zimmerman at the Ten O'clock Scholar and influenced his harmonica style.

Before disconnecting the ten-dollar long-distance call, however, the Boston-based impresario Manny Greenhill casually dropped the name of yet another teenager that he felt would fit into the La Cave lineup, "if Stan could find a slot" for him. It truly was a favor Stan would be doing, because while he was reasonably certain that all of Manny's other stable dwellers would earn his club a profit, no one outside of Massachusetts had ever heard of Woody Guthrie's son, the unrepentant litterbug Arlo. Stan immediately filled the only open spot left in his spring schedule, the last weekend in March. It was one of those rare afterthoughts that once in a very blue moon alchemically turned lead into gold.

Arlo

An extremely short list of people has made a successful career out of littering, but the almost twenty-minute song-story that evolved into the "Alice's Restaurant Massacree" did just that for Woody Guthrie's son Arlo. The song started life as a commercial for Alice's restaurant, but the tale that Arlo spun during the song about littering and resisting the draft got longer and funnier with each retelling. The iconic line "You can get anything you want/at Alice's Restaurant (excepting Alice!)" began life as "You can hide out from Officer Obanhein/at Alice's Restaurant." For a couple of years, Arlo would workshop the song, slowly massaging it into shape. In early 1967, after one performance on Bob Fass's radio show, listeners called in demanding to hear it again. Bob, ever the iconoclast, was only too thrilled but to oblige, playing it over and over. Arlo began to play out regularly at places like Club 47 in Boston, his sets anchored by the "Massacree."

By the time the now-twenty-year-old singer/songwriter pulled his ancient Volvo into the driveway of Stan's pad in late March '67, his charismatic, homespun-humor persona had already begun to acquire him some popularity that had nothing to do with dear old dad. Arlo played a total of nine sets over the weekend, opening each one with a beautiful ballad he wrote, "Highway in the Wind" and ending each set with either "Now and Then" or "I'm Going Home," all three of which would make it onto his debut album released about seven months after his stop at La Cave. Sandwiched in between was a different version of "Alice's Restaurant Massacre," a couple of them far exceeding twenty minutes. In between those shows and his album release, Arlo got himself invited to play at the '67 Newport Folk Festival in front of 20,000 folk music fans, where he hit it out of the park. Chosen to close the festival, Arlo was joined onstage by about 50 other performers who chimed in with the refrain to the Massacree each time it came around on the guitar.

And days before Arlo's debut album hit the streets, Woody died on 3 October, 1967.

A Command Performance

No sooner did Arlo beat it on down the line than a surefire, bona fide La Cave attraction, Josh White, returned for 8 sets over 3 days on the first full April weekend. If Arlo could draw about 420 paid customers while commanding a meager $250 for his weekend, Josh would have to draw that many plus another two hundred fans to justify his $1,200 performance fee. He did that and more, with over three hundred fans paying their way down the stairs on Saturday alone. And while Sunday was a relative bust with only sixty-three paid denizens, Josh put on his usual high-powered gospel-influenced blues and impressive guitar licks, along with the powerfully deep tenor voice that drilled home his subversive messages of love and brotherhood. Sunday brought the gross take for the weekend up to a cool $1,775 on admissions alone. If you're keeping score at home, you could safely add another eight- or nine-hundred bucks in beer and food sales and notch up yet another fruitful weekend for Nelson, Stan and the small staff that kept the 3.2 beer flowing.

Each night, Josh regaled the rapt audiences with his between-songs patter. He reminisced about the time during the most recent world war when his song protesting racial segregation in the Armed Forces, "Uncle Sam Says," reached President Roosevelt's attention and Josh was summoned to a command performance. Rightfully so, Josh was nervous, as he knew he was the first African-American to give a Command Performance. "Isn't that song aimed at Mr. Roosevelt?" his equally-nervous wife asked. When Josh got to Washington and met the President and First

Lady, the President asked Josh directly, "Am I 'Uncle Sam' in your song?"

To both Roosevelts, he answered in the affirmative. To FDR, he said he had written the song after visiting his brother and seeing that while the white soldiers slept in barracks, the black soldiers slept in tents. Furthermore, the black soldiers were treated separately and definitely not equal in other ways.

Impressed with Josh's courage and candor, the Roosevelts and the Whites became close friends, with the Roosevelts becoming godparents to Josh, Jr. in 1940, and Josh Sr. being hired as a goodwill ambassador or, as Roosevelt sometimes referred to him, "The Presidential Minstrel."

"And that's how the two "White" houses got together," Josh concluded to the rapt audience in the crowded basement room. And he winked.

Is There a Doctor in the House?

Doc Watson's style of playing guitar and banjo was mesmerizing. His fingers would fly over the strings so deftly that it was almost impossible for other flatpickers to copy, try though they might. In 1985 Arlen Roth, a columnist for *Guitar Magazine,* wrote that "...we can attribute an entirely new style and a whole generation of pickers to [Watson's] inspiration. He was the first rural acoustic player to truly 'amaze' urban audiences in the early 1960s with his dazzling, fast technique, and he has continued to be a driving, creative force on the acoustic music scene."[xxxix]

Doc went on to release over fifty solo albums and compilations in a 60-year career, but at the time of his La Cave appearance he had four LPs to his credit. But, and it's a big but, would Doc draw more than flies? He wasn't folk. He wasn't rock. He wasn't even country. He played a proprietary blend of traditional, old timey, bluegrass, blues and even country swing, with one thing being a sure bet: any song Doc played instantly became a "Doc Watson song." Stan had signed Doc to play nine sets over three days with these contractual considerations: Doc would receive a guarantee of $350. As a bonus, he would receive 50% of the gross door take if the door took in $750 or more.

LA CAVE DE CAFE, INC.
10615 EUCLID AVENUE
CLEVELAND, OHIO 44106
PAID
2544
April 17 1967
PAY TO THE ORDER OF Doc Watson $392.10
Three hundred Ninety-Two 10/100 DOLLARS
DOAN OFFICE
CENTRAL
NATIONAL BANK OF CLEVELAND, OHIO
LA CAVE DE CAFE, INC.
Stanley Kain

Doc Watson's pay, 13-15 April, 1967

Stan's luck held. The La Cave door haul for Doc's three-day stint came to $788 on the strength of 394 paid admissions. After a one dollar, ninety cent deduction, Doc pocketed $392.10, a cool forty-two bucks over his guarantee. Ironically, he made more playing in front of fewer than four hundred fans at La Cave than he would by playing in front of more than 12,000 fans four years earlier at Newport '63.

Rumor has it that Doc enjoyed the snack Stan had deducted from his paycheck.

Chapter 10:
The Only Thing That Stays the Same is Change

1967 was shaping up as the year that La Cave shed its folk music cocoon for the electrified beauty of '60s-style underground rock. But neither Stan nor Nelson was foolish enough to abandon their many ties to early-60s folk acts and management. Consequently, in May and June they inked folkies Judy Roderick, Patrick Sky, José Feliciano, Brainsneeze,[xl] Jim & Jean, Candy Forest and Gusti & Sean. At the same time, slipping through to fill the cracks in the schedule were local heroes The Terry Knight Revue, and The Munx, a band of indeterminate musical genre hailing from Sandusky, an hour west of Cleveland on the Lake Erie shore. The Munx's main claims to fame were two singles released on Clevetown Records in '67 and '68, and the fact that for the nonce it was home to future Peter Laughner collaborator, drummer Robert Bensick.

Also slated to appear were the Paul Butterflied Blues Band, the James Cotton Chicago Blues Band, and relative newcomers to the folk-rock scene, the Stone Poneys, a trio that included an unknown twenty-year-old harmony singer with stunning vocal ability and equally memorable appearance named Linda Ronstadt.

The James Gang Rides into Town

Drummer Jim Fox of the James Gang doesn't specifically remember the first time the band he helped found played La Cave,[xli] but he does recall that Glenn Schwartz was the band's guitarist for the first gig, and also recalls that Glenn left the band in late '67. His memory lapse is not due so much to the notion that that the performances weren't memorable but rather that he spent practically every night he could spare by going to La Cave, and a half century later, well, memories get intertwined. One aspect he remembered about his many treks down Euclid Avenue ended up with him and a pal or two hanging around the door waiting for the right moment to see if they could cadge Larry Bruner, who worked the door those days, into a free pass for the evening. "I was broke. Stan wasn't always around, but Larry was," Jim recalled. "He was always very kind to us. He knew we had a band and needed as many breaks as we could get. [Larry] and I had to confront each other every single night because I wanted to see the show and I didn't have any money and Larry knew that. He wouldn't even look at me until just before show time, then wave me in. I found out later that he had been following [the Gang] in the newspapers, and for our first gig there we might have repaid Larry by agreeing to being a last-minute replacement for some cancellation."

It was likely that out of this mutual respect that Jim and the rest of the Gang repaid the debt by putting on two nights of kick-ass blues-tinged rock and roll for a piece of the door. It sure beat robbing trains like their namesakes. The Gang's haul that first weekend was a cool $240, slightly over two grand in today's buying power. No one could ever accuse the check signers at La Cave of being skinflints.

"There just weren't that many really great guitarists in Cleveland – not like today," remembers Jim Fox with a smile. "When Glenn [Schwartz] plugged in, everything else just kind of stopped." After going through a Who's Who of local guitarists with varying amounts of success, Jim and the Gang were on the lookout for a plank spanker that had "it,' whatever "it" was. No one could define "it," but no one could miss it when it showed up. And that was the band's missing ingredient. It. Guitarists Domenic Troiano, Greg Grandillo, Ronnie Silverman, Dennis Chandler, "Mouse" Michalski, and one or two stringbenders whose names Jim may have never even known took their turns in the lead position. The band was pretty tight, but…not quite there yet.

And then it happened. Word spread that local six-string legend Glenn Schwartz was back home from a stint in the Big Green Mother[xlii] and predictably, Glenn soon showed up to dig a Gang gig. Jim Fox: "At one point, he came up on stage and started playing Jeff's Boogie with us. He was phenomenal." When Glenn accepted an offer to join the band, "that was a major grab for us." Second guitarist Mouse Michalski was less than enthused at his reduced role and caught a hat for greener pastures. When the band picked up Bill Jeric for the second guitar spot, sparks flew. Jim recalls, "[Bill] was a tremendous asset for us. Those two guys (Bill and Glenn) would sit in a room, on two folding chairs with their knees touching and their eyeballs in contact and they'd play for, like, eight hours. Bill was the perfect guy for Glenn to bounce off of. That was the special sauce."

That was the lineup for the Gang's first La Cave appearance: Glenn and Bill on guitars, Tom Kriss on bass and Jim perched on the drummer's stool. It was a gas.

After sardonic folkie Patrick Sky with his explicit lyrics and sarcastic sense of humor and the duo Brainsneeze rounded out the merry month of May, summer came to La Cave with the promise of hot bands, warm nights, and cool friends to get each other into some innocent trouble. And in some cases, not so innocent.

For the fifth year in a row, José Feliciano made the trek from the east coast to La Cave. He arrived with a couple of measures of his growing popularity, not only in Cleveland, but internationally. One clue was that Stan inked him for a ten-day residency, correctly estimating that there would be more rear ends than seats available. Another hint was that the days of signing José for a couple hundred bucks and a crash pad were gone. This time around, José asked for and received $1,500, meals, transportation and lodging for himself and his driver, who happened to be the Missus. And his guide pooch. It turned out to be a great investment. Not only did a total of well over a thousand local music lovers bring the house down night after night howling at José's clever but risqué 'tween songs patter and virtuosic strumming, many in the nightly throngs came night after night to see the virtuoso guitarist with the razor-sharp wit, each time dragging new friends with them.

Folk music was Wendy Patillo's thing. So much so that having descended those stairs to see the show so often, she felt right at home in the cozy confines of La Cave. One evening, in between jobs at the moment, she impulsively asked Stan for a job. It was not part of any well-thought strategy; her mouth just opened and out spilled the words. He had one question: Can you make espresso? Fifteen minutes after her affirmative fib, she was working tables and, six months or so into that job, she graduated to "manager," meaning she had more duties but not necessarily more pay. But she didn't have to wait tables except in a pinch. She could make espresso and pour pitchers of watery beer while – at the same time! – getting paid to hear live folk music instead of the other way around. Sometimes, life is good. For Wendy, at the time, life was really good, as it was for many of the cave dwellers, at least when they were within those dark walls covered by darker curtains.

Marci Zabell had an even better reason to drop in to La Cave than Wendy did: her boyfriend was in a band[xliii] that opened for a number of acts including the Velvet Underground, Canned Heat,

Blood, Sweat and Tears, Terry Knight, and others. She recalls: "Back in the '60s my life was pretty typical of a girl my age and [socioeconomic] status; my dad was a dentist, my mom worked at home. In 1967 I was 15. Spent time with my girlfriend at the mall, walking around, exchanging looks with the boys, listening to our transistors. When I wasn't doing that, I was babysitting. Lots of babysitting. Working in my dad's office, doing school plays, and going out with boys, mostly to hear local music or to movies, it would seem. I only dated older guys, so we drove everywhere."

"I remember La Cave was dark, and the floor was sticky. I don't know what they served; I got in with a fake ID, so probably beer. The first few times I was there, I was with my boyfriend's band, so no one checked my age. I have vivid memories of being in the green room at La Cave, sitting on my boyfriend's lap on an overstuffed chair behind a curtain, making out. And there was a niche backstage from where I could watch him play keyboards. But it was just a typical backstage area. The walls in the green room were signed by all the bands, and that was quite cool. The furnishings were just old couches and beat-up tables. And chips and pop and maybe some other stuff..."

"La Cave was a really great place to go in the late '60s. The vibe was totally laid back and everyone there was friendly to everyone else. I missed the folk years, and really wasn't paying attention while I was there, to be honest, but everyone who was anyone played La Cave and I'm glad I was there the little I got to be."

1967 was the heyday of AM radio. For kids and their music, radio was the only game in town. First aired in 1965, WIXY-1260 (now *there* was a catchy name) was tops, even though at 5,000 watts their signal wasn't in the category of WKYC's 50,000-watt clear channel signal. But until WIXY hit the scene, the most popular station in town wasn't even in town. It was Windsor, Ontario's

50,000-watt powerhouse CKLW that ruled Cleveland's airwaves until three enterprising entrepreneurs, Norman Wain, Bob Weiss, and Joe Zingale realized what an opportunity this chasm in Cleveland radio presented and bought WDOK, a stick-in-the-mud station perched at the 1260 frequency. By December 1965 it morphed into WIXY and began a ten-year run of relentless promotion and publicity centered around newly-breaking bands and their admiring listeners. A crescendo of sorts was reached when the station sponsored the Beatles' second Cleveland appearance at cavernous Cleveland Stadium on 14 August 1966. That, of course, was an effort that would never be matched.

Like Butter

With Candy Forest, Dick Wedler, and Gusti & Sean handling most of the duties of show openers, Jim & Jean, the Butterfield Blues Band and Sandusky's The Munx all held court over the next three weekends in June. For the Butterfield troupe, their first appearance in Cleveland was something of a sensation. The goings-on that weekend were merely a prelude to the most raucous month in La Cave's run, because – besides the Butterfields - Stan had also agreed on La Cave hosting the James Cotton Blues Band out of Chicago, and an unknown trio from California, the Stone Poneys. Both groups had just released albums and were beginning work on their next long player, so extended tours in the summer of '67 were de rigeur.

The Butterfield Band was on a roll. They had burst upon the scene at the infamous '65 Newport Folk Festival, being slated as the weekend's opening act. Their inspired set drew the rapt attention of the soon-to-be the next Bad Bob of Folk, Bob Dylan. It was the first time that many of the mostly folk-music fans had heard a high-powered electric blues combo. Bob, of course, had his own plans for the festival. All he needed were a handful of co-conspirators in the guise of an electric band. Amazingly, just such a collection of musicians fell into his proverbial lap when the Butterfield Band amazed him, and after an impromptu late-night rehearsal, members of the band Paul Butterfield, drummer Sam Lay and bassist Jerome Arnold, along with Al Kooper and Barry Goldberg, accompanied Bob on the short electric set that changed the course of musical history.

At La Cave, Paul Butterfield's crew found their mojo. Their new sound, incorporating brass with a blues band, was groundbreaking. Having virtuosos in the unit certainly helped: Paul himself was one of the greatest harpists ever to blow a blue note, Michael Bloomfield had few, if any, peers on guitar, Sam Lay was one of the most in-demand session drummers on the scene, David Sanborn was already world-class, and Jerome Arnold played a funky bass that was rarely heard outside the records being cut in Detroit at Hitsville USA by Motown guru Berry Gordy and the Funk Brothers. At least one set – and likely all the sets – included a stretched-out jam on the band's signature song "East-West" from their 1966 album by the same name. The song was a truly groundbreaking amalgamation of jazz- and Indian-influenced riffs and the virtuoso playing of Bloomfield and his bandmates. It was, for the band, a stop on their journey to the Rock and Roll Hall of Fame.

Another almost-unique facet of the band was that it was racially integrated, something that was still far outside the mainstream in 1967, the year of many race riots that contrasted starkly with the "Summer of Love" ethos that struggled to compete with the darker forces of the American social fabric. It cannot be stressed too strongly that with the Vietnam War as a backdrop to all the other pressures of modern living, the country was splitting along lines of racial and generational differences. This dichotomy was creating sparks that would soon catch the nation on fire. And music was the match that lit the blaze.

Linda and the Poneys

As a teenager in Tucson in the early '60s, Linda sang in a folk trio with her brother and sister and billed themselves as "The Three Ronstadts" for reasons obvious. Bobby Kimmel, a friend and sometimes bandmate of Linda's, moved to California and in 1964 began cajoling her to come on out and join him to make music. Linda, now all of seventeen, quit high school and did just that, merging forces with Bobby on rhythm guitar and folkie Kenny Edwards on lead guitar. Linda remembered their vision for the group in a 1976 interview: "It was going to be five people. We had an electric autoharp and a girl singer, and we thought we were unique in the world. And it turned out the Jefferson Airplane and the Lovin' Spoonful had beaten us."

The group stayed a trio and named themselves the Stone Poneys, intentionally misspelling the name a' la the Beatles and Byrds. The Poneys became instantly popular and picked up steady gigs at places like The Troubadour in Hollywood and The Insomniac in Hermosa Beach, eventually travelling cross country to play at the Bitter End in Greenwich Village. Linda was so mesmerizing that it was almost painful, in the best of ways, to see her onstage barefoot, bra-less and miniskirted. She was everybody's girl next door, sexy in an innocent way – and then she started to sing. It was only a matter of time until she hit it big.

The Stone Poneys' stay in Cleveland was not without its share of extracurricular activities. By this time, Stan's pad off of Murray Hill Blvd. near Cedar was an open secret. Most nights, and *every* weekend night, the cognoscenti knew that an hour or two after the last D chord rang out from the stage and the last pitcher of three-two pisswater had been drained, the beautiful people would begin to gather at Stan's to continue the movable feast that was otherwise known as living the dream, Sixties-style. The "Free Love" movement that had smoldered below the surface of society for a generation now burst into flame during the Summer of Love.

It was against this backdrop that Stan's pad became *the* place for after-hours debauchery. One member of the La Cave community, Richard Shack, was a musician, playing in the popular local band The Case of E. T. Hooley, and later The James Gang. He put simply: "Our goal was to play loud and get laid." Stan recalls, "On my way in to work each morning, I'd stop by [my "pad"]to drop off coffee and doughnuts. The first morning I didn't expect to see anyone up, but when I walked into the house there was a naked girl standing at the kitchen sink, washing dishes. Before I knew it she was right there in front of me. It shocked me because I didn't recognize her. I almost panicked cuz she looked like a teenager and I thought, "Oh, no." When she spoke, I realized it was Linda. She smiled sweetly and said, "Oh, don't mind me. I hate wearing clothes." Stan barely noticed blankets here and there covering some of the landscape, but only some of it. Ashtrays full of roaches, cigarette packs and matches were strewn about, and the usual several bottles of beer and booze graced the view, mostly empty and laying unceremoniously wherever they had rolled or been kicked. The smell of weed was strong, but Stan barely noticed it. Nor did he pay much attention to the other remnants of the previous evening's joy scattered about. His attention had been diverted.

David Budin, who opened as a solo and a band performer at La Cave for numerous acts, and opened for all six of Linda's nights, recalls: "I did have a lot of conversations with [Linda] backstage. "Different Drum" and its album, their second, was about to come out and Linda told me, more than once, how much she hated the song. She said, incredulously, that 'Nicky [Nik Venet] put a harpsichord on it.' She couldn't understand that. The story ended with the other two, very talented, guys being unceremoniously dumped by Capitol Records.

Once again, Stan and Company had hit one out of the park. But if Linda was a home run, the next act to rattle La Cave's stage would – eventually – hit the equivalent of a game winning grand slam, granting the little club its own measure of immortality.

The Velvet Underground

A recurring theme in La Cave's limited lifespan is the superpower of Stan Kain, and soon, new Resident Wizard Larry Bruner, of spotting talent earlier than almost everyone else; so much so that it often seems like they're working backwards from the future successes of musicians and bands to the days when those bands toiled in obscurity in front of a dozen fans (or fewer) at a time. But as of this writing time travel remains the province of science fiction. These stories are much too strange not to be true.

In June 1967, the Wizards of La Cave brought an unknown New York City band called the Velvet Underground to Cleveland for the first of what are now many legendary concerts in the tiny basement club on Euclid Avenue.

How influential was the Velvet Underground on twentieth century, and beyond, popular music and culture? Brian Eno, Rock and Roll Hall of Fame Inductee as a member of Roxy Music, in a 1982 interview, said, "I was talking to Lou Reed the other day, and he said that the first Velvet Underground record sold only 30,000 copies in its first five years. Yet, that was an enormously important record for so many people. I think everyone who bought one of those 30,000 copies started a band!"[xliv]

The concerts the Velvets put on at La Cave were mesmerizing, hypnotic, loud as hell, and transformative. Few, if any, denizens came away from the experience unchanged. For many, the dark room, the otherworldly sonic products of the band, the barely intelligible but still moving lyrics, the appearance of the band, and the fact that you could smell the band's sweat from across the room left few people unimpressed.

To one attendee, it felt like an attack by space aliens. Judy Rossman remembers, "I had no idea what they would be like. We didn't even go to see any particular band play that night. We just went to be with friends and listen to some music, you know, just to hang out." An upperclassman at Case, nothing in her stodgy New England upbringing had prepared her for the sensory assault that she experienced in spring of 1968. "We were folk music fans. We liked the Kingston Trio and Peter, Paul and Mary. We knew from friends that La Cave was a folky club that served beer to kids. I'll never forget that first night seeing the Velvet Underground and realizing that there was this whole culture that none of my friends knew about. I kind of became like, you know, an evangelist for them for a while."

But what did Lou Reed, a founding member of the band, have to say about their pre-fame days as starving artists in search of an audience?

In an era when charge cards were still somewhat a novelty, Lou gave credit where credit was due. In 1989, Lou told a number of us, "When we were in the Velvet Underground, we practically lived out in Ohio because, you know, La Cave. Like, between La Cave and the Boston Tea Party, those two clubs supported us for about three years, so I feel a real nice thing about out here in Ohio." Later that same evening, from the stage of the Palace Theater on Euclid Avenue in front of an SRO crowd, Lou followed that interview with this remark: "Maybe you remember a group I was in called the Velvet Underground (thunderous applause ensues). We used to play out here at a place called La Cave (the decibel level increases). They supported us for about three years, lemme tell ya, so I have a real love for this [city]."

It's a simple proposition: according to Lou Reed, without Stan, Larry and La Cave, there would likely be no enduring Velvet Underground, and a there would be huge cultural hole in our shared musical heritage.

The Midwest Version of the Summer of Love

The month of June was in the books and while the Summer of Love was well on its way into oblivion out west, it was just taking hold in the Midwest. Most Clevelanders were looking forward to that most patriotic of holidays, the Fourth of July, and in '67 the 4th fell on a Tuesday, making for a short work week. The tragicomic folksinger Tim Buckley, scheduled to perform from the 4th through the 9th, managed to somehow make his way to the wrong city and consequently left a hole in the schedule the size of a holiday week. It wasn't the first time he would no-show somewhere and it wouldn't be the last. Once the smoke cleared, Stan and Larry had filled the first two dates with the ubiquitous Gusti, she of the operatic-level vocal abilities, who heroically abandoned her children to the care of her husband to headline the first two dates, and The Third Bardo pinch hit for the final three Buckley dates, earning a cool five hundred for their weekend sets. David Budin hitchhiked down the hill from Cleveland Heights and played to open the band's sets, knocking down forty bucks for his efforts.

Gusti, who by this time was reverentially known as La Cave's "house band," for her willingness and availability to open, close, or headline, not to mention employing her mad managerial skills, sealed the deal with two wild nights of both spiritual and ribald Irish tales. The Third Bardo was a psychedelic quintet out of New York City whose two main claims to fame were their only single, "I'm Five Years Ahead of My Time," released in May of '67, and an appearance on Cleveland's Upbeat TV show to lip-synch the song. It all went up in pot smoke when radio stations correctly perceived the lyrics to be thinly-disguised references to illicit drug use and placed the song at the top of the Do Not Play stack. The band, whose careful choice of their name came from the Tibetan *Book of the Dead,* soon disbanded, apparently joining those Tibetans in their eternal slumber.

No sooner had the Bardo abandoned the heights of the La Cave stage that the next band began the laborious process of hauling their equipment down the stairs in order to rehearse for what would be their biggest show biz break yet, a two-day "trial" residency. The band was the Bill Miller-led Mr. Stress Blues Band, who had the home field advantage, having two of their number also employed as waiters at La Cave – Kenny Klimak and Rich Dzurik. Excited to play what would be their biggest dates yet, they began rehearsing on Monday the 10th, a weekday on which La Cave was typically closed for its weekly "cleaning."

Mr. Stress Blues Band at La Cave, July 1967

Bill Miller, the aforementioned "Mr. Stress," had begun putting together a band in late 1966 to accompany his prodigious harmonica talents. Inspired by performances from harp legends Paul Butterfield and James Cotton, Bill and has merry band of music makers never met with mainstream success, but he nevertheless shepherded his band through numerous lineup changes and continued to perform full-time until 2010. Many luminaries in the music world passed through the band on *their* way to spots in nationally-acclaimed outfits. A few of these names are Chuck Drazdik (It's A Beautiful Day), Anton Fier (The Feelies/Golden Palominos/The Lounge Lizards), Alan Greene (Breathless/The Innocent/Humble Pie), Chrissie Hynde (The Pretenders), Peter Laughner (Pere Ubu/Rocket From The Tombs), Vito San Filippo (Tower Of Power/The O'Jays), and Glenn Schwartz (Pacific Gas & Electric/James Gang). As Nick Blakey tells it on the band's Facebook page, "While visually it was pretty obvious that the MSBB were a bunch of white boys from Cleveland, if you closed your eyes when they played, you could be convinced that they were a well-oiled machine of veteran bluesmen from Chicago's South Side."[xlv]

The band comported itself well. Waiters/Guitarists Rich and Kenny designed, printed and handed out flyers to anyone with a spare hand, which packed the house with old and new friends, and the band worked hard enough to earn an invitation to play a longer residency in November. They would return numerous times to enthrall rowdy crowds until La Cave's demise in the summer of '69, and go on to become long time regulars first at The Brick Cottage ("The Brick") and later, the Euclid Tavern ("The Euc").

No sooner had the boys of Mr. Stress stored away their amps and drums in back than the man with the pleasing baritone voice and master of between-songs patter, Tom Rush, pulled into the Versailles Hotel to check in on his way down Euclid to La Cave and a four-day stint starting on the 13th. In a reflection of Tom's growing stardom, his remittance for his stay in the cave skyrocketed from the $400 he had received just this past February to a lofty $750 with a bonus rider for selling out the room, which he promptly did. That feat brought his end of the handle to $875.

Buck-naked Buckley

Meanwhile, all was forgiven, regarding the absent Tim Buckley, when he agreed to play six days for $400, with a bonus rider sweetening the pot. But it was the extra-curricular activities that made his stop in Cleveland memorable, at least for several of Cleveland Heights' finest, a few pissed off tenants in need of sleep, and a gaggle of lucky music fans. And, of course by "lucky" I mean unlucky.

It was Saturday night and the concert had just ended. People began to straggle out of the club a little after midnight, but some few stayed behind. Two of them, David Budin and Walt Mendelssohn, were musicians who sometimes played together, sometimes solo, and often with others, anytime and anywhere they could. This particular night found them unpacking guitars for an impromptu jam with Tim, in front of a scattered collection of bodies too exhausted or stoned to exit the dank and muggy basement, whose air conditioning valiantly fought a losing battle with the elements.

Heights resident and cool guy-wannabe John Stark Bellamy II, his brother Christopher, and a handful of their friends had tried to see Tim play on Thursday night, sans funds, and got the bum's rush from Stan, but not before hearing Tim's tantalizingly languorous cover of The Supremes' "You Keep Me Hanging On." Late Saturday/early Sunday found them at loose ends, wandering the deserted grassy median strip of Euclid Heights Boulevard, which connected La Cave's neighborhood with The Heights. To their delighted surprise, the quintet ran into their friends David and Walt traversing the same wobbly route, with a very stoned Tim Buckley in tow. "Try to look cool, guys," thought John, neither quickly nor profoundly. It quickly became obvious to the entire entourage that

Tim wanted, no, Tim *wanted*, to go swimming. But first he wanted, no, he *needed,* to get even higher than he was.

John and Christopher had the solution: their parents' nearby backyard. Almost before you could utter the words "nickel bag," the gang was behind Dad's garage in his rose garden and fired up a corncob pipe filled with the good stuff. Highness accomplished, it was revealed by the brothers Bellamy that a solution to Tim's other obsession was readily available in the form of a nearby apartment complex swimming pool in which local youths, including the brothers, had enjoyed midnight swims, at least until the security lights came on. Scaling the wooden fence and shucking their clothing in the clumsy manner of the stoned, the laughing, giggling group dove head first into the water. In what seemed like mere seconds later, a security guard rounded the corner, shone his flashlight on the squealing youths – by this time Tim was singing lustily – and demanded an explanation.

The explanation came in the form of the octet barely stopping to retrieve their piles of clothing as they hightailed it back over the fence and, not stopping to bother dressing, laughed their way back to the rose garden. When John and Christopher regained a portion of their senses, they noticed that David, Walt and Tim had either been swallowed whole by the earth or had taken off in another direction. Years later, none of the combatants could remember putting their clothes back on, but we can all rest assured that, sooner or later, they did.

That Week Jimi Hendrix Didn't Play La Cave

The Velvet Underground was not the only unknown-but-soon-to-become-immortal act that Stan booked during the spring of 1967. To this day, conjecture on Jimi Hendrix's activities and whereabouts still exists, although these are documented seemingly to a degree reserved for the Beatles, or perhaps, people on FBI Most Wanted lists. Most of his moves during the Summer of Love are well-documented due to the number of corroborating witnesses, but that still leaves all of Jimi's private or unobserved movements to spice up the story.

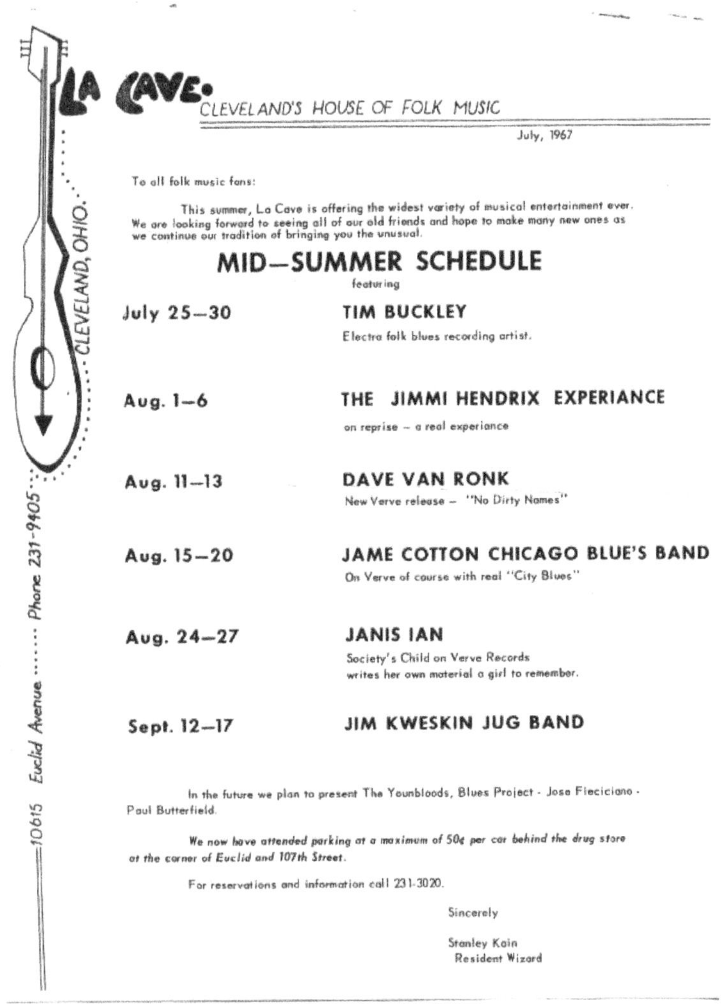
LA CAVE. CLEVELAND'S HOUSE OF FOLK MUSIC

CLEVELAND, OHIO.

10615 Euclid Avenue .... Phone 231-9405

July, 1967

To all folk music fans:

This summer, La Cave is offering the widest variety of musical entertainment ever. We are looking forward to seeing all of our old friends and hope to make many new ones as we continue our tradition of bringing you the unusual.

MID—SUMMER SCHEDULE

featuring

July 25—30 **TIM BUCKLEY**
Electra folk blues recording artist.

Aug. 1—6 **THE JIMMI HENDRIX EXPERIANCE**
on reprise – a real experiance

Aug. 11—13 **DAVE VAN RONK**
New Verve release – "No Dirty Names"

Aug. 15—20 **JAME COTTON CHICAGO BLUE'S BAND**
On Verve of course with real "City Blues"

Aug. 24—27 **JANIS IAN**
Society's Child on Verve Records
writes her own material a girl to remember.

Sept. 12—17 **JIM KWESKIN JUG BAND**

In the future we plan to present The Younbloods, Blues Project - Jose Fleciciano - Paul Butterfield.

We now have attended parking at a maximum of 50¢ per car behind the drug store at the corner of Euclid and 107th Street.

For reservations and information call 231-3020.

Sincerely

Stanley Kain
Resident Wizard

La Cave handbill, Mid-Summer 1967

This much is true: sometime in early March, Stan Kain spent several days in New York, talking up La Cave, visiting agents and attending concerts. He vividly recalled seeing Jimi perform on someone's recommendation. Who exactly made the recommendation is lost to memory, but Stan recalled that the club was Steve Paul's The Scene. The records of Stan's trip to NYC and Jimi's jams at the Scene intersect in that first week of March, and their agreement is dated 13 March, which is the first work day after Stan returned to Cleveland. He wasn't all that hot about going to a rock & roll club, but upon witnessing the human hurricane and seeing the effect Jimi's playing had on everyone in the room, he ended up signing the still-anonymous guitar god to a six-day residency beginning 1 August, for the bargain basement price of $600 plus expenses. Included was a rider granting Jimi 50% of the gross over $1,200. This would give Jimi plenty of time to return to England to put the finishing touches on his debut album and presumably play a number of club dates while there, and also, importantly, he'd have a chance to visit his new girlfriend, Kathy Etchingham, whom he had met on his first British club date at the Scotch of St. James venue, where Kathy was manager.

Between March and August, a little festival took place in California: the Monterey International Pop Festival. Jimi's performance was incendiary and propelled him into instant stardom. Not a whisper of any of these hijinks made the Cleveland newspapers. Jimi's debut album had yet to be released in the States, and the music magazine industry was still in diapers. *Rolling Stone* magazine was all of one month old in June of 1967. There was no buzz on the street. If anything, at this point both Nelson and Stan were wondering if maybe the six hundred bucks they promised the seemingly unknown guitar slinger was too steep a fee. The overwhelming interest Jimi attracted in New York had faded somewhat in the months between Stan's visit and initial exuberance in signing the still-unknown performer.

Then the 30 June edition of *Time Magazine* hit the newsstands. Buried in a small article, their mention of Jimi's performance might as well have been screamed into Stan's ear by a town crier. Jimi's music was secondary to the story: setting his guitar on fire was the hook. Stan was simultaneously shocked, dismayed and excited. In other words, he didn't know what to think. Regardless, Jimi had just priced himself out of La Cave's financial reach.

Perhaps, in retrospect, it was all for the best that Jimi detoured around La Cave in August 1967. Most of the accoutrements of La Cave were extremely flammable.

Summer, Continued

The first of August was, in the parlance of our times, a clusterfuck. In those pre-internet days, there was no easy (read: free) way to alert the populace that Mr. Hendrix had cancelled his appearance. In fact, about a week prior it was decided not to answer the phone to take reservations, as was the custom, because virtually all of the calls were for a Jimi date. Fortunately, the house band, as in Gusti, was available and David Budin also filled in. But it was larger-than-life Gusti who stilled, and then thrilled, the uneasy audiences that first week of August. To say that the force of her personality saved the day is barely an exaggeration; she had the ways and means to shush even the unruliest of crowds without getting her Irish up. And she had plenty of Irish if needed. Eschewing the stage, she traversed the spaces between the tables to serenade every last person in the room, including the waiters. Gusti was that teacher you had in junior high who could freeze you in place with a wicked glance. If she wanted you to have a good time, you simply had a good time. You never wanted to find out what the "or else" might entail. Things were so much easier that way.

Dave Van Ronk rolled into town for a three-night stint starting 11 August, but it just might have been Joan Baez's concert downtown at Music Hall that weekend, where she sold every last one of the three thousand tickets offered, that kept things rather sedate. It might also have had something to do with the buzz about Hendrix's no-show that still rattled the rafters. In any event, it was a hell of a musical weekend in Cleveland, with Ms. Baez and the Mayor of MacDougal Street Van Ronk, Wilson Pickett, Ray Charles with his Raelettes, and Ramsey Lewis all vying for the city's entertainment dollars.

La Cave resumed activities on the Tuesday after Dave split town, with the James Cotton Blues Band back for an encore week. The *Plain Dealer* devoted almost ten column-inches to singing the praises of Cotton's crew. This time around, James found himself exactly one drummer short of the required number. But he had clout and besides, like all good bluesmen, he knew every other good bluesman and they traded musicians the way young boys traded baseball cards. Sam Lay, everybody's first-call traveling drummer, was at loose ends and agreed to meet the band in Cleveland. Their popularity was such that they agreed to another six-day stint the first week of September, after a week back in Chicago to wow the hometown crowd. Unfortunately, Sam Lay would not be available that week. And that, it so happened, was gonna be a big problem.

Janis Ian...Society's Tuned-In Teen

Teenager Janis Ian's audition, held one day after school at producer Shadow Morton's office, was met with indifference by the mogul, who spent the time with feet on desk, reading the New York Times. Never at a loss, the precocious Janis produced a cigarette lighter and set fire to Morton's newspaper. And promptly left. That got his attention, even if her singing hadn't. Shadow saw the light and caught up to her at the elevators, intrigued at what he might be passing by. She returned to his office, played him "Society's Child," and a week later recorded the song.

Unlike Shadow Morton's meteoric rise, Janis's climb was much more pedestrian. After someone at Atlantic Records, who had cut the track, actually took the time to listen to the lyrics, they returned the master tape to Morton, passing on the controversy they knew would ensue. Twenty-two other record companies also passed on the song. Then MGM, who had just opened the subsidiary Verve Forecast and was looking for some tax write-offs, took the bait, believing the song would never sell. Their feeling was that it was a tremendous song that nevertheless would never see the light of day. Then an angel appeared in the form of conductor Leonard Bernstein. Leonard had a Sunday night special coming up on CBS, and on it he featured Janis and "Society's Child" in a fifteen-minute segment. The next week, bam! huge ads appeared in all the music rags, and slowly, city by city, the tune began climbing charts.

Janis Ian's message to La Cave

By the middle of June it hit number two on the local Cleveland charts, besting everyone except The Association's "Windy." It was at one of her Gaslight appearances that Stan inquired as to her availability, and signed her to a four-day weekend at the end of August. Her fee included enough funds to cover her chaperone's expenses. By all accounts, her shows were amazing. "She looked all of thirteen, and acted and sounded like a 40-year-old," recalled one attendee. Her four nights at La Cave saw just a smidge under a thousand Clevelanders pay their way in, many for multiple nights, and earned Miss Ian not only her $950 asking fee, but also a $117 bonus for selling out Friday and Saturday nights.

Tragedy Strikes

For the third time in less than two months, James Cotton's blues crew agreed to earn another cool grand for six nights of harmonica-fueled boogie. They were immensely popular with the La Cave crowd for their inspired high-energy act, and adored by Nelson and Stan for their never asking for an override to their basic contract, which would have earned them a nice bonus. As it was, they had consistently filled the house. Richard Shack, who later became the James Gang's lead guitarist, remembers one performance in particular: "At one point, [Cotton] did a somersault on stage. No kidding. There was no room to do one on that stage, but yeah, he did and somehow, I remembered that." Sue Crutch, known by all as "Suzy Creamcheese" after the fictional Frank Zappa character,[xlvi] was working the door and also remembers how loud and popular the band was. "I just loved them and the Butterfield band, too. They were all very nice to us."

But there was an issue: drummer Sam Lay had to boogie back to Chicago to begin a short tour with Paul Butterfield's group. Not to worry, according to James, who knew pretty much everybody who was anybody who labored in the blues idiom. "I got a guy."

James's "guy" turned out to be Billy Stepney, a talented journeyman drummer who had also played with countless combos. Born in 1930, by the mid '60s he had occupied the drummer's chair for Willie Mabon, Memphis Slim, Muddy Waters, Eddie Boyd and Little Walter, among many others. He slid into the lineup effortlessly. Unfortunately for Billy, the gig at La Cave lasted one day too long.

It was a Sunday night, 10 September, getaway day. Unusual for the day of the week, La Cave was crowded, a testament to the band's popularity. Sue Crutch was working the door. Kenny Klimak and Rich Djurik were waiting tables. Richard Shack was at a table with friends. Stan was hanging out, keeping a twinkling eye peeled. The band was ready to rock the house. Then something weird happened, according to Sue. Up to the table at the door came a man who almost defied description. He said he was a guest of the band. "He looked 'French.' He was tall and had a silk scarf and an earring, which was quite unusual in those days. As odd as he looked, he said something even more bizarre: 'Give the drummer some.' Sue dutifully recorded his name and his host's name, and then he 'blended into the crowd.'"

Memories differ in details, but these details are not in dispute: Sometime during the late set, no one remembers the specific song, people in the crowd could not help but notice that the drummer was slowing down the beat, not keeping up with the song. It was loud, dark and crowded. Everyone knew something was amiss, but what? Almost on cue, in answer to that unspoken question, Billy slowly stood up behind his drum kit, stayed almost motionless for a moment that seemed to last a lot longer than it probably did, and then slowly pitched forward onto the drum kit and disappeared behind it as cymbals and drums crashed crazily toward the crowd. Some people, thinking it was a part of the act, applauded. That lasted only a couple of seconds as the band, one by one, stopped playing. Sue Crutch said, "It was bedlam. Chaos. Nobody knew what happened. But I had become friends with Gordon, the band's manager, who was staying with me at my apartment on Hessler. I knew he'd tell me, if I could find him. But I couldn't, at the time." At the time, nobody knew. That would change momentarily.

Chaos did indeed reign as a large crowd began to congregate in front of the stage, despite shouted pleas from Stan and others. Billy was carried offstage into the green room. The next thing anyone recalls is a contingent of firemen descending the stairs with a stretcher and spiriting an unconscious Billy Stepney away. Some people, mostly those who had been in front, were horrified and quite a few left the club in tears, shock, or both. Those souls who had been farther removed from the action milled around in wonder, debating whether to hang around or skedaddle. But then, while chaos still reigned, the first sounds of a guitar overwhelmed the muted conversations. Lo and behold, the band, with its leader James Cotton in the drummer's chair, sticks and harmonica in hand, began to play! James, it turns out, had started his musical career as a drummer. He was also a veteran show business performer and he had no intention of letting the last thing Clevelanders remembered about his band was seeing their drummer die onstage. But the magician was out of tricks and the magic just wasn't there anymore. After a couple of songs, the band petered out and Stan bid everyone a good night.

When Sue got back home, she contemplated the events of the evening, especially the cryptic message from the "Frenchman." It wasn't until many years later that she learned that the phrase had begun life as black jazz slang for slapping hands, like giving a "high five." But by 1967 it had come to mean "Watch out, the drummer is about to really put on a show."[xlvii] Little did anyone know Billy would be putting on his *last* show. Then Sue heard the expected late-night knock on her door on Hessler Street. It was the band's manager, Gordon, with the news: "Billy had an aneurysm. He was dead before he hit the floor."

The More Things Change...

It was a good time to take a deep breath and assess things, so Nelson did just that. He had recently realized that Stan, or anybody, just wasn't up to managing the now-brisk business all by themselves. He needed an assistant. Nelson let Stan know that they needed to be on the lookout for someone competent but affordable. They wouldn't have to look very far.

The More They Stay the Same

Meanwhile, to coin a phrase, the shows must go on. And so they did. The next act in the barrel was the Jim Kweskin Jug Band. While jug band music – acoustic-based music using often homemade instruments like washboards, washtub basses, jugs made primarily from stoneware - along with harmonica, guitar, Jew's harps, combs, spoons and kazoos, never ascended to the top of popular American music genres, it played a vital preparatory role for both musicians and musical styles. Kweskin was idolized, and imitated, by the likes of the Grateful Dead, the Lovin' Spoonful, and the Nitty Gritty Dirt Band, among others. This obscure but delightful combo had released six albums by 1967 and played upwards of 300 dates per year.

Jim Kweskin knew how to hold an audience in his hand; it was his gift, as was his influential guitar-picking style. He peppered his sets with old timey favorites like "Sheik of Araby" along with covers of songs like Dylan's "I'll Be Your Baby Tonight," and inserted his own wit and wisdom between the tunes. Thankfully, his week's stay at La Cave was uneventful, if enjoyable. Everyone needed a rest, and Jim's jug band was just the balm to calm the frayed nerves of the staff.

Next up on the calendar was the Left Banke, a baroque-rock New York city band that began life in 1965 when a gaggle of sixteen-year-olds got together to jam at the studio of one member's father, who was a popular session violinist. In '66 the band scored two major hit singles, "Walk Away, Renee" and "Pretty Ballerina" and were well on their way to stardom. But there were simmering tensions among the band members. After all, the song "Renee" was a song of unrequited love written by the keyboardist about his mad boyhood crush on the bass player's girlfriend. It came as no surprise when, in the summer of '67, the band broke into two factions, neither of which ever toured. In late '67 the band reconstituted itself, much too late to benefit the denizens of La Cave.

Luckily, there was enough time to find a suitable replacement act in the form of Wildflower, a psychedelic San Francisco outfit that had formed in 1965 as part of the vaunted "San Francisco Sound" with contemporaries Jefferson Airplane, Quicksilver Messenger Service, the Dead, Sopwith Camel, and Big Brother & the Holding Company, to name a few. They played the Fillmore, the Avalon Ballroom, the Matrix and the Trips Festival alongside these other purveyors of psychedelia, and travelled extensively up and down the California coast. But their main claim to legitimacy was their 1966 residency at the Red Dog Saloon, alternating weeks and sometimes jamming with a young Janis Joplin and Big Brother & the Holding Company. Wildflower was one of those original San Francisco Sounds bands who missed out on the big record contracts that other west coast bands were getting.

Their six-day stop at La Cave was part of their only tour outside the Golden State. For a solid month, the band played at The Ambassador Theater in D.C., The Trauma in Philadelphia, the Garrick Theater in New York and the Boston Tea Party. That left a ten-day-sized hole in their travel plans, as they had no bookings until their next concert in San Francisco on the 28th of September.

The music of the Wildflower painted pictures of mental experimentation, kicking off their set with their "Look Out Your Window," after ironically noting that there wasn't a window to look out of in the basement room. "Please Come Home," "Message to You," "In My Mind," and an extended jam on "Wind Dream," followed. As the first set ended, Stan attempted to clear the club for the next set, running into a large contingent of evidently very comfortable patrons, who refused or were unable to budge. It took all of his considerable charisma, and maybe a free espresso, to regain control. Many of those reluctant exiters turned right around to get in line for the next show, some of them grumbling about the good old days when La Cave was largely deserted, while others reveled in the ambiance of this youthful oasis where they could let it all hang out, so to speak.

When the last inert human form had been dislocated from its dank and smoky interior, La Cave's fearless Resident Wizard tallied the score: one thousand, eight hundred and forty-eight paid admissions spread over the fourteen sets the band performed. It remains one of the club's top ten best-attended week-long residencies for which records exist.

I Can't Believe It's Butter, Again

Having introduced the Butterfield Band to throngs of their Cleveland area worshippers, Stan had once again rolled his imaginary dice and came up seven, at least in the eyes of Irwin Arthur, the band's New York agent. He signed them to a six-day stay during the final week of September. Stan fondly recalled their recent stay and the profits that the little basement room produced as a result. This led to signing them, again, for an astounding $2,750 against 60% of the gross. In terms that we mere mortals can understand, that amount calculates to *each person in the band* receiving the equivalent of two weeks' income for the average American worker *each night.* By the end of the six-day residency, each band member received what you or I might have taken three months to earn!

No one could see it at the time, but this was the high-water mark for profits. The inexorable move away from solo acoustic acts was in its adolescence; soon the soloists would be eclipsed in popularity by full electric bands, sending the cost of running small clubs into the stratosphere. Few smaller clubs would survive into the Seventies.

Chapter 11: Larry Bruner

The decision to hire Stan some competent management help arrived with the timing of the U. S. Cavalry as led by Phil Ochs's hero John Wayne in *Fort Apache.* It came at the most opportune time possible. The bills were mostly paid and there were a few untapped funds in the till. Plus, and this weighed heavily on Nelson (not so much on Stan, who always had a sense keen of the inevitable), there were even larger bills on the horizon, as Nelson had begun to clearly see the direction that popular club music was taking. They could hire an up-and-comer like Janis Ian for around a fourth of what a full band with the same curb appeal cost, have fewer expenses and problems, and keep almost as much of the take as they would after a full band's stay at the club. Those costs often included feeding and sheltering the band and keeping them supplied with…stuff. Traveling with…stuff…could earn someone a felony stretch in a state or federal pokey, so it was often an unwritten rule that the clubs provide for the aid and comfort of the entertainers. Having a larger club could help absorb those extra costs. But Nelson didn't have one handy. He also knew that Stan was, and probably always would be, a soft touch. What was needed was some serious bean-counting, and a serious bean counter was what they got.

Larry Bruner picks up the story: "As a college student, I loved going to La Cave as a customer.

I saw Odetta and Tom Rush and Judy Henske and I was just entranced. I graduated from John Carroll [University] in August 1967. I'd worked overnight in hotels to put myself through college so far, and at that time I was at the Versailles Motor Inn. Channel

5, the home to the nationally syndicated Upbeat show was nearby. Many of the acts playing on the show and many record promotion men would stay at the Versailles, which also featured name entertainment in both a first-floor lounge and Penthouse Supper Club. I'd won a scholarship to law school and had in mind I'd work in civil rights and entertainment law. I started to look for a job in entertainment and Nelson heard about it somehow and gave me a call. He and Stan Kain interviewed me over lunch and said La Cave would have to close if they didn't find someone to take it over. I was enthusiastic in expressing my fondness for the place, and said I could turn it around."

"I was hired. Afterwards, Stan said to Nelson, 'I don't understand why someone like him would want to come to work with us.'"

"One of the first things I did was to tighten the La Cave door and insist that folks pay to come in. To say 'I'm a friend of Stan's' was no longer enough to escape paying for a show. I adopted bean counting protocols of keeping track of income and expenditures. Pitchers of beer had to be paid for. I started keeping meticulous records, tracking all income and expenditures. I also started to put my own stamp on the club mailing list. I redid the club logo with a '60s flair and started to personally design monthly postcards. Before I knew it, I'd become one of the social engineers of the local counterculture."

"At the Versailles, I'd seen a lot of acts that were slickly well-rehearsed, like Jerry Vale, the Temptations. Those acts I was used to had the same dance step moves and banter every show. It was quite different in this new underground world. Often a performer stood alone on the tiny stage, and if you were at the front tables, you often sat less than 10 feet away from the act. I was enthralled by the spontaneity I found at La Cave that Judy Henske or Arlo [Guthrie] would ramble for 10 minutes before a song with an introduction totally different from the night before. I even once asked Arlo why he didn't do "Alice's Restaurant" like it was on the radio. He said, simply, 'That's what the record is for.'"

For the first few months of his tenure, Larry worked at La Cave part-time, in order to be affordable, to learn the ropes, and to continue his law school studies. But the club was seductive.

"Six months later I dropped out of law school."

The Longest Journey Begins with the First Step

Larry was a quick study, bright in general and motivated in particular. Said he, "I was stopping by almost every week at the *Cleveland Press* to see Bruno Bornino and Harriet Peters and at *The Plain Dealer* to see Tom Davis and Jane Scott. These newspaper writers very rarely, if ever, came by to visit, but proved invaluable in mentioning who was playing. I kept a couple file cabinet drawers of paper, including 8x10 glossies and performer bios. It was a time of massive progressive social change and experimentation. Many of our performers were providing a soundtrack for the changes. La Cave featured acts throughout the '60s that were on the edge of something bigger than any of us knew. Many of them became widely known. Our tiny 300 seat disheveled club, known as Cleveland House of Folk Music, also became a stage for lots of blues and progressive rock music."

During his three-day stint from the 13th to the 15th of October, Dick Wedler attracted a total of 174 paying listeners. Sunday was the biggest bomb. Instead of pulling Larry's fat from the fire, it poured gasoline on it instead, with only thirteen patrons ponying up the required two bucks' admission price. In total, the club grossed a paltry $479 on admissions, food and drink for the weekend. Subtracting Dick's two-hundred-dollar wage and the other operating expenses netted the club nothing. The saving grace was that only one waiter was needed. On Sunday, that waiter was Kenny Klimak and he handled the embarrassing amount of $11.80 in food and drink sales. For the entire performance. There is no record of whether or not any spare change found its way into his tip jar.

However, to give credit where due, Larry was already beginning to play his long game. As soon as it had become apparent that The Fabulous Pack's weekend showing (Larry's first weekend on the job) was somewhere south of fabulous, he realized that the band's previous draw had been the name "Terry Knight," which came as no surprise, since the man had always been a relentless self-promoter. Larry got on the horn and asked, no, demanded, that Terry make things right. Terry, to his credit, agreed to a little horse trading: Terry Knight would return with the original Pack on the last weekend of November for a flat $1,500, *and* the first weekend of December for only a piece of the door, thereby guaranteeing that, overall, La Cave would see black ink by the end of those engagements. The Pack, with Terry's name attached, was a proven fan fave.

Nobody Said It Would be Easy

The road to success is littered with the remains of the has-beens and the never-was. Getting to the top was almost impossible; staying there was even harder. Larry was quickly learning that there was a little more to this booking game than meets the eye. In fact, one aspect of the business he was quickly gleaning was that if a club promoter landed even ten percent of the acts he or she wanted to sign, that was par for the course. It was even harder to book bands than soloists, for obvious reasons. But it was what the concertgoer wanted, more and more, and the customer was sometimes right. On the other hand, La Cave *had* built its reputation on solo acoustic performers, and many of them had not yet reached their sell-by dates.

Even before Larry began helping with the managing and booking for the club, Stan had hired some great acoustic acts to fill in the remainder of '67. Those names included, after Dick Wedler's poor draw, a New York up-and-comer with one Verve-labeled album under his guitar strap named Richie Havens, all of twenty-six years old and able to play his guitar in only one open tuning. Nevertheless, he was turning heads and ears, with his rich, soulful, booming baritone. Then there were the Youngbloods, veterans of La Cave and "owner" of the decade's theme song, "Get Together," Linn County and the Siegel-Schwall Band, two midwest blues-based combos that had proven very popular, more so as horns began to be integrated into rock music. Linn County boasted as members guitarist Steve Miller, later leader of his own wildly successful Steve Miller Blues Band, and Clark Pierson, who went on to accompany Janis Joplin.

Pulling out all the stops now, feeling Larry's metaphorical hot breath on the back of his neck, Stan also quickly promoted two very popular local outfits that knew La Cave well, the Mr. Stress Blues Band and the Tiny Alice Jug Band, to headline status. Both groups had large, enthusiastic local fan bases. Bill Miller of Mr. Stress and David Krauss of Tiny Alice could hold their own with the harp greats of the day like Butterfield and Cotton. Many felt them to be superior to the national names: they had home field advantage.

Rounding out December, Stan inked Dave "The Mayor of MacDougal Street" Van Ronk, the living legend Odetta, Jim & Jean, and was on the prowl for a suitable act to ring out the old and bring in the new year. Larry would beat him to it.

The Turning Point

A strong case could be made that the final three months of 1967 proved to be the artistic and financial high-water mark for La Cave. There was the internal conflict brewing between Stan and Larry for managing supremacy. Stan was soft-spoken but relentless with the charm, while Larry was headstrong, confident and well-spoken. Their conflicting styles were always threatening to collide, but somehow each man took the other in stride. It's not known if this conflict was the conscious construction of Nelson Karl, but whether it was or not, it certainly generated a lot of energy that was used constructively to move La Cave forward. The effect was to book more well-known (and *more expensive*) bands, which increased both La Cave's visibility and expenses. In the end, it wasn't sustainable.

Vietnam, Flower Power, and The Fugs

October 1967 would prove historic both nationally and locally, and the public did not see it coming in either locale. On 21 October, a massive anti-war demonstration, the largest yet, took place in Washington D.C., and the next day the entire world saw clearly the political fracture lines in American politics. And all because of a photograph that would ultimately cop a Pulitzer nomination. The March on the Pentagon was a massive protest that involved over a hundred thousand anti-war demonstrators in direct confrontation with armed members of the 82nd Airborne, famously known as the All-American Division.

The climax of the demonstration occurred when poet Michael Bowen delivered two hundred pounds of daisies to be passed out to the protestors. Bernie Boston, photographer for the *Washington Star*, was on hand to snap a picture of a young protester putting a daisy into a soldier's rifle barrel, while other rifles nearby also sported daisies. When published the next day all across the country under various incendiary headlines, the photo became an instant icon of the antiwar movement, which adopted the term "flower power" to send a nonviolent message to the rest of the country.

Larry used the occasion to La Cave's advantage. In his first week at La Cave (and before the March on the Pentagon was well-known) he had lobbied for booking a band that fit the description "obscenely radical leftists with an agenda." For reasons undiscovered, both Stan and Nelson signed off on Larry's signing The Fugs, a satirical band with a political slant, not to mention lewd and scatological lyrics. The group is mentioned in an FBI file; an excerpt mentions that the songs from *The Fugs First Album* are "vulgar and repulsive and are most suggestive."[xlviii]

The band's often frank and humorous lyrics about sex, drugs, and politics occasionally generated hostile reactions from listeners. How could they not? Those people were their target.

The band's participation in the March on the Pentagon is chronicled in Norman Mailer's book *The Armies of the Night.* Fugs member Ed Sanders also wrote a fictionalized account in his novel *Shards of God.* Mailer reminds us that the term "fug" is merely a slightly more acceptable version of the word "fuck." Larry strongly felt that an appearance by them would begin to put his own stamp on the La Cave mystique.

On 10 October, Larry, using Stan's name on the contract, signed the Fugs to perform on the first weekend in November for a staggering $2,500. On 21 October the band played at the March on the Pentagon. On 22 October, the same day everyone else heard about The Fugs, the shit hit the fan once again at La Cave.

All You Need is Luvs

The next exciting mishap during Larry's eventful first weeks at La Cave occurred when Herb Gart, one of Stan's valued New York connections, thought La Cave might be just the place to showcase his latest obsession, an all-female rock band. Back in spring he had mailed Stan the 2 May 1967 edition of Look Magazine, drawing his attention to a feature article on the Luvs, a Connecticut-based quartet of feisty eighteen-year-olds brimming with untapped sexual tension. Supposedly, they could play and sing, too. They were attractive and they knew it. It was going to be their ticket to stardom, or so the article explained. Stan had ignored or overlooked the article, but Larry, hungry to learn the ropes, had been rifling through Stan's disorganized collection of correspondence and chanced upon the article. He penned an impassioned plea to Herb's office on West 54th Street in the City and got an immediate reply. Herb explained that the band had two extended tours under their mod belts, one of them a month in a North Miami nightclub, and an extended residency in New York at actress Sybil Burton's posh discothèque Arthur, a place frequented by celebrities and their hangers-on. For a kicker, he casually mentioned that the quartet was just about to sign recording contract. In so many words, "This is your big chance to make a splash, kid."

Larry was smitten, partially by being able to talk freely with a big shot like Gart, and a little bit by the power of saying either yes or no to Herb's proposal: "The gals have a hole in their busy schedule. You can have them for four days at the end of October for the low, low price of $750, but kick in 60% of the gross if they do well." Larry was reasonably secure that he understood the terms and readily agreed. Contracts were exchanged and signed, and a couple of newspaper ads were submitted to the local rags.

The fall schedule continued apace, with Richie Havens drawing a large, respectful attendance and earning himself and the club a cool grand each for his four days of peace, love and strumming. Richie didn't so much play the guitar as attack it, his long, thin fingers flying up and down the open-tuned frets while he strummed with all the speed and vigor he could muster, his impassioned vocals more of a plea than poetry, although poetry was at the heart of his lyrics. Next, the Youngbloods had been slated to perform, but for some reason a contract had never been concluded, so the Luvs got chalked in in the schedule, slated to arrive on 26 October. It was that arrival that was problematic. Oh, a band showed up, on time and ready to play, it just wasn't the Luvs. This outfit called themselves The Enchanted Forest and contained exactly one member of the Luvs: lead singer Sanna Groseth. Rehearsals during the day proved to be less than acceptable, and Larry was in a fix. He'd been had, as somebody had pulled the old switcheroo on the neophyte talent buyer, and there was no time to make a change. Stan was told, and he placed a frantic call to Nelson, who placed his own frantic long-distance call to Herb Gart. Nelson was adamant; he'd pull a local act out of his magician's hat or close the club for the weekend, he threatened, nicely but firmly, as was his style. Anyone close to Nelson knew he rarely bluffed.

When the smoke from Nelson's ears cleared, the agreement was to pay the Enchanted Forest half of the previously agreed-to fee of $750, should they manage to survive their four nights on La Cave's stage. Evidently they did, because they left Cleveland, never to return, with the lower fee in their clutches. Lessons were being learned. The music business was exactly as Hunter Thompson described it – a shallow money trench filled with pimps and dogs.

Things began to settle back into some semblance of normal disorganization, the kind the club owners were accustomed to. Nelson had met with Stan and Larry, and made it clear that for the time being Stan was numero uno and Larry's bookings needed to be cleared through him. Terry Knight's group then had a couple solidly profitable weekends. The Siegel-Schwall Band was in top form, and even the locals who had been pulled into headline status along with Dick Wedler, the Tiny Alice Jug Band and the Mr. Stress Blues Band, were wildly popular and filled the club respectably, averaging almost two hundred fans per show. December had arrived and it looked as if the boys in the cave might just make it through one more year.

Onstage, December produced a flurry of great performances. Dave Van Ronk was back for a weekend, packing the club to capacity Friday the 8th and the next day, too. The next weekend, living legend Odetta held court and sold a thousand tickets, with Dick Wedler opening, and the ever-popular Jim & Jean crooned their way into youthful hearts during the week preceding Christmas. The bottom fell out and the year ended with a crash, however, when the Steve Miller Band cancelled and Linn County was pressed into service. And while they soldiered on professionally for the final six days of '67, the temperature, like the glittery Times Square ball, plummeted below zero to ring in the new year. It kept almost the entire city away. Those who were prone to premonitions, like Stan Kain was, shuddered, and not only from the cold.

Chapter 12:

1968 - Storm Clouds Gather

Even considering the breakneck speed with which society was being propelled into the future, as 1968 took its place atop the calendar, time and events accelerated beyond the population's ability to keep up with changes. The War in Vietnam was a daily dinner-table and water-cooler topic; everyone had a strong opinion by now, with antiwar sentiment beginning to gain the upper hand.

January of 1968 was also to be the moment that the United States government got crushed under the weight of their miscalculations as to the order of battle in Vietnam and their lies about it to the public. Last November, U.S. Ambassador to Vietnam Ellsworth Bunker, Commander of Forces General William Westmoreland, and President Johnson supported each other's conclusion that the war of attrition was working splendidly, as evidence by the high daily body counts of enemy dead. General Bruce Palmer Jr. claimed that "the Viet Cong has been defeated." Westmoreland was even more emphatic. At an address at the National Press Club on 21 November, he reported that, as of the end of 1967, "I am absolutely certain that whereas in 1965 the enemy was winning, today he is certainly losing. We have reached an important point when the end begins to come into view."[xlix]

Then, on 21 January, two regiments of Marines were overrun at a place called Khe Sanh, and it would take three months for those Marines to recover and prevail. But that was just a feint by the North Vietnamese Army (NVA). On 30 January, a campaign of surprise attacks known as the Tet Offensive began, striking at over a hundred cities and provincial capitals. It was the largest military operation of the war so far.[l] And while the battle was ultimately a military defeat for North Vietnam, their ability to strike in such a massive and unsuspected manner gave the lie to the U.S. government's rosy reports and turned many of the formerly staunchest war supporters into doubters. Even news anchor Walter Cronkite, known as "the most trusted man in America," visited Vietnam and came back home disillusioned, stating in February that the war could not be won. General Westmoreland demanded 200,000 more soldiers to knock back the attack, causing even more blowback from a war-weary populace.

Never again would the war enjoy widespread popular support. Secretly, the Johnson administration began seeking negotiations to end the war. It would take over five years and many more casualties to accomplish. It would also destroy Johnson's chance at a second term as President.

It would take another eighteen months, but La Cave would become one more casualty in the culture wars. Before the year could really get rolling, something akin to panic gripped the staff, and not because the New Year's Eve weekend was a bust. It was widely known that La Cave had been under surveillance for some time by the Cleveland Police Department. Its rise in popularity had brought with it a corresponding scrutiny from the authorities, who were stopping by nightly, following patrons to and from their cars, frisking the odd pedestrian, and making it clear that something was, sooner or later, going to give.

Sacred Mushrooms and Apple Pie

It's hard to overstate the influence that drugs, particularly hallucinogenics like LSD, had on the music of 1968. It was an era of wild experimentation. At this point few if any musicians envisioned making much money or having a lifelong career in music, and consequently could experiment with trying to recreate, musically, their "trips." In a couple of years this would change, when the moguls of music discovered that kids were willing to hitchhike halfway across the country to sit in the rain and mud for three days without ample food, clothing or shelter – all to listen to otherworldly music. But for now, there were still no arena acts, few festivals, and small, struggling clubs like La Cave, trying to adapt to the lightning-fast changes in musical tastes.

Some clean-cut, good old American as apple pie entertainment was just the ticket, so the Apple Pie Motherhood Band made the trek from the east coast to occupy La Cave's stage for four days beginning on 11 January. Of course, the band's name was pure misdirection. They had recently signed a recording contract with Atlantic Records, but only after taking their manager's good advice and changing their name from Sacred Mushroom, which sounded downright druggy. The nom de musique worked and they got the contract, releasing an album later in '68 and another in '70 before disbanding.

The band opened their sets at La Cave with a song they had recorded, to no acclaim at all outside of their native Boston, where it charted on WBZ radio, "Long Live Apple Pie." The song had been produced by Atlantic house producer Felix Pappalardi, who had also produced the English band Cream. The song was sung by the entire band, minus one – lead singer Anne Tansey. As the scattered applause faded, she burst onto the stage and began to belt out the band's trippy song "Ice." Anne's voice, strong, bluesy and melodic, has been compared favorably to another hippie chick. She was described as "a powerhouse, kind of a Janis Joplin with a sweeter voice, but sultry dynamic energy."[li] After the song and applause ended, she shouted out, "Anyone want some LSD?"[lii] Sometime during their set, they broke into an extended jam on Albert King's "Born Under a Bad Sign," an obvious nod to Felix and Cream. They would end each set with a long psychedelic jam they called "Ultimate." The audiences for their four-day stay were appreciative, if sparse. The long weekend was a plus for a couple hundred fans, but a net loss for Nelson and Company.

The Apple Pie band and the next band, the Fallen Angels,[liii] also a trippy quintet, were two of Larry Bruner's attractions. The erstwhile college student, now assistant to Stan Kain in booking La Cave, was also a folkie – but he had a keen eye for the changing trends. Plus, he had a connection with the local ABC-TV affiliate Channel 5, which hosted the nationally syndicated Upbeat Show, through his many nights working at the nearby Versailles Hotel, where many touring stars stayed while in town to film the show. Getting onto a nationally-syndicated show like Upbeat was a cherry atop the sundae that appearing at La Cave was. The Apple Pie Motherhood Band had taped a segment to be aired on 20 January, the same day as the Fallen Angels' appearance was scheduled. The timing was serendipitous, since the Angels weren't scheduled to play in the club until the 25th. By then, word had spread that this was a band not to be missed. And all because of a little toy doll.[liv]

It seems that the band, recently signed to Roulette Records, had been in conflict with their label's marketing gurus. They were ready to release their tripped-out single "Hello Girl," when, unbeknownst to the band, Roulette decided to re-record it with a more "pop-friendly" sound. For a band whose main musical inspiration was Frank Zappa, that was a call to arms, so to speak. But it wasn't the arms that the band pulled off the little doll they brought to the Upbeat set. It was the head, and it was during the taping of their song "Hello Girl." A major editing job was needed.[lv] Meanwhile, Larry's accounting of the Angels' La Cave stint was an even 450 paying customers, enough to eke out a profit.

Just Us Folkies

February witnessed an invasion of folkies at La Cave. In quick succession Tom Rush, locals Donnery & Rudd, the Times Square Two, Mike Seeger and Dock Boggs, and Woody's kid Arlo held down the stage, with only the psychedelic band Tiffany Shade to present a contrasting sound.

Tiffany Shade had several minor claims to fame in 1968. They released their only long player on the psych-heavy Mainstream label (where Joplin and Big Brother, and the Amboy Dukes got their start), opened for Big Brother and the Holding Company and the MC5 in Detroit at the Grande Ballroom in March and again in April, and, later in '68 took over the care and feeding of Stan's pad, but that's getting ahead of the story.

The folkies of February held their own, financially speaking. Larry's scrutinous records indicated that Tom Rush had sold 868 tickets, the Time Square Two attracted 192 paying patrons, Tiffany Shade brought in 280 payers and youthful Arlo Guthrie, recently declared "The new crown prince of folk music" by New York critics, garnered 792 fans. Arlo's 18-minute antiwar tale "Alice's Restaurant" had explosively zoomed into international polls of best-selling albums. To top off the offbeat marketing campaign, WIXY-1260 radio DJ Jerry Butler informed lucky listeners that sending him a postcard marked "underground" would give ten radio fans a chance at a free ticket to see Arlo at La Cave. Butler claimed to be the first AM DJ to play "Alice's Restaurant" in its entirety."

La Cave lived to fight another month.

1968 brought a sea change of local, national, and international events. On January 22nd, the Rowan and Martin Laugh-In Show debuted on NBC. Along with the Smothers Brothers Comedy Hour on the CBS-TV network, the youth "counterculture" was invading American living rooms in prime time. Along with the growing popularity of FM radio, which was still largely commercial-free, suddenly there were new outlets for the experimental sounds of what people were calling "underground" music. Local AM stations began to sponsor weekly segments featuring non-pop music. In Cleveland, that meant the Doc Nemo Show and The Perlich Project. FM radio was quickly becoming the 800-pound gorilla in the room, with avant-garde DJs like Martin Perlich holding court overnight, playing music that would otherwise have never sniffed a radio station turntable. Record companies were signing bands by boatloads, in hopes that a pearl would appear among the swine.

Overseas, on the 7th of February, after a battle for the Vietnamese village of Ben Tre, an American officer told Associated Press reporter Peter Arnett, "It became necessary to destroy the town in order to save it." The quotation, printed in newspapers nationwide, became a catchphrase for opponents of the Vietnam War.

The war was primary on minds of voters in this election year. The Tet Offensive had badly damaged LBJ's standing with voters, and a groundswell of support for Robert F. Kennedy (RFK) to challenge the incumbent bore fruit when on 16 March he declared his candidacy for the Democratic nomination. LBJ could plainly read the Texas tea leaves and two weeks later, declared he was dropping out of consideration. This instantly put the antiwar candidate RFK in the pole position for the upcoming Presidential race.

What Could Possibly Go Wrong?

Then Stan got a call from an old pal of his, Al Kooper, formerly of the Blues Project. Stan and Al had gotten close during his band's Cleveland stops, and Al considered La Cave his home away from home. Al's big idea, which was to marry a rock band with a horn section, had met with a big thumbs down from the Project's leader Danny Kalb. So Al formed his own group, which he named Blood, Sweat and Tears, after the Winston Churchill remark.

Al then used his industry connections to get Simon & Garfunkel's producer John Simon at Columbia Records to produce the band's debut, and Columbia was nothing short of happy to pry Al away from Capitol. By the end of 1967 the album was in the can and Columbia announced the date of the record's release: 21 February of '68. Which meant the band had to get on the road to promote it.

So Al continued his own version of working the phones, meaning that he called Stan to have La Cave fill the hole in their touring schedule. The hole was the first weekend in March, which happened to collide head on with the weirdly-nicknamed members of the Canned Heat troupe, who were contracted for that weekend. It was Larry Bruner who came up with what everyone thought was an amazing solution to the scheduling snafu.

Larry had been rather relentless. It was just his way. He jumped in with both feet on many causes. After his stint at La Cave he would continue working for peace, running or assisting neighborhood non-profits, booking concerts and rallies, publishing a counterculture alternative newspaper, and spend a lifetime promoting local folk music. But now, he massaged his local relationship with local chain Disc Records, while Stan and Martin Perlich hatched the rest of the plot.

When the weekend was finalized, Canned Heat *and* Blood, Sweat & Tears would play alternating sets on Friday and Saturday night. On the Friday the bands were to open, 1 March, Larry got both bands to agree to make an afternoon personal appearance, sign some autographs and generally act rock star-ish at Disc Records in Cleveland Heights. Stan got the bands to agree to stick around La Cave after their last sets in order to play live on Martin Perlich's "Perlich Project" overnight underground radio show on WCLV-FM. They would play until 4am, reportedly.

Crucially, Larry induced Disc Records to place a three-quarter-page newspaper ad and pay for it, sharing the formidable cost with WCLV, which also broadcast a few announcements on the air. While these announcements were of no cost to La Cave, they constituted some of the very first advertising spots on the formerly pristine FM radio band. And Disc passed costs along to Liberty Records and included their logo in the ad.

And finally, Stan got the label to cover the band's cost for the weekend meaning, in essence, they were playing for free as far as La Cave cared.

What could possibly go wrong?

Stan arrived around noon on Friday to oversee the cleanup and setup, and worry a bit. His main concern was that way too many people would arrive, congregate outside and cause disturbances both in the club and out on the street. Which is exactly what happened. Then the police showed up. The crowd quickly became the least of his worries.

Stan picks up the story: "Two cops in uniform and two in plain suits came into La Cave and asked for me. I was in back, so someone came and got me. The cops offered me a deal. They said they knew the traveling musicians would be carrying drugs with them. They wanted me to find out who had what and when the police came in, I could point out which ones had the drugs and they'd take it from there. I refused. 'What about the customers? We know a lot of them come here to buy drugs. Point some of them out to us. We won't involve you in any way.' So I asked them how long they thought I'd stay in business if word got out that La Cave was a good place to get busted?"

"Yes, for the first time I was scared. But I refused to, you know, rat on anybody." Stan didn't remember any specific threats being made, but it was well understood that somebody's days as a free man were numbered, and that somebody was him.

The bands were a huge success all around. They attracted throngs of young worshippers at the record store, many of whom went to camp out on Euclid in a line that stretched around the block by 6 o'clock. Dozens or more clutched newly-purchased albums in hopes of having autographs applied to them. When the door opened, it was mayhem. But Stan, Larry and the staff quickly regained command of the terrain, and everyone was seated, with their thirst temporarily slaked, and when the first boogie beat of Canned Heat's soon-to-be top ten hit "On the Road Again" filled the club, mayhem resumed. It was happy chaos, and when the dust settled, 464 paying customers and at least 50 freeloading "friends" had experienced a real happening. Blood, Sweat and Tears ended the evening's festivities with their soulful "I Love You More Than You'll Ever Know," and, to their delight, dedicated it to the cave dwellers who then lined up for autographs.

The friskings and arrests began the moment the crowd began to disperse.

March of '68 proved to be one of the more offbeat set of bookings La Cave had seen yet. After BS&T's and Canned Heat's weekend, Mike Seeger popped in the next weekend and played to sparse crowds, not quite 200 for his three days onstage. Mike was an accomplished musician, musical historian and musicologist. He usually showed up for gigs with the better part of a music store in hand – he could play a dozen instruments. As one of the musical Seeger family, Mike garnered six Grammy nominations and received four grants from the National Endowment for the Arts, including a 2009 National Heritage Fellowship, which is the United States government's highest honor in the folk and traditional arts.

Mike brought with him as his banjo accompanist 70-year-old Dock Boggs, whom Mike had "discovered" in 1963 when Mike, who knew all about his old timey recordings, traveled down Virginia-way specifically to find him. Through Mike's efforts, Dock played before an estimated 10,000 folk music fans at the Newport Folk

Festival that year. Also due in part to Mike's efforts, the Dock Boggs Festival began in 1968 and continues through today.[lvi]

And yet, because of the times, no amount of old-time acoustic talent was going to outdraw the next great thing in music: loud, experimental, psychedelic rock. As a result, the two living legends, Mike and Dock, split five hundred bucks for their weekend at La Cave.

The next band due in town was Orpheus, a baroque-rock band from Massachusetts that Larry had heard one late night on Martin Perlich's radio show. The band hit the scene in '68 with a charting song "Can't Find the Time," and released their self-titled debut album at the same time. The band was part of a slick marketing campaign called the "Bosstown Sound," a bald-faced attempt by east coast promoters to cash in on the success of the San Francisco psychedelic scene. But due to a scheduling conflict (which, along with "illness in the band" was one of the two standard excuses for no-showing), they had to withdraw. This was fortunate, as it opened up a spot for a band that had been relentless in requesting stage time at La Cave, going so far as having a number of fans write letters, some of them fairly legible, to Stan to hire one of the strangest – and as it so happened, one of the most popular in La Cave's history – bands in existence in 1968 or, for that matter, any time, The Hello People.

Hello, People

"Weirdly deep" is how Allmusic website contributor Fred Thomas describes the Hello People.[lvii] Of course, in 1968, "weirdly deep" was something close to normal. As was "deeply weird," and both phrases describe in elegant precision pretty much every aspect of the band. To call them unique would be an understatement. In 2013 the Dangerous Minds web reviewer opined, "In a genre unto themselves, one we can all be thankful never took off, the concept of 'mime rock' and The Hello People sprang from the mind of longtime manager and record producer Lew Futterman."

What singled out this collection of Ohio transplants to New York was the fact that they played in whiteface, a' la Marcel Marceau. Further, they acted in mime between songs, never uttering a single word. Topping off their stage act was a decidedly antiwar theme to many of their songs, the song "Anthem" being particularly incisive. It opened their sets and was sung from the point of view of a draft resister.

Their performance began with a John Philip Souza martial drum beat remindful of a firing squad cadence. One by one, in mime, three guitarists aimed their instruments like rifles at the audience and "fired" them to a snare drum rim shot. But the fourth guy looked sad and slowly lowered his guitar and shook his head "no." The drumbeat stopped and a mournful flute passage was played. Then the lyrics began: "They say I was born/in the land of the free/But the home of the briefcase/is all I can see/With fine houses and highways/we cover the land/But freedom's a fable/if the conscience is banned/So I'm going to prison/for what I believe/I'm going to prison/so I can be free."

Their ten-song set lasted about forty minutes in front of a slightly amazed roomful. Polite applause, an automatic reaction, followed each tune, as the listeners caught onto the mime segments between songs. The final song ended with the same drumbeat as, one by one, the band "marched" offstage until only the drummer, "Thump Thump," remained behind the drum kit. Then, theatrically, the band returned to take a bow – to thunderous applause and demands for an encore. Word quickly spread and Friday's middling crowd turned into a standing-room only affair on Saturday, with many fans from Friday returning for a repeat performance.

Before the end came, they played La Cave six more times in the twelve months following their debut and became one of the most endearing – and enduring – memories of many cave dwellers.

Another "Bosstown Sound" band was the next act to show up, Ultimate Spinach. They sported a gimmick for the times, a female guitar player, Barbara Jean Hudson. She could also belt out some powerful vocals. Another advantage the band had was that MGM, their record label, was willing to spend beaucoup bucks on promotion. This made Larry very happy. His opinion was that almost anyone could draw a full room of fans with enough promotion. He asked for, and got, large posters, signed album jackets, albums (the band had already released two LPs, with their self-titled debut reaching number 34 on the Billboard album chart), and a batch of glossy 8x10s to plaster around town. It worked. Their three-day stop at La Cave starting 22 March attracted over six hundred paying souls.

Stan had only scheduled two waiters, so the result was another black ink weekend for the club. It didn't hurt that the band also had a strong antiwar message to their music. That theme had become a surefire winner with the fans of the "underground" scene.

He would schedule a total of ten waiters for the following weekend, and he'd need them all.

All We Have to Offer You is Our Blood, Sweat & Tears

The buzz surrounding Blood, Sweat & Tears' encore engagement for the last week of March was palpable. Everyone who was anyone planned to go, to be part of the scene as well as to hear a band with a growing national presence. After their first stint at La Cave, they had been featured on Cleveland's syndicated music showcase The Upbeat Show. It was designed to build on the first stop. This band meant business, literally. Part of the scheme included a repeat stop on Upbeat after this La Cave weekend, on 6 April, to gauge the band's progress.

Larry, his value to the club only increasing, got Columbia Records to give away fifty of BS&T's debut album *Child is Father to the Man*. The *Plain Dealer* was only too happy to relay that touch of marketing genius. On the other hand, the band's management insisted on a $2,000 fee, with a sellout bonus, as opposed to the first appearance when Columbia picked up the tab.

Sandwiched between these two stops in Cleveland, BS&T travelled to the Grande Ballroom in Detroit, Kiel Auditorium in St. Louis, the Fillmore and Winterland in San Francisco, the Whisky a Go Go in Los Angeles, back up to Frisco and the Avalon Ballroom, and then back east to the Electric Circus in Greenwich Village before decamping to La Cave again. Afterwards, they'd hop back to NYC to the Café and Electric Factory again, and the Garrick Theater, upstairs from the Café Au Go Go at 152 Bleecker Street.[lviii]

In other words, discounting their many east and west coast appearances, they performed at only three clubs in the heartland, including twice in Cleveland. An "underground railroad" of sorts had been established for progressive bands and La Cave had become an essential stop on that circuit. Like BS&T, La Cave would soon be recognized as such by the music industry. The events of that final weekend in March were memorable. Especially to Stan.

La Cave Earns National Media Attention

This book has mentioned Billboard Magazine several times, the reason being that it is considered "the bible" of music news, ads, gossip, industry hijinks, and all other things musical. Billboard had been a company with progressive ideas for generations. They made huge societal news in 1920 by hiring the country's first African-

American journalist James Albert Jackson to write a weekly column. Billboard also established a policy against identifying performers by their race. The company achieved numerous other industry firsts and to this day publishes the most trusted, respected music charts in the country.

Billboard Magazine was the weekly periodical that found its way onto the desk of every music impresario in the States. Chairmen of multi-million-dollar record labels and starving agents working on a client's next gig, and everyone in-between, took notice of every word in the mag. Even the agate type. *Especially* the agate type.

That's why the magazine's 23 March 1968 edition was of such intense interest at La Cave. In a lengthy article, the magazine explained that a string of "underground" clubs had risen to the top spot showcasing and breaking new recording groups, as important as radio.

This was sweet music to Nelson, Stan and Larry. It alerted them to the fact that clubs like La Cave had achieved, through lots of hard work, worry, and luck, the kind of prominence that they had only imagined for themselves. Until now, life at La Cave was a daily struggle to pay the bills, sign the acts, shepherd the hired help, fill in the scheduling holes on an ad hoc basis, deal with regulating authorities, and generally just try to make it through the next concert. The article raised their consciousness about their part in the scheme of things to a higher level for the first time. It was heady stuff.

The article continued on page ten, and that's where the bombshell dropped. The comment listed seven clubs on the coast: four in Boston and New York, and three in Los Angeles and San Francisco. That was to be expected and was really no surprise to anyone in or out of the trade. Included however, representing the rest of the country, were two heartland clubs no more than a two-hour drive from one another: Detroit's Grande Ballroom and

Cleveland's La Cave. That's it. That was the sum total of clubs that Billboard considered "taste-makers and trend-setters."

The effect was immediate. The phone began ringing regularly. the days of begging acts to perform and the sleepless nights juggling the bills were over. Or so it seemed at the time.

An Offer You Can't Refuse

One person who read the Billboard article was the manager of the Hello People, Lew Futterman. He dashed off a Special Delivery letter which began "I have been waiting for you to get back to me regarding a new booking for the Hello People." Farther down, "[T]he people at Philips were quite pleased with the way everything went and would be most willing to cooperate with you thoroughly on a replay."

He continues the letter, almost on his knees: "Our anxiety to play your club again is based on the fact that we do feel one more appearance in Cleveland will break the boys through in the market."

Then came the "offer you can't refuse:" Lew offered Stan future options to host the band at the same fee as before. "As you know," Lew continued, "options can be lifesavers the way the money of these groups tends to escalate." As a final inducement, Lew asked Stan to watch the band on the Tonight Show on 12 April, the unwritten message being that the band was about to "break" nationally.

Stan, Nelson and Larry may have done a celebratory dance. For a club the size and location of La Cave to begin receiving this kind of offer, and there were many more, was simply outstanding. You could count on one hand the number of non-NY, LA or SF clubs that were held in such high esteem. Being no fools, the cave men signed the band for six more appearances. They also might have imagined needing buckets to shovel their money into.

La Cave had finally "made it."

Tragedy, Again

April of 1968 was a banner month for the boys in the basement. For one thing, the increasing focus on the Vietnam War and its detractors in the underground political movement was gaining traction and slowly exploding into daily front page stuff. The kind of person who felt at home at La Cave was feeling increasingly empowered, and being part of "the scene" was a crucial desire for more and more young people. On the third of April, "The Mobe"[lix] held a nationwide draft card burning day, which would have made much more of an impact but for the news that fractured the nation the next day. Breaking into the regularly scheduled six o'clock news programs on every television set and radio receiver, newscasters scrambled for details, but this much was known: at about 6pm in Memphis, Dr. Martin Luther King, Jr. was assassinated at the Lorraine Motel, where he was staying after delivering his famous "I Have Been to the Mountaintop" speech.

In Cleveland, Mayor Carl B. Stokes, the first elected African-American mayor of a major American city,[lx] pleaded for calm. Nationally, Presidential candidate Robert F. Kennedy, on the campaign trail in Indiana, broke the news to the African-American neighborhood to screams and wailing of pain and disbelief. His words were a balm to the stunned crowd. He was met with applause instead of anger, and the listeners quietly dispersed. The rest of the country didn't fare as well. A wave of riots rocked the nation on the 4th, with some historians opining that it was the greatest wave of social unrest the United States had experienced since the Civil War.

It was going to be a long, hot, violent summer, and Cleveland would not be spared.

Before the heat, however, came a definite chill in the air. It wasn't atmospheric, it was emotional. People of all shapes and sizes were stunned by the assassination. As riots broke out all through the country, and denunciations flew in all directions, nobody was in the mood to go nightclubbing. Entertainers cancelled their weekend gigs to hole up and contemplate their future. La Cave, situated on the very edge of one of the country's poorest neighborhoods, felt particularly vulnerable. Stan had no headliners to play that weekend, so he called stalwart Dick Wedler, who ultimately declined, and then Stan had a thought. A local band had been hitting him up for a chance onstage. They were an outrageously loud pre-punk psychedelic garage band named, appropriately, Spontaneous Corruption. They came complete with a bad reputation. The members of the band were guitarist Greg Giancola, drummer Ken Hamlin, and bassist Danny Sheridan. All three would go on to have lengthy careers in music, Greg as a manager, booking agent and other sundry duties, Ken, who later became a VP of sales at Elektra/Asylum Records in New York, and Danny, perhaps the most well-known of the trio, who helped pioneer the nascent "outlaw country music" genre by founding the band Eli Radish, became an influential rock bassist, and managed the career of Nina Blackwood, his girlfriend and MTV's first video jock (VJ). He later managed and toured with Bonnie Bramlett of Delaney, Bonnie and Friends with Eric Clapton. But at the time, he was all of seventeen. Stan snapped them up for the weekend.

The band played to sparse crowds on the 5th and 6th of April, which was not unexpected – only 132 paying customers for both nights. Nevertheless, they put on a show for the ages. Loud as hell, they ran through their repertoire of original songs, among them their only regional hit "Freaky Girl," which was either a reverent homage to or blatant rip-off of Hendrix's "Purple Haze." At one point in the festivities Ken decided to douse his cymbals with lighter fluid, and moments later they were engulfed in flames, to the delight and horror of the fans. Fortunately, according to Greg, it just took "a few towels" to extinguish the blaze. When Greg mentioned to his Dad that the band had played in a dangerous neighborhood, the fatherly advice he received was "Tell your mom you played at the Holiday Inn."

Once again, fate stepped in to ruin things. Phil Ochs, scheduled to play for a weekend, was a no-show. It wasn't Phil's fault this time. Phil's brother Michael, acting as his manager since Phil had alienated his previous handlers with his often-bombastic style of communication when not on stage, fired off a furious letter to Stan. Phil had his demons, but he also had acquired some clout since the days when he busked for spare change at La Cave and elsewhere. The collect call Phil made from Cleveland Hopkins Airport to Michael singed the younger brother's ear, so much so that he fired off the following diatribe under the Aquarian Age, Inc. letterhead:

"Dear Mr. Kain,

Michael and I feel that your failure to arrange for someone to meet Phil at the airport or to contact us regarding it was entirely avoidable and quite unprofessional. We regret your lack of organization and professional and personal courtesy; therefore, it appears likely neither Phil nor any of our other artists will be appearing at your club in the future.

Regards,

Michael Ochs & Robert Emery"

"Fuck me," thought Stan. He knew exactly why he had become so distracted.

After The Blues Project cancelled their appearance for the next weekend, Dick Wedler agreed to sit in and drew about 150 attentive but subdued patrons. Furious muted conversations circled the room. But it was the following weekend that made La Cave, and Cleveland, history.

Harumi

Mid-week at La Cave – Wednesday the 17th, witnessed one of the weirder and more obscure performances in the already weird but no longer obscure club. Harumi, a 21-year-old Japanese performance artist made a one-day, two-set stopover on his way from Boston to Honolulu. He was in the midst of his only career concert tour, a five-week affair funded by his label, Verve Forecast. His self-titled album had just been released and he was traveling cross country in its support. With him came a four-piece combo whose identities have been obscured by time.

Harumi's specialty was spoken word. He may have been the world's first "rapper," as he wrote poetic lines like "sugar in the tea/just to hide the flavor of reality" and "sang" them in both English and Japanese. His twenty-five-minute ""Twice Told Tales of the Pomegranate Forest" was in spoken word, while the equally lengthy "Samurai Memories" was a slow-motion freakout that probably was much more enjoyable to the acid-dosed crowd than to mere mortals.[lxi]

In an interview, Harumi said, "Some write for one kind of group, like r&b. When I write I hope everybody will like it. There's a little bit of everything." The interviewer added: "Which might just be the understatement of April. Who else has poetry, a Japanese dialogue and a dog on his records?"

It was a great plan to bring him to town on Verve's dime, because, with little advance promotion the crowd was sparse – only 13 drink checks were issued.

An extensive search failed to find out anything about Harumi in the years afterwards. His life and assumed death are shrouded in mystery. There are several conjectures about him, but none are confirmed. The same could be said about his dog, "Misty."[lxii]

Like Velvet

In the early morning hours of 26 April, the ad in the *Plain Dealer* depicted the Velvet Underground holding their most recent release, "White Light/White Heat." This was undoubtedly the most anticipated concert of the year, since those attending the band's previous stopover in Cleveland had been spreading the Gospel of Lou, and everyone wanted to see this group for themselves. Knowing the ad was in Friday's paper, and needing some distraction from his personal problems, Stan came in around 9am to a ringing phone. And it didn't stop ringing until he finally left it off the hook. The reservations had reached, actually surpassed, the room's capacity. And with Verve picking up expenses, the Velvets had agreed to play for a mere $1,100 for the weekend.

Early arrivals to Friday's sets could hear the band noodling around backstage, warming up, improvising. Expectations were heightened. While the band was still firmly in the cult category, it was in the air that they were going to break out nationally any time now. Something about Lou Reed made whatever space he was in come alive.

Suddenly, it was showtime. The band sprinted onto the crowded stage, with barely enough room for them and their equipment on the platform. The crowd was beside itself before a note was played. Moe Tucker's drum kit was set up to Lou's right to make room for the keyboards that John Cale would play when he wasn't on the electric viola. Lou sported his hot-rodded Gretsch White Falcon (with a decal shouting "Caution! K-9 Corps") and Sterling Morrison hoisted his Gibson. Scattered around them were their double cabinet Vox amps. As befitted her style, Moe brought no cymbals.

Friday and Saturday nights were tours-de-force of ear-splitting bliss for lovers of the Velvets, but a large minority of fans crammed into La Cave needed a little time to adjust. Lou alternately insulted and complimented a couple waiters and fans, and was generally what he would become: arrogantly talented. It was all in good, clean fun. Stan & Co. put 426 paying fannies in seats and standing room on Friday, and 466 were shoehorned in on Saturday.

Jaime Klimek taped the Sunday matinee, and while the setlists of Friday and Saturday are still in dispute, the Sunday set included a 39-minute "Sweet Sister Ray" segueing into "Sister Ray," "Mr. Rain," "Venus in Furs," and "Heroin." Somewhat amazingly, fewer than a hundred fans showed up on Sunday. Then again, it all made perfect sense.

A few weeks later, the *Plain Dealer* had a lot to say about Lou and his cohorts, and disputed the band's detractors, defending the avant-garde, experimental sound of the group. As popular as they were with the underground crowd, few at the time could have predicted the bands would eventually gain immortality with their election to the Rock and Roll Hall of Fame, not to mention Lou's additional induction as a solo artist.

Cleveland's Underground Poet Laureate

On Saturday, 27 April 1968, underground poet d.a. levy was comfortably installed on the floor, Buddha-style, directly in front of the La Cave stage, awaiting the much-anticipated appearance of headliner Velvet Underground. He was early enough to witness local band The Mind Garden (they had not yet changed their name to the even more psychedelic Mynd Garden*)* play their early set as the evening's opening act.

Mind Garden. There's a band name that conjures the '60s. Sowing psychedelic seeds, as it were. The Mind Garden was a collection of high school students from Cleveland's eastern suburbs. As Jeff Joseph remembers, "All [of us] were high school kids from Cleveland. Me, Bob Finkle, Art Penner, Roger Sherman, Paul Caron, Wally Waffel, Linda Gilliland. We were all 17 at the time. Bob and I went to Mayfield High, the others [to Cleveland] Heights [High School]."[lxiii]

Linda Gilliland, now Linda White, today lives in Florida, where many Clevelanders take their winters, not to mention their sunset years. As one of the band's vocalists, she remembers "how friendly and kind Al Kooper and Blood, Sweat & Tears were when we opened for them in March. They told us we were welcome to use any of their equipment that was up onstage, and we partied with them after the show. The Velvet Underground barely noticed us when they were [at La Cave]."

The Mind Garden may not have survived the '60s as a band, but they made a deep impression on d.a. levy that late April night at La Cave. Finding inspiration in their performance as well as their appearance, he put pencil stub to paper as he published his review of their musical effort on his own hand-crank press in his own publication, Cleveland's first underground newspaper, the *Buddhist Third-Class Junkmail Oracle,*[lxiv] praising their formidable talents:

THE MIND GARDEN – wrathful deities of the UTP?

d.a. levy 1968

LA CAVE Sat 27 april/ I was blasted into the ocean of the universe by seven, 17-year-olds (Clevelanders) who were doing (perhaps through naïve inexperience) one perfect song after another. IT WAS UNHOLY! ECSTATIC!

"Even after one too many glasses of beer, I think it was my 2nd, I can still hear & record music from the other shore. i sat on the floor in front of the group but I was flying & transmitting like an electronic computer – ZAP ZAP screaming in the vortex – they seemed to have dredged the sound of psychic warfare from the genetic memory banks of the Underground Thought Patrol. The Music like a lesson in survival, learning how to kill for peace (unseen) rolling in the currents of inner-space – thought rides into the emptiness of the Ohio night & the lonely echoes of the ephedrine sulfate (and/or) ritalin (and/or) preluding run – flight of vultures through transparent space – humping & stomping on GROUND ZERO as if to say 'We are not the targets, we are the bombs dropping" The MINDGARDEN explodes in your brain – giving you a 'clear' space to reconnect with the universe – reminding you to survive as you search for love. Like they are saying it, flower children armed with the eye of Horus.

Listen to them whenever they appear again. Listen to them before they are scattered and disillusioned by the whores of the establishment…the UTF is listening o you……."[lxv]

d.a. spent several seemingly pleasant evenings at La Cave during the remainder of 1968 according to a number of patrons. But as far as can be determined, he was never so inspired as he was that magical, at least to d.a., night.

A sad postscript to this tale is that on November 26, 1968, several months after having his mind blown by The Mind Garden at La Cave, d.a. levy committed suicide, alone and broke, in his rented East Cleveland home. But not before he immortalized, sort of, the now lost-to-the-mists-of-history band Mind Garden.

Michael and Tom and the Enemies List, Eventually

You might be asking yourself how a nice guy can meet a lasting partner while out on tour? According to Tom Shipley, it's a process. Tom, born, raised and educated in the 'burbs of Cleveland, began busking around while attending Baldwin-Wallace College in Berea. Michael Brewer, an Oklahoma native, began troubadouring around the same time. In 1964, during their travels, they met at the Blind Owl Coffee House in Kent, Ohio, an hour south of Cleveland. By '67 they had both migrated to Los Angeles in search of their respective muses, and as it happened, ended up living around the corner from one another. Tom picks up the story: "You get a couple of young musicians together, they both have guitars, what are they gonna do? They're gonna play, right?"

Michael had picked up a gig as staff writer for Good Sam, A&M Records' publishing arm, and put in a word about Tom, who also joined the staff as a writer. It turned out that their writing was top shelf, and soon Good Sam was selling their tunes to The Nitty Gritty Dirt Band, Glenn Yarbrough, H.P. Lovecraft, Bobby Rydell and others. Their songs were so well-crafted and popular that someone at A&M suggested the boys team up as players and release their own album. While writing and performing, the duo, besides their own gigs, opened for bands like The Byrds and Buffalo Springfield (who got their name from a bulldozer parked in front of Michael's house). May of '68 found them together on the road, writing songs and playing concerts in anticipation of their album's release, "Down in L.A.," which happened in October.

That merry month also found them at La Cave for weekend dates on the 3rd through the 5th. Both had performed separately in and out of Cleveland, including at La Cave, and now, in May of '68 they were finally a harmonious duo. Both were above-average guitarists and vocalists; together, well, their styles and talents were multiplied. To this day, fans revere their two-part harmonies. They were never flashy; they were consistently very good, with nights of greatness.

They were still six months away from having an album released, and in fact they were still a couple months away from being Brewer & Shipley, since this time around the circuit they were billed as Shipley & Brewer. Combined, the two made a great impression everywhere they played. It was obvious that they had already spent years in becoming an overnight sensation. A recording of Michael's first La Cave appearance exists, and it's obvious he already had a charismatic stage presence. He was closing for Saline Fjeld (pronounced "field"), a popular local folkie. It was a sparse Sunday night crowd of perhaps three dozen, when Mike appeared on stage to light applause. "Oh, thank you very, very much. I'm sure Saline Fjeld said it once before, but I'm going to say it again. Welcome one and all (pause for effect) to La Cave. (another pause) Big Sunday night, right here... in Cleveland, Ohio. Lots of fun. Oh well, hey, before I go any further, I want to tell you something right now. If anything really terrible happens while you're here tonight, especially while I'm on stage, don't think anything of it because terrible things happen everywhere I go. Because I am a jinx. I really am. Terrible, terrible, horrible things happen to me everywhere I go. So if anything really drastic happens, just don't think anything of it."

Michael launches into several examples of his jinxiness, each example more and more improbable, to more and more laughter, and ends his spiel with, "So I'm going to dedicate this next song to me. This song is sort of become my theme song, it really has. I could never get on any stage and not sing this song. The song is also dedicated to the fine people that I had the opportunity of spending the day with. Crazy things happened today, folks, but I'm not even going there. The song is called, "That's the Bag I'm In."[lxvi]

The applause Michael received afterwards sounded more like three hundred than three dozen.

Chapter 13:

The Beginning of the End

Stan had been distracted for a while. That was evident to everyone. The only other person who knew what his problem was, was Nelson Karl. It all changed on Monday morning, 13 May, after the Canadian r&b outfit The Mandala had played La Cave in front of a total of 218 ticket-buying fans on the just-ended weekend. The band was one month shy of releasing their debut – and only – album on Atlantic Records. Internal discord would tear apart the band before any real success could be attained. Interestingly, their guitar player Domenic Troiano later became lead plank-spanker for Cleveland's own James Gang.

In an unintentionally ironic way, the band's implosion closely resembled La Cave's slow-motion implosion. Just at the point that La Cave had broken out of the bush leagues to become a national player on the club scene, the Feds executed an arrest warrant on Stan and three others early Monday morning, 13 May. Nelson was able to bail him out immediately, but the charge was a federal crime: conspiracy to violate the Drug Control Act of 1966. The chaos that was engulfing the country on several fronts overtook the day-to-day dealings of the club. And on Tuesday morning, the entire city knew what had happened, thanks to local reporting and 48-point font, all-caps headlines.

THE PLAIN DEALER

CIRCLE AREA LSD RING SMASHED

No Shift in Positions

U.S. and Hanoi Trade Views

Fisher's Plans Chicago Merger

Stanton Raps Stokes'

If the reporting was accurate, Stan and three co-conspirators had either "obtained or manufactured stimulant, depressant and hallucinogenic drugs and distributed them to pushers." A front-page story wasn't enough, evidently. Stan's picture graced page one also, along with his home address and description as "part owner of La Cave."[lxvii]

This was no penny-ante bust of local druggies. This was, according to the authorities, a bust that included over a million dollars' worth of LSD, ready for distribution to area "pushers" for sale to users. They also identified the University Circle neighborhood as "the [city's] main peddling area."[lxviii]

The *Cleveland Press,* the city's afternoon daily, followed up the scoop on the same day, under the headline "LSD Charges Denied by 4 Nabbed as Drug Suspects." At least the headline wasn't in all caps. The article quoted Stan, as told to a reporter, distancing himself from the charges: "'No LSD was ever dispensed at La Cave,' said Stanley Kain, 32, part owner of the Euclid Ave. folk-rock night spot." The reporter then averred that Stan "did not deny that drugs of the amphetamine group had been exchanged there," thus giving Stan an opportunity to incriminate himself. Stan didn't disappoint him, being quoted as saying, "They're just diet pills, aren't they?"[lxix]

U.S. Attorney Robert J. Rotatori stated, "This was a business-oriented ring in the sense that they weren't interested in using the drugs. They were interested in selling it for profit. The market for these people was mainly pushers. They very seldom sold to users themselves."[lxx]

The police department, along with their FBI cohorts, had made good on their promise of retribution for Stan's refusal to rat out his performers or patrons.

Nelson sprang into action. He and Stan agreed that Stan should lay low and not be seen at La Cave, a promise Stan readily made but couldn't quite keep. He then asked Larry Bruner to step up as full-time manager. Larry had already kept the books as well as hired some bands, recommended others and had shadowed Stan quite a bit, so it wasn't a cold open. Jim & Jean were already scheduled to play the upcoming weekend, the ads had been placed, flyers printed, and post cards mailed. That provided a modicum of breathing room. Stan would stay on as the main talent buyer unless a prospective act's management demurred.

Larry got to work. A quick inspection of Stan's bookings took longer than expected – it turned out that Stan had no central location for his contracts and correspondence, and that's putting it kindly. "Scattered" was more accurate. However, Stan had booked the west coast band Moby Grape for Wednesday the 22nd and

Thursday the 23rd, with locals The Tiny Alice Jug Band opening, New York-based folkie John Hammond, Jr., for the weekend, psychedelic folk-rockers Arthur Lee & Love for the 29th and 30th with the Hello People in support, and then the Hello People headlining the final weekend in May and to 2 June. But no ads had been placed, nor had any other promotional duties been discharged. No waiters were on the schedule, no payroll had been completed, no bills paid. These were the kind of chores that were firmly in the uber-organized Larry's wheelhouse. He was, by everyone's reckoning, a "bean counter." He was also as honest as Stan was disorganized.

La Cave was staggered by this body blow but stayed on its feet, ready to fight another round.

What's Big and Purple and Lives in the Ocean?

Moby Grape was a huge band in 1967, and in 1968 was quickly devolving back into the ranks of the has-beens, largely a result of their manager Matthew Katz's series of blunders. However, their sets at La Cave proved to be a big hit with listeners, with more than respectable attendance figures for their two mid-week days. 238 fans crowded into La Cave on Wednesday; word quickly spread and on Thursday almost 400 fans paid their way in to one or the other of the band's two sets. Stan tried to talk them into staying for the weekend, promising them headliner billing over contracted John Hammond, Jr. but the band had business elsewhere.

Life is fickle. John Hammond, no longer "Johnny," who had been signed almost three months prior, found out that the quickly changing music scene at La Cave and elsewhere was diminishing the popularity of solo singer-songwriters, and while his sets were enjoyable, humorous and touching, he only attracted four hundred people to his three-day weekend ending on the 26th. It's possible that people were saving up for the following weekend, when the

Hello People returned, supporting the psychedelic/folk-rock west coast band Love.

Meanwhile, local faves Tiny Alice regaled the crowd as the opening act each night with their unique blend of old timey instruments and clever contemporary lyrics.

All You Need is Love

It was a wild five-day ride for newly-minted manager Larry Bruner and his crew to begin June. The newspaper ad that Larry placed for the band Love misspelled their name as "LUV," an embarrassing mistake, but understandable in 1968. In an extreme case of irony, the ad was placed directly next to a larger ad that screamed "L.S.D." at the top. That certainly garnered attention. Closer inspection informed the reader that the initials stood for "Let's Start Dancing," and was an advertisement for the new Fred Astaire Dance Studio in downtown Cleveland. No one has ever confessed to purposely placing the ads adjacent to one another.

Love was scheduled for the last Wednesday and Thursday of May. Larry said, "I tried to stay aware of acts playing the circuit, especially in New York, with an occasional notice of the west coast. Booking agents would call daily. A major change I made was scheduling rock acts mid-week, when they were traveling to or from New York for the weekend. It allowed us to negotiate a lower fee."

Love was the quintessential cult band that made it medium, not big. However, in later years, their 1967 long-player *Forever Changes* became regarded as one of the greatest "underground" records of all time and in 2011 was added to the Library of Congress's National Recording Registry.

The Hello People arrived in town early for their weekend gig, and when they met with Larry Wednesday morning, he invited them to open for Love before starting their own three-day stint, and they happily obliged. The shows were a huge success, attracting 703 paying souls mid-week, a record for the club. Conversely, the weekend was a relative bust, with the quirky Hello People only managing to pull in 367 fans. For some reason, you either loved or hated the People. These fans *loved* them. All in all, the week was a success, grossing almost four grand. Within that number lay the seed of La Cave's eventual demise, however: the bands' fees came to $2,458, so after expenses, the black ink only amount to about $500. The high cost of bands versus solo acts was going to become an albatross draped over Nelson's checkbook. The saving grace was the money that the record labels were throwing into the promotional pot, otherwise, even sellouts might not produce profits.

RFK

The Hootenanny tradition continued as planned. From spring onward, Tuesday night was still the night to screw your courage to the sticking place and ascend the lofty stage to offer your two or three best songs to sparse crowds consisting mostly of family and friends. In a sign of the times, more and more combos showed up try their luck, and from this roster sprang some really good, tight bands: Mr. Stress Blues Band, the Tiny Alice Jug Band, The James Gang, The Rich Kids, The New Group, Donnery & Rudd, Leatherwood and Lisa, Toni Dell, Scott Fagan, SRC, the Mind (or sometimes "Mynd") Garden, Tiffany Shade, stalwarts Gusti & Sean or Gusti solo, and others with unremembered names.

Tuesday night, the 4th of June, began slowly. A sparse crowd awaited whatever act would appear. La Cave had grown from the days when the performer was all-important to turn a club into a hangout, secure in the knowledge that the music would be good. Nobody remembers anything that happened that day, because events on Wednesday would eclipse anything in recent history. Robert F. Kennedy, Presidential candidate, was shot several times at point-blank range in the kitchen of the Ambassador Hotel, where he had just spoken to adoring fans before attempting his exit through the work area, away from the throngs in front. A fan, Juan Romero, cradled his head as he lay on the floor. Others wrestled shooter Sirhan Sirhan to the ground. Kennedy asked Romero, "Is everybody OK?", to which Romero replied, "Yes, everybody's OK.[lxxi]

America's long summer of discontent got longer. The decade of peace and love had just witnessed, within the recent five-year stretch, four of the most significant assassinations in the country's history: JFK, Malcom X, Dr. King and now, the guy everybody called Bobby. The guy who kept the peace in March when Dr. King was gunned down. The guy who would have brought our boys home from Vietnam.

Now who was going to be the voice of maturity, of peace? Who would speak for young people?

Nelson had made a career of reading between the lines. It's one talent to see something for what it is, and much more profound to see what that something foretells. The small profit from the Love/Hello People sellouts signified the financial ceiling Nelson was facing. No longer could the club gross $500 or a grand in an evening and still make money. There were two other factors worrying him, one being Stan's situation. Like it or not, La Cave had become somewhat a cult of personality, and that personality was Stan's. An offshoot of Stan laying low was that word quickly spread, mistrustful agents smelled something rotten, and calls with offers began to dry up. La Cave, which had worked so hard for so long to become a "happenin' place," was slip-sliding away. Streets in major cities were bursting into flames; Americans were dying trying to claim their rights as citizens. And La Cave was nestled on the corner of one of the most volatile neighborhoods. Brotherly love was quickly being replaced by fear, mistrust and violence. There were a number of skirmishes at La Cave, mostly guys descending the stairs, scooping up the money drawer, and disappearing back up the stairs.

There was no use calling the police; they wanted places like La Cave to fail. They especially didn't want a white-owned establishment to do well with an integrated crowd. The police were a constant presence inside and outside the club, and it had as chilling an effect on the mood as did Stan's absence. It gave Nelson a lot to ponder. He began developing his exit strategy.

Nelson knew that Stan was the beating heart of the entire La Cave mystique. He wasn't called The Resident Wizard on no account. Larry Bruner later said, "[Stan] was no businessman, but he was a creative genius." Without Stan, the mood at La Cave slowly darkened.

In the meantime, the shows must, well, you know. Larry had a daring idea – why not sign up advance ticket sale outlets, partner with local record stores and radio stations? It would be a departure from the tradition of only taking phone or in person reservations. Reservations didn't always turn into sales; a percentage just didn't show up, but once a ticket is sold, it is sold forever. By simply phoning the outlets, Larry could get an advance read as to the popularity of an act. This was important when deciding how to schedule and advertise the acts. So, in short order, he bought serially-numbered ticket books and passed them out to his new sales locations at Westgate Disc Records, Music Grotto, Severance Disc, Tommy Edwards' "Hillbilly Heaven," Downtown Disc, Summit Disc, and Discount Records at 221 Euclid. There would be others. Larry also befriended La Cave supporter DJ Martin Perlich, who liked few things better than cramming a band like

Blood, Sweat & Tears into his main air studio at WCLV and letting them wail.

Martin, however, was playing both sides of the fence, unbeknownst to Larry.

These Vizitors

Rick Curtis was a musical prodigy. The man could write, perform and sing better than just about anyone else. Seven years after Rick's band recorded the original at Sound City Studios, accompanied by unknowns Stevie Nicks and Lindsey Buckingham on backing vocals, Stephen Stills bought a half-interest in Rick's song "Seven League Boots" and rewrote it slightly into his mega-hit "Southern Cross."

Rick's band, These Vizitors, was a family affair, comprised of Rick and his siblings Tom, Michael and Patty, with a friend on drums. Even though they caught a major record label deal with Capitol, their total recorded output was one single and a few demos. What they didn't catch from Capitol was a commitment to an advertising blitz. And while their performance fee was covered by Capitol, no promotional events or materials were, and since the La Cave crew knew next to nothing about them, their weekend in June turned out to be a dress rehearsal for next weekend's show featuring Canned Heat, with Mynd Garden opening. Rick and his band drew little more than flies, which was a shame, because the band was top-notch. The three-day total paid attendance was just under 250. Only the fact that expenses were low made the weekend not a complete bust.

Rick didn't seem to mind. He, like his family members, were artists, in the best ways. They just wanted to make music, and in that ethos they were quickly becoming dinosaurs on the music scene. Popular music was becoming more manufactured and less spontaneous by the day. Musicians with record deals were discovering that those deals offered little advantage towards fame and fortune. The winds of change might be blowing with gale force, but the record companies were still lusting after that next #1 smash hit.

Bring on the Boogie

Canned Heat was a study in marketing contrasts. They were a good band – a *very* good band, tight, well-rehearsed and possessed of high energy. These Vizitors were so much better, musicianship-wise, but they lacked Canned Heat's secret weapons: national distribution and a hip marketing scheme. Half-page ads in the main newspapers in every town were de rigeur, as were personal appearances and album signings at local record stores. Late night stopovers on free-form radio shows helped a lot. This time around, the band stopped by the local ABC-TV affiliate to tape segments for three upcoming Pat Boone shows, as well as getting in a taping on the Upbeat Show. Canned Heat did all of these; These Vizitors did none. Plus, the brouhaha surrounding their previous stop at La Cave certainly solidified the club's reputation as the place to be. Playing mid-week, which was becoming Larry's booking preference, did nothing to keep away 940 similarly high-energy, raucous fans. No one seemed to notice, or care, but the concept of a "listening room" where patrons sat in respectful silence during performances, was on life support. No amount of shushing could still the pent-up emotions of the mostly draft-age crowd.

Adding to the excitement, the popular local group Mind Garden, that aggregation of 17-year-old classmates, put on quite a show, covering bands like Cream, Jimi Hendrix, and a half dozen other faves, to tremendous applause. They had obviously invited a hundred or so of their closest friends to regale one another in the dingy basement club with them.

Nelson Karl was a perceptive man. He saw the direction the booking business was going, and that direction was away from small clubs, multiple-day residencies, and solo acts. He correctly perceived that La Cave's days were numbered. From June through December 1968, events bore witness to his attitude, with no less than nineteen bands cancelling bookings to play larger, more lucrative venues.[lxxii]

Instead of fighting the trend, Nelson decided to play along. If larger venues were the next thing, it was time to get involved in that niche of the music business, or fold up the tent and go home. With six years of hands-on experience, he was confident that he could pull it off. But not by himself; he needed a creative genius.

The next weekend brought the Loading Zone to town, supported by local faves Tiffany Shade. The Loading Zone may have had an uninspired name, but they were years ahead of some other psychedelic outfits. Not only did they play at the Trips Festival in January of '66, they also were chosen to play at the very first Family Dog production, "Tribute to Dr. Strange," three months prior.[lxxiii] They also played many times at the Fillmore West, opening for the likes of Cream, The Who, The Byrds, Big Brother & the Holding Company, Grateful Dead, Howlin' Wolf, Sam & Dave, Chuck Berry and Buddy Miles.

In 1967, they picked up their secret weapon – Linda Tillery's magnificent voice. Soon after, they struck a recording deal with RCA Records. She was only 19 and yet bested all other applicants for the audition. Linda recalled her audition day with humor. The band's guitarist went to her house to pick her up. "My mother saw a hippie at the door and refused to let him in." The *Plain Dealer* adorned a full half-page of newsprint about the band, gushing about Linda's vocal prowess.

The band was spectacular Friday and Saturday, drawing 618 patrons over the two days. The group had an Achilles' heel, however, in that they lacked a songwriter. That numbered the band's days, and in a couple of years they began to fade from memory. Linda, however continued a singing career that spanned the next half century, winning a Jammie (Bay Area Jazz Award) as Outstanding Female Vocalist for her 1970 solo album *Sweet Linda Divine*, and a Grammy nomination in 1998, among many other accolades.

Larry Bruner picked up James Cotton's band for mid-week, and Stan recommended the Watson father and son, Doc and Merle, for the weekend of the 21st. But there was tension in the air; everywhere, it seemed. There was rampant speculation about the upcoming 4th of July and whether or not the streets of American cities would explode in racial strife. The performances seemed a little strained, and yet Cotton's crew sent 808 fans home happy, and the Watsons drew 696 patrons. Try has he might, Larry could not find a headliner for the final June weekend, a harbinger of booking problems to come. He filled the slot with a local band, the Rich Kids, sandwiched between two hootenanny nights. And the turnout was satisfactory: 696 customers paid their way in over the 7-day period ending 2 July. A long summer waited in the wings.

Say it Ain't So, Joni

Tucked away neatly on page 13 of the 28 June edition of the *Plain Dealer* was an ad for La Cave's upcoming schedule. Way down there in the agate type, somewhere below The Paupers and somewhat above hootenanny night was a notice that someone named Joni Mitchell would appear to regale the cellar dwellers on the second weekend of July. The folksinger had released her debut album on the Reprise label, but evidently she was held in such low esteem that the album cover was misprinted, and nobody caught the flub. Consequently, the album was listed as *Joni Mitchell,* or *Song to a Seagull,* or even *Untitled.* None of those choices were accurate, and few people bought it. That was a shame, since she had already written numerous hit songs for other artists: “Both Sides Now" and "Chelsea Morning" for Judy Collins, "Eastern Rain" for Fairport Convention and "Urge for Going", "The Circle Game" and "Tin Angel" for Tom Rush. Nobody paid any attention to details like who wrote the songs, and she recorded none of them for her debut. Consequently, she would have to wait until 1970 for fame, fortune and her first Grammy.

So that’s probably why no one really noticed when she stiffed La Cave as a last-minute no-show. What was worse was that, like Jimi Hendrix before her, she made it big enough in the next twelve months to achieve a hat trick in La Cave no-shows, duplicating the feat two more times. The weekend was salvaged after frantic phone calls found Spider John Koerner on his way to Detroit and point west. He played the three nights in front of a total of 470 folk-music-loving folks.

Many years later, Larry Bruner had this to say: “We booked Joni Mitchell three separate times in 1968, even advertised her once, but her appearances were always cancelled. I had the opportunity to go to the Miami International Pop Festival that December. It was the predecessor to Woodstock, but of course no one at the time knew that. I was backstage talking to Albert Grossman about [The Band] when I spotted Joni and went over to talk to her. I had brought with me one of her signed booking contracts and pulled it out as I introduced myself, saying we’d booked her three times. She was with two men and introduced them, Elliot [Roberts][lxxiv] and Graham [Nash]. She looked at the contract and said, ‘Elliot, do you know anything about this?” He and I started talking and…[he] sidestepped why he’d cancelled her, but we did establish a relationship that resulted in my bringing Neil Young to Cleveland twice in the next six months.”

While antiwar and racial protests continued to flare up, and nobody felt safe from harm, the Hello People decamped to La Cave for the long Fourth of July weekend, and succeeded in taking young minds' focus away from their troubles. From Wednesday the 3rd through Saturday, the People regaled almost 1,500 fans[lxxv] with their offbeat but socially conscious mime-plus-folk-rock act. It was good practice for the staff at La Cave, because the doors were about to be blown off the building three days hence.

The Jeff Beck Group & Rod Stewart

Kathy Buhovecky and Loreen Rote were teenagers and besties. On weekend nights, they could typically be found at a dance in one of the many schools or dance clubs that featured local bands. It was always loud, and almost always a good time. The music was passable, as were most of their dance partners. What they were *really* into was the British music scene, and one early summer day in 1968 they heard the news: the Jeff Beck Group was coming to town, to La Cave. This was another one of those Larry Bruner mid-week specials, minimally advertised but word of mouth driven.

Jeff was already well-known as the bad boy of the Yardbirds, having replaced Eric Clapton in the band, before his attitude and unreliability got him fired. Clapton himself had become disgusted with the Yardbirds abandonment of the blues, and when "For Your Love" hit #1, he knew there would be no going back, so he bolted to John Mayall's band the Bluesbreakers. But as he did, he recommended his replacement: a young session guitarist named Jimmy Page. Page, in turn, nominated his friend Jeff, and two days after Eric's exit, Jeff played his first Yardbirds' gig. He didn't last long, and the divorce was announced in November 1966. He mainly hung around recording studios, sitting in on the odd session, until he and his pal, a virtually unknown vocalist named Rod Stewart, decided to form a new band, the Jeff Beck Group.

They went through numerous incarnations of a rhythm section until settling on bassist Ronnie Wood and drummer Mickey Waller.

Jeff Beck at La Cave

Kathy and Loreen had no idea what they were in for, and in that uncertainty they were joined by just about everyone. A tipoff might have been the seven Fender and Marshall amps and Mickey Waller's humungous drum kit being wrangled down the stairs. Nicky Hopkins was touring with the band and down the steps his keyboards also descended.

Kathy remembers: "In 1968 my friend Loreen and I were teenagers and very much into the British music scene. We heard The Jeff Beck Group was going to be appearing at a place called La Cave. Our most outstanding memory was that it was pretty small and rather dark, very much a nightclub atmosphere, so different from the places where we were accustomed to seeing rock groups. It turned out to be one of the very best venues ever, just for that reason, as it made it a more personal, up-close experience."

"We arrived early and picked a table near the front. We'd never been that close to any band before! At the time we were only familiar with Jeff Beck of Yardbirds fame, and he was the main reason we were there. But we were really impressed with Rod Stewart as well, having not known much about him at the time. It was amazing later on to realize that we'd seen not only Jeff and Rod but also Ronnie Wood who eventually joined the Rolling Stones. The drummer was Mickey Waller. We do remember how much we loved the show - especially having been so close to see them perform in that small club - and I am so happy I'd brought my camera to memorialize the event!"

Loreen lived an hour south of Cleveland in rural Medina County, but her grandmother "lived on West 35th near Lorain, so we took the bus down to La Cave. We were 16 or 17 at the time." When asked how they thought they'd get into an 18-and-over club, "We didn't even know [it was over 18], and we had no trouble getting in."

"Kathy and I went to concerts together all the time. We went to both [Cleveland] Beatles' concerts. For La Cave, my grandmother was concerned. She said it was a bad part of town, but of course we went anyway. We went to see Jeff Beck, and boy was he great!"

Richard Anderson, whose three-piece combo Frog opened for the Fugs at La Cave, was there, too, for all three nights. "They had just released their album called Truth, and the band was in excellent form. The acoustics at La Cave were really good because the low ceiling stopped it from being just a complete echo chamber, and all the people in there could hear everything really well, including me, and I was standing in the back of the room, where I liked to stand - right at center stage in the back. And the lead singer was really good but I couldn't see him. I'm looking, where's this singing coming from? and I thought, man, this guy must really be short. I can't see this guy anywhere on the stage. Then I finally spotted him and he was off to the side of the stage hiding kind of behind one of the PA speakers while he was singing the whole time. Apparently, he was a little shy, but boy, he really had a good voice and he really belted out the singing."

Rod Stewart hiding out at La Cave

The band was indeed a smash hit, the stuff memories are made of for the 896 mid-week paying patrons and another hundred or so "friends" of someone or other.

The Tinderbox Smolders

No sooner had Jeff Beck's outfit loaded up and left than down the stairs came the popular folkie Spider John Koerner again, followed mid-week by the psychedelic folk-rock band HP Lovecraft, many of whose songs were as hypnotically spooky as their names suggests, having been named after the venerable horror writer. Neither act crept into black ink, Koerner garnering 470 patrons over the weekend of the twelfth, and HP attracting a disappointing

280 souls on Wednesday and Thursday, after inexplicably no-showing on Tuesday. Larry called in the local group The Hempstead Incident to cover for them, but by the time they took the stage, all but about 60 customers had gotten their refunds.

The next weekend was the calm before the storm. The summer had been running hot, as had racial tensions and mutual mud-slinging by politicians, activists, rioters, and youthful demonstrators continued their overt acts of public outrage. But for three days in mid-July, a kind of truce descended over a surprisingly upbeat gathering for the triumphant return of one of the most popular acts in La Cave's brief history: Al Kooper's Blood, Sweat & Tears. By now, their album *Child is Father to the Man* had been on store shelves for five months, selling well enough to break into the top 50 albums on Billboard, and was played incessantly on FM radio stations and college campuses everywhere.

On that steamy Cleveland summer weekend in July, in the dark and damp confines of an obscure (to the general public) basement listening room, BS&T roped in 1,446 paying customers, making it one of La Cave's biggest residencies ever. It couldn't last.

The Shit Hits the Fan

La Cave was closed for cleanup and restocking on Monday the 22nd of July. Waiting in the wings to play Tuesday was the Earth Opera, a band fronted by two bluegrass virtuosos, Peter Rowan and David Grisman, both of whom went on to highly successful, lengthy careers after moving in different musical directions. At this time, they felt that the country had left their genre behind, so they formed Earth Opera as one of the "Bosstown Sound" bands coming out of Boston. They were closer to an eclectic chamber orchestra than a rock band, and psychedelia was the order of the day.

Unfortunately, only a couple dozen Clevelanders got the chance to see the Earth Opera perform, and only for a brief time. Patron

Richard Anderson recalls the reason: "Earlier in the day we had driven down Liberty Blvd. (now Martin Luther King Blvd.) and saw Army men lined up on both sides of the street with jeeps, and we were wondering what the heck is going on. We were a little paranoid and thought they're gonna pull us over and have us arrested, just 'cause we had long hair or something. Later that night we found an alley that went behind La Cave and we found a parking spot."

"We were walking in the dark [and saw] these two men coming towards us, and then as they got closer, we noticed they were both carrying bricks in their hands. And again, we're thinking all this is trouble, you know? So we got a little scared and we thought about running, but we just stopped in our tracks and the two men got a little bit closer and one of them said, 'Please help us.' We're like, whoa. We saw that their faces were bruised and bleeding. They told us they've been attacked while walking down Euclid Ave by angry rioters."

"So we got them in La Cave and the ladies who worked there, they cleaned and patched up their wounds and a bit later two policemen came in because the doors were still open and they told us to lock all the doors. There was only a handful of people in the club, but we stayed inside for several hours and we could hear loud noises outside, like shouting and banging. We didn't hear any guns go off, but you can hear crashing and yelling and stuff. Eventually the police came and let us leave. They escorted us to the car and we went back [to Stan's pad]."

The Glenville Shootout

The following morning's paper screamed in large capital letters the news that 3 cops and 3 civilians had been killed on the streets, and that the National Guard had been called in. To this day there are a wide range of opinions as to who started what came to be known nationally as The Glenville Shootout, with several sides casting blame at one another. For the better part of the decade, violence had been simmering just beneath society's surface, and ever since the nearby Hough Riot of 1966, the neighborhood around La Cave, the former Doan's Corners, had been hollowing out, with many residents and businesses who could afford to moving elsewhere, leaving behind a poverty-stricken hellscape that even the Cleveland Police Department had "redlined," meaning that once darkness fell, only emergency and fire department vehicles would serve the area.

Mayor Stokes pleaded for calm, breaking into a televised broadcast of the Cleveland Indians – Baltimore Orioles game. It was to no avail. The shootout developed into a full-fledged four days of rioting in the neighborhood. Bus service to the area was stopped; the National Guard and police withdrew to a perimeter around the area. Two blocks north of La Cave, an entire city block burned to the ground. Alcohol sales in the city were banned. Resentment grew volatile between the nation's first black mayor and the predominately white police force. Rioting continued unabated until Friday morning, the 27th, when a semblance of calm returned.

Nelson and Larry met the following day to try to figure a way out of the latest existential predicament. They had rolled with the punches every time, but the fix they found themselves in this time was outside their abilities to solve. The city was on fire both figuratively and literally. Politicians and police were powerless. From this point on, attracting customers to 10615 Euclid was going to become more and more difficult, a fact which only strengthened Nelson's resolve to initiate his and Stan's Plan B.

Tedd Browne

When things could not have looked worse, more calamity befell Cleveland and its music community. As a direct aftermath of the Glenville rioting, someone decided to take racial matters into his own hands. Early on the morning of the 28th, beloved African-

American folksinger Tedd Browne, he of Faragher's and national fame, was found dead behind his steering wheel at the top of Cedar Road hill with a .45 caliber bullet in his brain. The murderer had left the bullet casing on the car floor with the "n-word" scratched into it. It took almost eight years of investigation, but in 1976 white nationalist Richard Robbins, a mere 17 at the time of the murder, and the son of a Cleveland police officer, was charged and ultimately convicted of the murder. At the time, he had proclaimed the he was going to kill the first black man he saw, using racist language in his statement.

But with the crime being unsolved at the time, life as known at La Cave it was no longer possible. What had taken 6 years to build threatened to be destroyed in six days. Even the Fugs coming to town for what should have been a raucous mid-week happening failed to bring any sense of calm to the crew at the cave. Three days of hosting the outrageous band, which should have attracted upwards of 500 fans per night, drew only 898 fans, meaning that a good five hundred people stayed away. Nobody felt much like partying, and the kitchen and bar only sold a paltry $700 worth of refreshments.

In short order, the next two headliners, folkie Tim Buckley and another of Larry's mid-week signings Big Brother and the Holding Company starring Janis Joplin, cancelled their gigs. In their place, Larry held hootenanny nights.

Butterflies of Iron

The next Larry Bruner midweek special floated into town for three nights beginning Monday, 12 August, and it was perhaps the most un-La-Cave-iest booking yet: Iron Butterfly. The band was riding high on the strength of their just-released 2nd album and, more specifically, the 17-minute jam that comprised all of side two, the title track "In-A-Gadda-Da-Vida." The song has become one of the most iconic songs of the '60s: the album became the biggest-selling album of 1969, crushing bands like the Beatles – and everyone else – and up to that time outsold every other record in history.

Larry Bruner recalls: "I had Iron Butterfly come in to play La Cave as their first gig away from the West Coast. 'Juggy' Gayles, the National Promotion Director of Atco Records, had never heard of them, and he thanked me for bringing them to his attention. Yet, they'd already had two albums on Atco by then and the second, *In-A-Gadda-Da-Vida*, eventually sold more than twenty million."

The band's three-day stint did a lot to raise the sad spirits around La Cave. They drew just south of 1,100 in ticket sales for their midweek appearance. Just as importantly, the gang in the seats plowed their way through $2,400 worth of refreshments, spurring several beer-chips-bread-ham runs by the staff. It made the band's $3,000 performance fee palatable.

Regardless of future events, the Iron Butterfly performances at La Cave stand out as highlights in the club's history.

.---

The rest of August at La Cave was low-key. However, political tensions were still in the red zone, both locally and nationally. The "Yippies," or Youth International Party, a large, loosely organized national group of antiwar and social activists, along with "The Mobe" and other activist groups and individuals, were planning a large demonstration in Chicago during the Democratic National Convention in late August. The city's mayor, Richard Daley, publicly promised, "Law and order will be maintained." Privately, he was prepared to go much further than maintaining law and order. Thousands of regular Army and National Guard troops were activated, and permits to gather by the protestors were denied. On 23 August, Jerry Rubin and the Yippies nominated their candidate for President, Pigasus, a plump pig. Phil Ochs sang protest songs from the back of a flatbed truck. The only moment of levity that week happened after "we were arrested and were in jail and went in to be booked," said Rubin, later on. "One of the Chicago policemen came in and shouted out all of our names and then said, 'You guys are all going to jail for the rest of your lives—the pig squealed on you.'"

Chapter 14:

"A Year of Turmoil and Change"

The National Archives describe 1968 as "a Year of Turmoil and Change."[lxxvi] The Smithsonian called it "The Year That Shattered America."[lxxvii] The night of 28 August, in large part, became the focus of that shattering. Protestors had gathered in Lincoln Park, which had an 11pm curfew imposed especially for the convention week, As the crowd in the park began to disperse onto city streets, it became inevitable that police and protestors would clash. Demonstrators chanted, "The whole world is watching," and the networks obliged. The police moved into the crowd and "The Battle of Michigan Avenue," described as a 17-minute melee in front of the Conrad Hilton, was broadcast into America's living rooms. Police cracked heads, pushed protesters through plate-glass windows, then pursued them inside and beat them as they sprawled on the broken glass. TV cameras recorded the police brutality.

A country that had been divided became, indeed, shattered. The war had come home.

August also saw Flatt & Scruggs play La Cave. Stan was bemused that the popular bluegrass duo, in a way, mimicked the country at large. They hated each other's guts, to put it mildly. One of their demands was to have separate dressing rooms. Stan said, "They couldn't even stand being in the same room together. The only place they did share was the stage, and they never uttered a word to each other. I even had to pay them separately." But acoustic music, even from virtuosos, was quickly becoming yesterday's news, and the future Country Music Hall of Famers attracted only 356 customers.

Larry was having trouble with bookings. Almost as suddenly as La Cave became a first-call venue for New York agents, the times and the changing tastes seemingly made the small, inner city club anathema to artists and agents alike. After Flatt & Scruggs hit the bricks, separately of course, Larry filled empty slots with local bands: T.I.M.E. ("Trusting in Men Everywhere"), Chrysalis, the Mr. Stress Blues Band, Leatherwood & Lisa, The Mind Machine, and the weird New York electronic duo Silver Apples filled empty dates, while headliners Tim Buckley, the Steve Miller Band, Joni Mitchell and Richie Havens all cancelled. The paid attendance for any one date cracked the one hundred mark only on Saturday nights, and then barely. But there were two silver linings among the many dark clouds: Blood, Sweat and Tears at the end of August, and the British psychedelic band Procol Harum in mid-September.

BS&T started a three-day stay on 30 August, a Friday, and suddenly new life was breathed into La Cave. Founder, band leader, keyboardist and vocalist Al Kooper had been ditched for powerful lead singer David Clayton-Thomas, with trombonist Dick Halligan taking over organ duties. It's a wonder that an eight-piece combo could fit down the stairs, let alone onstage, but by now they were old hands at the chore. They were a smash hit, attracting 1,422 Clevelanders and raising the rafters with Clayton-Thomas's booming voice being heard blocks away. Larry had a full staff on duty for the first time since the band's stint five weeks previously. Leatherwood and Lisa provided the opening act, earning $35 in the process. BS&Ts take, including their override, hit $2,132.00.

The following weekend, just to prove wrong everybody who thought acoustic singer-songwriters couldn't draw flies, Tom Rush doubled La Cave's one-week winning streak, pulling in 1,253 fans.

It was an enjoyable, reminder of "the good old days:" no humping tons of equipment down and up the stairs, no lengthy setup and sound check, no outrageous food or lodging bills, no multi-page contracts with technical riders galore, no ridiculous demands by stoned musicians, nothing to break except perhaps a guitar string. Rumor has it that Stan Kain snuck in to enjoy one evening's entertainment, sitting demurely at a table with Nelson Karl and Nelson's wife Alice. And after all was sung and done, Tom Rush knocked off a $1,250 piece of La Cave's checking account. It seemed to Larry, Nelson, et al, that there might just be a little life left in the club. Larry was going to see to it.

The band that showed up two days after Tom split town did nothing to break La Cave's temporarily-charmed existence. Procol Harum was yet another Larry Bruner midweek booking. The band from Southend-on-Sea had already experienced the heights of success, even if it hadn't translated into arena bookings yet. Their 1967 classically-inspired baroque rock single, "A Whiter Shade of Pale" had reached a level attained by very few singles: it had sold ten million copies and become an instant international success. In its first three weeks it had become UK history's fastest-selling debut single. Their sound was experimental, psychedelic and somewhat opaque. The band combined the sounds of a piano by Gary Brooker and a Hammond B3 organ operated by Matthew Fisher, and added to that combo the incredible guitar skills of a 23-year-old prodigy from Catford, England, Robin Trower.

Now, a year later, here they were at La Cave. It seems that their star was quickly fading overseas, but in the States they were still red-hot. Consequently, management booked them on a lengthy American tour, and their second album, *Shine on Brightly* was released the same week as their appearances at La Cave. It also became a huge hit in America, outperforming *Procol Harum.*

One of their biggest fans was the Cleveland guitarist Richard Shack. He went to see the band on their first night, and came back for the second and third. As he remembers it, "I remember that well. I had a band called the Case of E.T. Hooley, and me and Donnie Baker, who's the other guitar player, we went to see Procol Harum. I had the unmitigated gall to go up to Robin Trower, their guitar player, and say in kind of an aggressive way. 'Hey man, do you want to jam?' and he just looked at us and said 'Piss off, you wanker.'"

The band attracted an acceptable 1,201 paying customers for their Tuesday through Thursday stop. Robin Trower soldiered on in a solo career that is still active and Richard Shack, the dedicated cave dweller who later became the James Gang's guitar-slinger, is also still active in writing, composing and performing original music.

Justice Delayed

The day after Procol Harum packed up and left was reckoning day for Stan Kain. He had a sentencing date with US District Court Judge Thomas D. Lambros. The judge delayed sentencing Stan and his co-defendants until they completed, under armed guard, a tour of the Cuyahoga County Jail "to understand incarceration" and "to see patients suffering the effects of LSD." Afterwards, he would hand down their sentences, looking for the best way to insure "they shall not again attempt to contaminate the minds of our youth."

As far as his control over sentencing was concerned, the Judge's hands were more or less tied. He considered the offenses serious enough to warrant the full punishment of a year in prison, but also strongly felt that a five-year probation period would better serve the public, in that, after a year's incarceration, Stan et al "will be back on the streets, with nothing hanging over their heads."

Notably, in the time between Stan's conviction and sentencing, Congress had raised his offense to felony status, which indicated a five-year prison term. So, as bad as Stan's near future seemed, it was a far sight better than if he hadn't been busted until a few more months had rolled by.

Three days later, in a lame attempt to appear "cool" to the nation's youth, President Nixon appeared in a five-second cameo on the top-rated Monday night variety show *Rowan & Martin's Laugh-In*, just long enough to issue what turned out to be an extremely prescient command: "Sock it to me." It was a popular catch phrase at the time, and the way he said it, almost as a question: "sock it to me?" instantly became a wildly hilarious way to mock him by repeating it that way. Democratic candidate Hubert Humphrey, perhaps recalling the adage about discretion and valor, declined an invitation to the comedy show.

On 16 October at the Summer Olympic Games in Mexico City, Americans watched as fellow countrymen Tommie Smith and John Carlos raced to gold and bronze medals, respectively, in the 200-meter dash. On the dais to receive their medals, both African-Americans raised their gloved fists in the "black power salute" to protest violence and poverty among other African-Americans. The following day, under intense pressure from the Nixon Administration, the International Olympic Committee banished them from the Olympic village and sent them home. The great divide in American society proceeded uninterrupted.

The remainder of September saw another downturn in attendance at the cave. Back-to-school shopping left students and young parents alike short of discretionary funds. After Tom Rush and Procol Harum hightailed it out of town, the Hello People attracted only 457 fans for their three-day weekend, and even with Elektra Records kicking in eighty bucks towards promotion, their stay was drenched in red ink. On Hoot Night, the door take totaled $15.00. The next weekend fared a little better, with PG&E garnering 887 folks, more or less breaking even at the bank. Even the underground heroes of distorted guitars and frantic stage antics the Velvet Underground could only attract 723 people. La Cave earned significantly less than the band, which took home $1,100.

One aspect of the Velvets' stay became the answer to the trivia question "where did Doug Yule first play with the Velvet Underground?" Another enduring reminder of this residency was a bootleg recording that became extremely popular among collectors of '60s band memorabilia. The early show was recorded in full, plus a couple songs from the late show, with the recorder presumably running out of tape.

The early show opened with "What Goes On," then "Waiting For The Man," "Pale Blue Eyes," "Foggy Notion," "Heroin," "Jesus," "Venus In Furs," "Beginning To See The Light," and "Sister Ray." The late show songs that were recorded were "That's the Story of my Life," "I'm Gonna Move Right In," and "I Can't Stand It." The Allmusic website had this to say: "The sound quality is low grade on this back-of-the-room bootleg cassette, but the Velvet Underground turn in a fantastic performance in this small Cleveland coffeehouse. Allmusic said, "There are only a few live recordings available from this key period, between White Light/White Heat and the self-titled third album. This alone makes La Cave 1968 a historic document worthy of exploration, even if it's a little difficult to penetrate. It is also worth noting that many of these songs were played live for the first time in this set, and this is Doug Yule's first live performance with the group, alongside core members Maureen Tucker, Sterling Morrison, and Lou Reed."[lxxviii]

The next act to ascend the stage was the Blues Magoos, whose record label Mercury Records was sponsoring their tour. A popular Bronx-based psychedelic outfit who started out as The

Trenchcoats, they hit the big time in '67 with their hit record "(We Ain't Got) Nothin' Yet," which topped out at #5 on the national charts. They were unable to repeat that success, even after an appearance on The Smothers Brothers Comedy Hour, and ultimately came to be one of the many one-hit wonders that littered the field of pop music. They also were unable to attract a profitable crowd midweek at La Cave, with a disheartening eighty-nine coming downstairs with cash in fist. Brewer & Shipley topped that on the weekend, attracting only 218, and did little to lift the flagging spirits of the staff at La Cave.

People were staying away in droves, almost like a spigot had been closed. That spigot was racial tension combined with being located in a high-crime area. If parents and music fans hadn't realized the danger before, the ongoing headlines about inner-city blues drove home the message.

José, Can You See, Part 2

Even as attendance took a nosedive, La Cave was being lauded in the city's newspapers as a hip, trend-setting club, as Billboard Magazine had already recognized. From August through October, large complimentary articles credited La Cave with being the first club in town to bring Blood Sweat & Tears, Big Brother & the Holding Company, Iron Butterfly, Tom Rush, Procol Harum, Brewer & Shipley, the Velvet Underground, and José Feliciano to Cleveland. The Feliciano article, published on 11 October, was especially painful in its damning La Cave with faint praise. The article lauded his appearance at La Cave, his Grammy Award winning record, an acoustic cover of The Doors' "Light My Fire," and noted his controversial singing of the National Anthem in Detroit before a World Series game. The problem was that this time around, he had bypassed La Cave to play the 3,200-seat Music Hall. Not only were the patrons bailing on La Cave, so were many performers, ironically many of those who used La Cave as a stepping stone to bigger and better things.

Something Old, Something New

For the remainder of October, Larry brought in the high energy band belonging to old friend James Cotton, and a Houston band called Fever Tree, who had charted a song in '68, "San Francisco Girls (Return of the Native)," as well as releasing their debut long player. Like the Blues Magoos, they ultimately became another one-hit wonder and quickly disappeared from the music scene.

Rockabilly guitarist Alan Cassaro, whose nom de stage was Alan Leatherwood, reminisced about the James Cotton dates: "I remember my duo, Leatherwood and Lisa[lxxix], playing warmup for the James Cotton Band. They played several times. Willie Dixon was playing standup bass, and he brought his wife along. A very nice man. I knew his name from the records, but I didn't recall which ones specifically. So we talked about foods we liked to cook and eat. Both Willie and his wife looked like they enjoyed eating. When I got home, I looked it up, and yep, he wrote "My Babe" and countless other great tunes for Bo Diddley. Yeah, man, he was a true legend."

Yet another newcomer to La Cave was a hard rocking British blues outfit called Ten Years After, led by lead guitarist/vocalist Alvin Lee. They had released one album at the time, and started touring the states to promote it. Deram Records, a subsidiary of Decca, was helping with promotional costs. The newly-formed Chrysalis Agency began booking them, and Stan had contacts there. They asked for, and received, the staggering amount of $2,500[lxxx] for a midweek appearance, and with 770 fans paying $3.50 each for a ticket, La Cave came up short, even though the record company kicked back $195 for expenses.

Maybe to quiet things down a notch, the next succession of acts to use La Cave's stage were a gaggle of folkies sandwiched around an obscure (read: inexpensive) psychedelic group featuring funky beats, fuzzy guitars, and the percussive genius of Ruth Komanoff: the Hamilton Face Band.

The cavalcade of acoustic players started with the popular folkie Eric Andersen. Since his previous visits he had become one of the hardest working, mileage-eating singer-songwriters in America, traversing the country many times in the '60s. At the moment he had already released four albums, the latest being *More Hits From Tin Can Alley* on the Vanguard label, where he would remain for two more records before signing with Warner Brothers. Although Bob Dylan and Judy Collins had both recorded his song "Thirsty Boots," he seemed destined to remain a cult figure. He had a warm baritone voice, pleasant delivery, and knew his way around a guitar. But he didn't have the sass of a Dylan or the impact of a rock band as folk music slowly faded in popularity.

Eric drew a disappointing 513 fans over his three-day stopover.

Nixon Wins!

On Wednesday, 6 November, the nation awoke to the news that Californian Richard Nixon eked out a victory over Democratic candidate Hubert Humphrey by a mere zero-point-seven percentage points, reversing his narrow loss to John Kennedy in 1960. It was the culmination of a bitterly contested election, encompassing assassinations and bloody riots, and his election did nothing to heal the ongoing fracture in American politics. LBJ's recent prediction that the Democrats had "lost the south for a generation" after his support of the 1965 Civil Rights bill had begun to come true as third-party candidate George Wallace of Alabama, with war hawk and former General Curtis LeMay as his running mate, carried most of the former Confederate states. The antiwar faction of the country was incensed. The prevailing opinion was that the United States would become entrenched in a "Forever War," as Joe Haldeman's Hugo Award-winning science fiction story of the same name described it.

Tim Hardin was the next act, and once again, Leatherwood & Lisa opened. In fact, as Alan Cassaro reminisced, "As best as I recall, Leatherwood and Lisa played on La Cave bills that featured Phil Ochs, Eric Andersen, Tim Hardin, NRBQ, Jim and Jean, The Youngbloods, Hamilton Camp, Bob Gibson, Doctor John, The Blues Project, Flatt and Scruggs, James Cotton, Buzzy Linhart, Neil Young and Crazy Horse, Tim Buckley, Odetta, and Blood Sweat and Tears. There were others." At thirty-five bucks a night, they were in great demand on the local circuit and a first-call booking whenever Stan or Larry needed an opening act.

Strangely, Tim was advertised as playing two separate concerts on Saturday, 9 November. He was opening for the Butterfield Band at Emerson Gym on the Case College campus, a five-minute drive from La Cave even if you hit all red lights, and then closing for Leatherwood and Lisa at La Cave. As part of their Plan B, Nelson Karl and Stan Kain produced both concerts, with Nelson ferrying Tim from Case to La Cave to finish his night of performing. The attendance figures for Emerson Gym are unavailable, but at La Cave, it was another lost weekend, garnering only 361 paying customers over three days.

The following weekend saw the aforementioned Hamilton Face Band make the only Cleveland appearance in their brief life. Almost as soon as the band had played their last song of the weekend, Ruth Komanoff left the band for a ten-year stint with Frank Zappa's band The Mothers of Invention. While in Frank's band, she played marimba, xylophone and the vibes. In '69 she married the band's keyboardist Ian "Motorhead" Underwood. At La Cave, her band's sound was highly reminiscent of the Mothers' style. With songs like "High Why and Die Company," "Chinese Guitar," and "Slippery Sweet," distorted guitars and Ruth's unconventional beat-keeping attracted a mere 160 listeners. The net loss for the weekend approached a thousand bucks, and only intensified Nelson's concern over keeping La Cave extant.

The Return of the Mayor

The downward spiral continued. Old pal Dave Van Ronk, who had sold out La Cave a year ago, could not attract more than 306 fans for his pre-Thanksgiving week stay. Fortunately, he only cost $600 as what star power he had a few years ago was fading. The weekend bled more red ink. Stan asked Alan Cassaro to wait a week to cash the $70 check for his previous two appearances.

Just when things were looking bleak, a break in the storm clouds opened up a brief ray of sunshine on the worried heads of the La Cave crew. Jesse Colin Young and the Youngbloods hopped onstage Thanksgiving night and stayed through the weekend. When the final strains of their soon-to-be-hit song "Get Together" faded to silence, the applause on Friday was so intense that the band repeated the song as an encore. Word must have spread, because Saturday was even better, and the band repeated their two-fer. When the counting ended, almost 1,100 fans had elbowed in, and even considering the two grand that Nelson paid the band, La Cave earned almost as much profit as Jesse's crew did.

The prosperity was temporary.

In the Bleak Midwinter[lxxxi]

Throughout the winter of '68-'69, Nelson Karl closely resembled the picture of a broke Mr. Monopoly with his empty pockets turned inside out. No sooner had most of November's bills been paid, or promised, the first two December weekends were busts. The Detroit-based psychedelic band SRC, another recommendation from the Chess Mate's Morrie Widenbaum, failed to crack 250 in attendance. Even though the band was voted into the Michigan Rock and Roll Legends Hall of Fame in 2010, the only other city besides Detroit where they made any sort of impression was Milwaukee, where they were affectionately known as "Striped Red Candy," a confection they would be pelted with by adoring fans.

John Hammond was another interesting singer-songwriter whose between-songs patter was right up there with the best. Nevertheless, he also underperformed his previous La Cave appearances when he stopped by mid-December. He *did* break 250 in paid attendance; however, but only by two admissions. Critically acclaimed in the coming years, John, a "barrelhouse" style performer, never did break into superstardom. But he did release thirty-four albums and garnered a Grammy Award in a long and distinguished career. He was considered a "musician's musician" by his peers. He's the only person to have Eric Clapton and Jimi Hendrix together in the same band, if only for five days at the Gaslight in Greenwich Village. In 2011, John was inducted into the Blues Hall of Fame of the Blues Foundation.

The appearance of the next band has been the subject of much speculation and dispute over the years. For decades people have sworn on their mothers' eyeteeth that they saw the Nazz at La Cave, while others are equally certain that could never have happened. But it did. On the weekend before Christmas, 20-year-old Todd Rundgren and his bandmates decamped to Cleveland for what would be a wild and woolly weekend. Todd's avowed goal was to become as big as the Beatles, and an important first step was taken in the summer of '68 when the band recorded a few demos for Atlantic Records, who then signed the band to their subsidiary label Screen Gems Columbia. The band had never been near a recording studio, and their assigned producer, Bill Traut, rushed them through their songs. Afterwards, Todd decided to re-mix the songs himself, and studio engineer James Lowe agreed to help him out. The result was their self-titled debut, which included the mildly popular songs "Open My Eyes" and "Hello, It's Me," which became the A and B sides of their first single.

Kenny Klimak and his buddy Rick Dzurik, former La Cave waiters and present Mr. Stress Blues Band members, had been storing their equipment at La Cave, which they used as a daytime practice space. Stan had the band members sign a statement holding La Cave harmless in case anything untoward happened to the equipment. Kenny still had the front door key Stan had entrusted him with. Excited to be the opening act, they got there early to hang out and watch the Nazz go through an early rehearsal. Acting as their own advance publicity team, Kenny and Rick had hundreds of flyers printed up advertising their band's appearance. "We went everywhere, and made sure to hit all the area girls' Catholic high schools," recalled Rick. "We knew a lot of flyers would be immediately torn down, but little did we care. You can imagine the surprise on the faces [of many La Cave patrons] when they saw the same two kids who had been putting up flyers a few days before [now onstage]." They were cranking out the blues, Kenny on lead guitar and Rick playing rhythm, and holding down the fort until the Nazz were ready to assault the eager clientele.

The weekend was a rare midwinter success, earning La Cave about fifteen hundred dollars in net profit. And the cashed checks paying the band stand today as mute witnesses to the fact that, yes, the Nazz played La Cave, no matter what Granny says.

1968 was going to end on a high note, thankfully. This late success only delayed the inevitable, but for the time being Larry's, Stan's and Nelson's spirits were buoyed by the fact that they actually ended the year in the black, if ever so slightly. The truth was that since the Glenville shootings, La Cave had hemorrhaged money. Had the first part of the year not been so profitable, Nelson would likely have packed it in by now. It was decided that for the first, and only, time, the cave would remain closed over the Christmas holiday. But the day after Christmas, into town chugged the Fugs for a triumphant return booking. The Fugs were perhaps the most offensive band on the scene. None of their songs were radio-friendly, and by a long shot. F-words, s-words, and vulgarities beginning with every other letter peppered their live concerts and their records. For some reason, young people have always gotten a charge out of hearing adults use salty language, and many in the audience were visibly thrilled, glancing around at friends to see if they were similarly impressed, every time an epithet escaped Ed Sanders's or Tuli Kupferberg's craggy visages, which was often. In fact, the band's name was itself a euphemism for "fuck," as Norman Mailer used it in his novel *The Naked and the Dead* and as every young fan knew.

Ed and Tuli, both antiwar poets of underground renown, were more like ringleaders of a scofflaw gang than musicians; in fact, musicianship was the least important aspect of their performances. An FBI file from 1969 revealed that the feds considered the Fugs "the most vulgar thing the human mind could possibly conceive."[lxxxii] Their fans at La Cave were fortunate: the band broke up in March 1969. In the meantime, they induced 1,703 mostly youthful Clevelanders to pony up three dollars and fifty cents on the 26th, 27th and 28th of December. Including the kitchen and beer take, the club grossed over $7,000, making it the biggest payday in club history and a late Christmas present to the owners.

La Cave wasn't through with the year, either. Longtime faves the Hello People, a groups as non-mainstream in their own way as the Fugs were in theirs, committed to the final three days of the year, culminating in a riotous good way. On New Year's Eve, when they passed out noisemakers to the crowd, 545 fans showed, bringing their three-day total to 1,046 insanely happy partiers, and swelling La Cave's coffers with another five grand.

The band ran out of noise-makers.

Chapter 15:

1969

The new year brought news from down south – the three-day Miami Pop Festival had just concluded on 30 December, sending an estimated 100,000 music fans home exhausted and deliriously happy. It would become a template for the Woodstock Music and Art Fair to be held in August in a muddy upstate New York cow pasture. Of the thirty-five acts that played at the outdoor fest, at least eleven had graced La Cave's stage – the Butterfield Band, the James Cotton Blues Band, José Feliciano, Flatt & Scruggs, Richie Havens, Ian & Sylvia, Canned Heat, Iron Butterfly, Buffy Ste. Marie, Pacific Gas & Electric, and Procol Harum. Joni Mitchell, Sweetwater and Terry Reid, three La Cave no-shows, also performed. Three other La Cave acts, H.P. Lovecraft, Terry Reid and Country Joe & the Fish, canceled. The music industry took note. So did Nelson Karl. Fully seventeen bands he had contracted with had a chance to play in front of an at-the-time unheard of number of fans. Without a doubt, 300-seat clubs were yesterday's news.

On New Year's Day, Clevelanders awoke to the headline "It's Zero" and minus-20 wind chills kept people home. The coldest month slowly thawed out over three weeks before the next cold snap. A mild spring was forecast. Mild, weather-wise. Nobody expected anything else about 1969 to be mild. In February, a new Gallup poll showed that fully 35% of Americans favored an immediate withdrawal from Vietnam. They went unheeded.

Beginning on the 2nd of January, James Cotton trudged his troupe downstairs for a three-day stay of virtuoso harmonica playing and plenty of loud blues riffs. Proving their popularity, 1,036 chilled but thrilled youths elbowed their way in to enjoy a respite from all the serious stuff happening out of doors. Once again, La Cave was able to pay off a few more overdue bills. The pile of debts was slowly diminishing in inverse relation to Nelson's concerns.

Mr. Bojangles

Everybody knows Bojangles. They met him in a 1968 hit song written and recorded by gonzo musician Jerry Jeff Walker. He called the song's character "Mr. Bojangles" after a homeless man he met while they shared accommodations in the drunk tank of a New Orleans jail. Jerry Jeff was busking there at the time, apparently unsuccessfully. This Mr. Bojangles, a white man who remains anonymous, borrowed the identity of Bill "Bojangles" Robinson, an African-American song-and-dance man who passed in 1949. Bob Dylan recorded Jerry Jeff's song for his 1973 self-titled album, and it became Sammy Davis, Jr.'s signature song.

Jerry Jeff hailed from New York, but quickly made the move to Texas and the burgeoning outlaw country music scene. Royalties from "Mr. Bojangles" kept him supplied with liquor and the opportunity to follow a laid-back lifestyle. He was becoming known as a sometimes no-show to concerts, but made it promptly to La Cave. Perhaps he needn't have, because he broke the string of winners, attracting a mere 187 fans, fewer even than the local Mr. Stress Blues Band on the following weekend. They tipped the attendance scale at 198. Furthermore. they did that in two nights as opposed to Jerry Jeff's three.

There was one bright spot, and that was nineteen-year-old local singer/guitarist Toni Dell, who opened for Jerry Jeff. Toni, yet to turn twenty, had amazing chops. Toni wanted desperately to entertain people from a stage; she was also "terrified" at the prospect. "People told me I had 'good time,' but that was just my knees shaking," she would later say.

Toni Dell at La Cave

Toni began singing at La Cave on various hoot nights. It took all her courage just to sign the performers' list, and there were times that "I'd be the seventh sign up, so I wouldn't get [to play] any songs." Observing the others, though, was an education for Toni. "I saw how they dressed, how they sang, how they played their guitar." She made her own stage outfits and improved her guitar skills. She also began songwriting, and peppered originals in among the standard folk songs of the day. Some of her songs were "What Price, Time?" "Gray Day in the City," "World of Your Love," "Pretend" and "Carousel." A trip to Paris in 1967 opened her eyes to the world, and the fact that she had five older brothers made her a competitor, a survivor. She also got to keep her brother's 12-string Gibson and soon mastered the instrument.

"I had a crush on Danny Kalb, so I wanted to open for Blues Project," admits Toni. Larry agreed, but Toni chickened out, maybe for the only time in her life. But with the encouragement of her family and friends, Toni soon made herself known as a sweet and talented stage performer, learning to play "Born to be Wild" on the 12-string. She also routinely played Jesse Colin Young's "Get Together" as a singalong, Richie Haven's "I Can't Make it Anymore," Donovan's "Catch the Wind," Ramblin' Jack's "San Francisco Bay Blues," Neil Young's "Flying on the Ground is Wrong" and John Sebastian's "Coconut Grove," every song a crowd pleaser.

Eventually, her list of concerts at La Cave came to include the opening slots for James Cotton, Arlo Guthrie, Hamilton Camp. The Hello People, Terry Knight's The Pack, and Brewer and Shipley. There were others, too.

Toni recalled in a bemused way how, when waiting backstage at La Cave with the headlining band also back there, it would suddenly get very crowded. "Girls from the audience would 'divvy up the band,' and plop down beside their chosen target, or even on their laps. There was nothing keeping those girls out. I was too terrified to talk with anyone backstage, but hanging with nice people like Al Kooper...," her voice trails off. Suddenly, she's back: "If only I knew then what I know now!"

Stan Takes a Vacation

On Monday, 13 January, Stan Kain had a date for sentencing before Judge Lambros to answer for his recent drug conviction. Judge Lambros sentenced him to the maximum allowable sentence, twelve months in a federal penitentiary. This came as no surprise, since the good Judge had already opined that he wished he could punish him more severely. He was upset because once the year was up, there was no provision for community supervision. He assumed that Stan would merely pick up where he had left off once free. And to tell the truth, the timing of the crime and the subsequent indictment were a stroke of luck because soon after the charges were handed up, Stan's misdemeanor became a felony and the penalty was raised to five years. Stan was convicted not of selling LSD, however. His charge had been amended to read "one count of selling prescription stimulant and depressant pills." The article that was picked up and carried by several area newspapers all described Stan as part-owner of the hippie hangout La Cave.

The next Friday Nelson drove him downtown to meet the bus that would take him to Lewisburg Federal Penitentiary in central Pennsylvania. This was the prison that would house John "The Teflon Don" Gotti and Henry Hill of *Goodfellas* fame in the years to come, among other celebrity criminals. In the old days, Soviet spy Alger Hiss had done time there. When Stan arrived, he was assigned to the medium-security wing, which concerned him. No sooner had he been issued his prison duds and been relieved of his personal effects, than he was met by a cadre of several tough-looking convicts. This wasn't going to go very well, he remembered thinking at the time. They marched him down a shadowy hallway and into an open cell at the very end of the hall. Behind what appeared to be a small child's desk sat a man not dressed like the others. He was wearing a white dress shirt open at the collar, and Stan could see freshly-shined shoes on his feet beneath the desk. A moment passed, then the man spoke: "I know all about you and your case. If you need anything, I'm the guy to ask." The words were said matter-of-factly. Stan was too nervous to speak; he just nodded, and soon it dawned on him that his audience with the mystery man had ended and was seemingly free to leave. He left. While at Lewisburg, no one ever bothered him.

The above is a story that Stan told many times, but it wasn't until decades later that he learned that the boss of that particular prison wasn't the warden. No, it was the man in the white shirt behind the desk, Jimmy Hoffa. Luckily for Stan, La Cave had always been a union shop.

As it so happened, Stan's "vacation" would last exactly three months.

Linn County had released their debut in 1968 and was working on a second LP at the time. One of the songs became an instant fan favorite when they introduced it. The band dedicated "The Cave" to the crowd and turned into a twenty-minute blues jam complete with fuzz, feedback and flashy guitar work. It got an extended ovation, so they played it during every set.

The following weekend, beginning 31 January, witnessed the triumphant return of the Velvet Underground for their third appearance at La Cave. Lou Reed and Sterling Morrison provided a swirling, intertwining guitar loop on "I'm Waiting for The Man," and the band launched into a thirty-minute version of "Sister Ray," including in it pieces of other songs in their repertoire, namely "Murder Mystery" and "Pale Blue Eyes." The highlight of at least one set happened when Lou lovingly lingered over the line, "suckin' on my ding-dong" for a few brief moments of hilarity. It was an amazing performance, and people remarked on how much the band had grown since their last stop.

Nelson and Larry, afterwards, sat looking at their shoes. La Cave was in a pickle. The times demanded that full, preferably loud, rock bands took the stage, but neither Larry nor Nelson (or for that matter, Stan) knew diddly about them. They were all folk music devotees. These bands needed a lot more in the way of payment and equipment. Also, they tended to treat the place harshly compared to an Arlo Guthrie or a Josh White. Not only that, but the folkies they helped popularize over the years were demanding higher fees, as befit their new status as well-known performers. Agents and managers were increasingly no help. Gone were the cooperative days. They wanted to get work for their up-and-comers, but nobody in Cleveland had heard of Linn County or the band to follow the Velvets, the Colwell-Winfield Blues Band. Colwell and Winfield's band had trouble drawing flies, with only 284 tickets bought for the three weekend dates. Nobody knew it at the time, but the coming months were going to become as well-known for the bands that *didn't* show up as the bands that did. In those months, a handful of weekends were going to be held down by last-minute local bands.

The writing was on the wall. The next five weekends, beginning with the folk-rock duo Hedge & Donna, should have totaled at least 3,000 patrons in order to squeeze out a little spending money to pay some past due bills down. Sadly, fewer than 1,600 heeded the call. ASCAP and BMI had their hands out, as did a couple of taxmen. The union was owed fees. The rent was half-paid. Everyone working the club was asked to wait a bit before cashing their checks. What had been, for a while, a walk in the park had become a high-wire act.

Another facet of La Cave's business model had become paying opening acts much more than they could make elsewhere. Donnery & Rudd was a prime example. The local duo, consisting of Jim Nice and Elaine Moore earned $100 for their opening sets. David Budin recalls having a good time accompanying Donnery & Rudd at various venues. He'd stand at the back of the stage, and said, "When I played bass behind them, there would usually be a spot where Jim would do a solo number, and then Elaine would [also solo]. In between those two songs, I would sometimes step up to the mic and say, "That was Nice. And now here's Moore."

"Dad jokes" were already in vogue, evidently.

"Shakey" and the Gang

For Larry's next magical trick, he pulled the author of the song "Birds" out of his hip pocket. Neil Young was not yet the star he would become later in '69. The former members of Buffalo Springfield, Neil, along with Stephen Stills and Richie Furay, had yet to become household names. For Neil and Stephen, that would change dramatically after their appearance with Crosby, Stills,

Nash & Young at the Woodstock festival in August, where Stephen famously declared, "This is only our second concert together. We're scared shitless, man!"

After leaving Buffalo Springfield in '68, Neil had kicked around doing some session work and some solo shows, and in January picked up Elliott Roberts as his manager and released his debut solo album, *Neil Young* on Reprise Records. Missing the interplay of being in a band, Neil picked up three members of the band Rocket, renaming them Crazy Horse. In only a couple of weeks they had recorded enough tracks to release *Everybody Knows This is Nowhere* on 14 May, 1969. It hung around the bottom of the charts until after his appearance at Woodstock, when it rose as high as #34 on the Billboard Pop Albums chart.

Neil's 1969 tour commenced at the Bitter End in New York, where he played for six nights. Then it was off to La Cave for three nights, and then on to the Troubadour. That completed the first leg of the tour, after which he spent most of the month of April in the studio working on *Everybody Knows*, which was released on 14 May. The second leg of the tour began in May and continued till the end of June, with La Cave and the Troubadour once again the final two stops.

By the time he first appeared at La Cave, Neil's musical feet were planted in two separate camps. He loved playing acoustically and connecting with his audience. He also loved to raise the rafters, turning his band up to "eleven" and shaking teeth fillings from their sockets. To accommodate him, his appearances at La Cave consisted of an opening, solo acoustic set, followed by an ear-bleeding Crazy Horse set. Most of the acoustic songs would appear on his third album, 1970's *After the Gold Rush,* while the Crazy Horse set played the entire song list of *Everybody Knows This is Nowhere.* A year after La Cave closed, *Gold Rush* would break into the Top 10 and eventually garner Grammy Hall of Fame status.

Nelson and Larry were hoping for a record-breaking turnstile count for Neil's La Cave stopover. They were severely disappointed. In the years to come, many more people took credit for seeing Neil at La Cave than actually did. Neil and the band sold 645 tickets, many of them to repeat customers for both nights. Leatherwood & Lisa, the popular local opening act, was responsible for a portion of that count, too. Nelson barely broke even, after hoping for at least three grand in net profit.

The following weekend was another financial disaster. While Stan and Nelson's new company Grape, Inc. hosted Judy Collins on Friday, 28 February at venerable Severance Hall, home of the world-renowned Cleveland Orchestra and almost within sight of La Cave, Larry's contracted headliner, the Florida outfit Leaves of Gold, failed to show up and for the first time in memory, La Cave was buttoned up tight on a Friday night. Meantime, a stunning 3,940 Judy Collins fans paid four bucks for seats and the gross take was well over $15,000. Showing up for Saturday's gig at La Cave, Leaves of Gold brought in a measly $390 in admissions and kitchen purchases. Opening act Toni Dell was more popular to the thin crowd than the headliner.

No one had any doubts as to the long-term viability of small, folky little clubs any more. But there still a few noteworthy concerts yet to be seen.

Larry scrambled to fill the remainder of March. He rescheduled folksinger David Blue from another date in order to fill the next weekend, and David could only muster 170 fans. More red ink. Next, the Charley Musselwhite Blues Band could only attract 511 fans for their weekend. Eventually, the band would be nominated for six Grammys, winning one, a Song of the Year Award, and fourteen Blues Music Awards for "Best Harmonicist" and other accolades.

Earlier in the week, the Ashley Famous Agency contacted Larry to consider booking one of their new acts, Frank Zappa's latest discovery, Alice Cooper. The agency's praise went so far as to say, "Alice Cooper is an electrifying 'freaky' in-person experience." Zappa's record label Bizarre Records, will provide promotional assistance, the agency added.

Larry declined to book Alice Cooper. Instead, the Hello People, a known success, were booked to play the next weekend, to be followed in a couple of weeks by the McCoys, a popular Columbus, Ohio band. But before the McCoys invaded, after the Hello People gave La Cave a little breathing room, attracting a rabid 1,100 fans, there was to be one more visit by a band obviously destined for bigger things, a band that considered La Cave and the Boston Tea Party as their home venues – the Velvet Underground. Nelson decided to hang his hat on the outcome of their performances. Their weekend residency would prove to be only an artistic success, failing to attract seven hundred fans to their six sets over three days.

It was on the Sunday morning after the Velvets Saturday night shows that Nelson knew for certain that the future of La Cave that it was no longer viable. He needed to pull the plug as quickly and painlessly as possible.

He knew it *would* be painful. One good thing happened, however, on the first night of Lou Reed's La Cave gig: Judge Lambros amended Stan's one-year prison term down to three months' incarceration to be followed by three years of supervised parole.

Hang On, Sloopy

Rick Zehringer was born and raised in western Ohio. He would later find lasting solo fame and fortune under the name Rick Derringer. But in 1968 when he was the leader of the southern Ohio band known as Rick & the Raiders, he traveled to the Big

Apple to record the pop classic "My Girl Sloopy." First, however, to avoid confusion with Paul Revere & the Raiders, they changed their name to The McCoys, and second, they changed the song's title to "Hang on, Sloopy." It was released in July of '65 and by August was number one on every music chart.

In a strange twist of fate, the song has achieved a kind of immortality, selling a million copies and going on to become the official rock song of the State of Ohio, the unofficial theme song of The Ohio State University, and is typically played during the 8th inning of Cleveland Guardians baseball games.

Ohio's House Resolution 16 designating "Sloopy" as the State Rock Song read, in part

> WHEREAS, "Hang On Sloopy" is of particular relevance to members of the baby boom generation, who were once dismissed as a bunch of long-haired, crazy kids, but who now are old enough and vote in sufficient numbers to be taken quite seriously..."
>
> and
>
> WHEREAS, Adoption of this resolution will not take too long, cost the State anything, or affect the quality of life in this State to any appreciable degree, and if we in the legislature just go ahead and pass the darn thing, we can get on with more important stuff.[lxxxiii]

For their La Cave appearance, the *Plain Dealer* tried valiantly to inform the public, even as popular local FM disc jockey Billy Bass continually played songs from their recent releases incessantly. The newspaper informed the curious public that the McCoys had changed from bubblegum to something a bit more edgy. The stylistic change didn't work for the band, and by the end of the year they were no more. It didn't work for their La Cave stint, either, and by the end of the week the club's checking account was overdrawn by exactly $2,339.75.

The End Draws Nigh

It had become evident that Stan Kain and La Cave were inseparable. His boyish innocence, twinkly eyes and quiet manner made him a charismatic figure around the club and around town. He often had the company of an attractive girl on his arm, and a nod or a smile from him at the bottom of the stairs often signaled that the recipient had free entry. As Larry Bruner said more than once, "Stan was no businessman; he was a creative genius." Larry, on the other hand, was perhaps *too* businesslike, not a person who smiled easily, or exuded a confident, relaxed manner.

All of Larry's tightfistedness was true and necessary, but it was the wrong time and place to enact such capitalistic attitudes. It was obvious that La Cave had become a "business" instead of a destination, a commercial concern rather than a hangout. Youths came to La Cave to escape "the man;" Larry *was* "the man." Stan's lassez-faire attitude would have no longer worked, either, so in the end their differing management styles were moot. But it was sad for many to see what the times were doing to La Cave, and people voted with their feet, staying away in bigger and bigger numbers. With no ability to expand, the club was no longer viable. Even with 300 fans per day, Nelson could hope for little more than breaking even.

Some good news spread in April: Stan Kain was home from prison. Unfortunately, the terms of his probation included a prohibition from associating with other "criminals," which would be impossible at La Cave. Several times, he "snuck in" to the club he used to call his own, but the thrill was gone. Keeping a low profile did not interest him, and besides, he was free to pursue his and Nelson's plan to become talent buyers and concert promoters at other, larger, area venues, without the responsibilities that came with club ownership.

In the middle of April, Pacific Gas & Electric, with incendiary guitarist and former Clevelander Glenn Schwartz out in front, hit the stairs for a sound check and a three-day weekend appearance. There were still sounds (and noises) of life left downstairs, and many of the 1,181 paying customers would have their last great fling, although nobody realized it at the time. Nelson put about two grand in his hip pocket, but had bills to pay. In a measure of the man, he had never once considered bankruptcy. He had seen its devasting effects from his lawyerly duties and knew all too well what kind of hit a businessman's reputation would suffer, and besides, his quiet pride cut off that avenue of escape. Before he was finished with La Cave, he would pay off every debt the club had incurred.

Meantime, La Cave's April through July calendar was full of holes. Bands were contracting and then cancelling those contracts every week, or so it seemed. Some gave notice; others simply did not show up. Buzzy Linhart held down the fort from 18 April through the 20th, with his enjoyable mix of songs and good-natured patter making almost everyone smile. Sadly, there were only 180 smiling patrons that weekend.

The 1st (and last) Annual Cleveland Pop Festival

Getting slapped in the face is how Nelson Karl felt upon finishing his morning coffee on the 18th of April. That's when he saw the ad – the huge ad – crowing about the "1st Annual Cleveland Pop Festival" to be held that very night at Cleveland's venerable Public Hall. But it wasn't just *anyone* who was featured, it was three acts that Nelson or Larry had been negotiating with for future dates. Headlining the "festival" was Blood, Sweat & Tears.

Compounding their misery, the opening act was the Iron Butterfly. The crowd of 8,500 delirious fans gave both bands standing ovations, with Iron Butterfly's ovation preceded by a volatile 23-minute jam on "In-A-Gadda-Da-Vida." And just to give the knife in their back a little twist, the opener to the opener was yet another former La Cave act, Tim Buckley.

To add a dose of irony to the proceedings, Tim Buckley was a no-show for the festival, prompting hurried phone calls to area bands. Tiny Alice answered the call, playing some fan faves like "Dr. Jazz" and closing with a spiffy version of Teresa Brewer's chestnut "Music, Music, Music."

And where was Tim Buckley, who had been seen lurking about town that very day? He was happily stoned at La Cave, having been added to the guest list at the last minute. Why did Tim pass up playing in front of 8,500 fans and instead watch Buzzy Linhart serenade 60 fans? All we can do is speculate. But it's well known that Tim had some serious addiction problems with alcohol and heroin, and La Cave *was* known as a place where a guy could get hooked up with his fave poisons.

After Buzzy finished his stage work, there were more open dates in La Cave's schedule than contracted ones. For the weekend beginning 18 April, three no-shows caused La Cave to close for the first full weekend since the riots. P.F. Sloan, Eric Andersen and future Woodstock performer Sweetwater all abandoned Nelson and Larry for greener pastures. The next weekend Raven, a blues-rock outfit hailing from Buffalo, just missed the 200 mark in attendance, ending with 199 by Larry's computations. Nor was he able to find a traveling band suitable for La Cave for the two upcoming weekends, instead bringing in the Mr. Stress Blues Band. They had the added advantage of storing their equipment at La Cave.

Even while the band was still shaking the stage with Bill Miller's stellar harp solos, a palpable feeling was shared by those working at La Cave that the club no longer had "it." Patrons likely could tell that things weren't all copasetic, too. Frantic calls to agents provided no relief, but when Jimmy Witherspoon cancelled last-minute, a bevy of angels in whiteface came to Nelson's rescue. Buried at the bottom of a page of the *Plain Dealer*, a tiny notice whispered that The Hello People would come to La Cave through Sunday. They noted that it was an unexpected change in schedule.

Unexpected, indeed. But highly appreciated. The folk-rock mime troupe was always a fan fave and, on Nelson's ninth or tenth desperate phone call, took advantage of a hole in *their* schedule to play from Friday the 9th through a Sunday matinee. It was bittersweet for Nelson and Larry. This was the same band that, just a year ago in March, showed the owners and the world that La Cave had "made it." Now, that seemed *so* long ago. One good aspect was that despite the last-minute nature of their performances, they drew almost twice as many fans as they did during their most recent, disappointing residency. Still, collecting $3.50 from 635 paying customers wasn't going to save Nelson's bacon.

Another La Cave favorite, the duo Brewer & Shipley, filled the next empty slot, the weekend beginning Friday, 16 May, in what should have been a victorious celebration, with the men having released their critically-acclaimed second album, *Weeds*. Kama Sutra Records, their label, had recognized their potential, and sprung for an all-star backing cast of session players to accompany them. Pianist Nicky Hopkins, guitarist Mike Bloomfield, pedal steel virtuoso "Red" Rhodes, fiddler Richard Greene, with Bob Jones keeping a restrained, elegant beat throughout, turned the album into a spare masterpiece. Their cover of Dylan's "All Along the Watchtower" and Jim Pepper's Native American chant "Witchi-Tai-To" became concert staples and college radio replays. But in a reflection of how poisonous the East 105th and Euclid neighborhood had become, they brought in a dismal 132 patrons over three days. Nelson' bank balance sunk deeper into an ocean of red ink.

A Possible Way Out of This Mess

Larry Bruner was furiously working the agencies and managers, many of who were still pitching acts to La Cave. Some bands that had shown interest were Neil Young, Chicago Transit Authority, NRBQ, Junior Wells, Sea Train, The Buddy Miles Express, Barry Melton & the Fish, Man, Eric Andersen, John Sebastian, the Chicago Blues All-Stars, Sweetwater, Otis Rush, Terry Reid, Dr. John the Night Tripper, Hamilton Camp, Doc Watson, the New York Rock and Roll Ensemble, Johnny Winter, Zephyr and a few others. His preferred method of communication was by Western Union telegram, a quaint way to avoid the expense of long-distance phone charges, yet quicker than mail by days.

Of these, he would sign contracts with all of them except Chicago, Junior Wells, and Otis Rush. And of those he signed, only six would ultimately honor their contract and actually show up.

Scrambling for ideas, Larry wrote to Richard Waterman of Avalon Productions in Philadelphia, a popular agency, who represented, among others, Junior Wells. Richard proposed a blues festival, and Larry's brain kicked into overdrive. He fired off a telegraph to Ira Blacker at Associated Booking proposing a three-week Blues Fest in August, and offered to sign Albert King, Bobby Bland, Canned Heat, Chicken Shack, Howlin' Wolf, and Savoy Brown. He also considered Buddy Guy and Lightning Hopkins, according to his handwritten notes. He was prepared to offer $1,000 to each act for six sets over three days each. He had calculated that the potential gross profit would meet or exceed $6,500.

Nelson, never a man to hide from difficult decisions, thought that although Larry's solution was creative, he had to tell Larry that his mind was made up. La Cave would close.

Reports of La Cave's Death are Only Slightly Exaggerated

Larry Bruner was devastated. Always ambitious, he had envisioned a career in law supporting social justice, and other forms of activism. And while he realized many of those goals later in life, at the time he was extremely happy with what he saw as another form of helping society by bringing to town many acts that he knew could influence young people in ways that a mere nightclub manager couldn't. He may have underestimated Nelson Karl's resolve, or thought that he could turn things around, but he didn't bail on La Cave when circumstances dictated that he should. He still had a few chances to redeem La Cave and, by extension, himself.

The next act to come to town was his first shot at redemption. Seatrain, the band that had been founded from the ashes of the Blues Project after their appearance at the Monterey Pop Festival.

Drummer Roy Blumenfeld and bassist/flutist Andy Kulberg were veterans of that band and by extension of La Cave, so they knew it would be a good tour stop. In their travels they had picked up virtuoso violinist Richard Greene and were in the midst of a tour to market their debut album *Sea Train.* But redemption would have to wait a week. Only 410 customers paid to see the group during its stay at La Cave.

Everyone held their breath for a few days, avoided walking under ladders, and kept an eye out for black cats. Their ancient superstitions were rewarded when the band Crazy Horse, with a wild-eyed Neil Young in tow, scrambled downstairs to unpack their equipment on 30 May, as advertised. There was no good reason why Neil and Company wouldn't pack the place to the rafters. In this thought, Larry was mistaken. The band played as they did the first time out, an acoustic set followed by a rollicking electric set, but the bottom line in attendance resembled their February residency, with only thirty more customers than the last time around. La Cave missed the 700 mark in weekend attendance. As the crew cleaned up after Sunday's matinee, Larry couldn't kid himself any more. He wondered if he should tell the faithful waiters and cleanup personnel. He figured they might already know.

If the attendance count for Neil Young was disappointing, the following week was near-suicidal. NRBQ, an acronym for the New Rhythm and Blues Quintet (they would soon become a quartet, eliminating the need for a name change), had formed in 1965 and had become well-known on the circuit for their high-energy performances and varied musical styles, playing and blending rock, jazz, the blues with pop and even Tin Pan Alley styles. With the Mind Garden opening on Friday night and Leatherwood and Lisa performing the same duty on Saturday, La Cave could only manage to attract a paltry 202 fans to show up. The Sunday show was especially depressing, with only 23 listeners paying their way downstairs. Even a surprise appearance by Don Adams, the zany Agent 86 on the smash TV show "Get Smart," disguised as a bearded rock and roll musician, couldn't save the day as he often did on the small screen. Don was the brother of band leader Terry Adams.

Among Larry's triumphs and tragedies, the next five weekends were particularly brutal. No one had worked harder to fill La Cave with quality stage acts, but he was swimming upstream and the currents were carrying him away from success. A baker's dozen of contracted performers either cancelled or merely didn't show up through the end of July, while only four did. Sweetwater and John Sebastian bailed for the 10th through 12th, Terry Reid and Zephyr missed the next weekend, followed by Doc and Merle Watson. Finally, what might have the biggest show ever to fill the club,

Johnny Winter, in cahoots with new concert promoters Mike and Jules Belkin, abandoned La Cave without notice for the 10,000 seat Public Hall.

Hamilton Camp showed up on 12 June for three nights. He was already an established cult figure in folk and rock music. He had burst upon the scene at the 1960 Newport Folk Festival, and his songs had been covered by an eclectic mix of recording artists. His apocalyptic warning "Pride of Man" was covered by Quicksilver Messenger Service, Gram Parsons, and Gordon Lightfoot. His song "You Can Tell the World" appeared as the opening track on unknown duo Simon & Garfunkel's debut album, *Wednesday Morning, 3 A.M.* Hamilton released a half dozen albums in the '60s, but in subsequent decades became known mainly for his acting chops, appearing in a couple of hundred movies until his death in 2005. Four or five years earlier it's likely he would have had the room crammed with appreciative folkies, but this time around could only manage to pull in 185 folk music fanatics.

Willie

Willie Dixon felt right at home at La Cave. He'd already played there as the bassist for James Cotton, and he and his wife had been shown a great time by Nelson. Willie was on his way to becoming a legend, as a multi-instrumental master, a songwriter a sideman, a band leader, and – most importantly, a fighter for justice and equity. As an added bonus, he had a booming bass singing voice. Without Willie in the fight, it's likely that the world would have been deprived of the talents of Muddy Waters, Howlin' Wolf, Little Walter, and other bluesmen. When the Chess Brothers opened their studio, they hired Willie as a songwriter for those legends, as well as for Bo Diddley, Otis Rush, and the entire Chess stable of players. When the 1960s rolled around, the Yardbirds and Rolling Stones were among the artists who covered Willie's songs. Cream had a hit with his song "Crossroads." Those famous song thieves in Led Zeppelin "borrowed" his "Bring it on Home" and

"Whole Lotta Love", and eventually had to provide a generous out-of-court settlement after Willie filed suit. In late '68 he formed his own band, the Chicago Blues All-Stars, and for the first time he became well-known in his own right. The All-Stars would go on to record thirteen albums, and Willie himself would eventually garner a Grammy Award and induction into three music halls of fame – the Blues Hall of Fame, the Rock and Roll Hall of Fame, and the Songwriters Hall of Fame.

The depressing news were the numbers 183 and 143; the paid attendance figures for the 21st and 22nd of June. The stage seemed more crowded than the tables and chairs.

La Cave was running on fumes. Even though Larry wisely waited until the last possible moment to place newspaper ads, more acts failed to show up than did show. John Sebastian, the Watsons, and Eric Andersen ignored their contracts to presumably play at larger clubs.

The two traveling acts that did put on shows were phenomenal by all accounts. Dr. John the Night Tripper had the last weekend of June on its calendar, and performed several of the most memorable sets ever to excite what few cave dwellers remained. Dr. John was the stage name of Malcolm "Mac" Rebennack, Jr. He was a small-time wise guy who had grown up bad: he had gotten into legal trouble. His musicianship became his ticket out of that trouble. After having a finger partially shot off, he moved to Los Angeles and worked his way up to being a first-call session keyboardist, playing on records as diverse as Sonny & Cher and the Mothers of Invention.

Looking for a unique way into stage performing, Malcolm, always interested in voodoo, created the Dr. John persona in late 1967 as an homage to his New Orleans roots. He wore a headdress and flamboyant costumes, put on shows that simulated voodoo ceremonies, and released his debut album, *Gris-Gris,* which in good time became critically-acclaimed.

All Dr. John did himself was to win six Grammy Awards, and become a member of the Rock and Roll Hall of Fame, inducted in 2011. Ironically, Larry didn't bother to advertise the good doctor's mid-week appearance, having been told by Nelson Karl that there were no funds to do so. Despite the high energy, mysterious, spooky sights and sounds of Dr. John's mid-week show, only 134 brave patrons ventured down La Cave's dim and dingy stairway to enjoy what are, today, legendary concerts.

As has been said many times about musical flops, it was an artistic success.

Chapter 16: I Heard It on the Grapevine

The whispers and slyly nodded heads had metastasized into full-throated, arm-waving speculation. "Is La Cave closing?" "Hey, what's up at La Cave?" "What have you heard?" To his credit, Larry was doing everything humanly possible to find a way to keep the club viable. Since he didn't have a headliner for the last weekend in June, he held "auditions," and listened to a bevy of near-competent singers and bands. All in all, he heard at least 13 acts, and ten of those thirteen had black lines crossed through their names in Larry's notes. Nobody could say Larry wasn't doing his all. For his part, Larry had no intention of throwing in the towel. That decision would have to be Nelson's alone. And Nelson's mind was firmly made up.

The end came with a whimper and a bang. Dr. John's turn at La Cave was the whimper; the New York Rock & Roll Ensemble's weekend, the last official concert at La Cave, was a relative bang. Unlike Dr. John, who came to town on the down-low, the Ensemble got a full dose of glowing reviews and plenty of printer's ink. The entire upper third of a page in the Fourth of July edition of the *Pee Dee* was devoted to singing the band's praises. Tom Davis, Jr.'s article explained that the band was so good that his column would not allow a full review.

In other words, ya gotta go see this band.

The Ensemble was just that – a collection of widely diverse but highly accomplished musicians. Davis, Jr., pulled favorable quotes about the group from the New York Times, while Leonard Bernstein referred to them as "mad geniuses."[lxxxiv] They were referring to the three front men, all having studied at prestigious Julliard, playing cello, French horn, harpsichord, oboe and other classical instruments in front of a rock and roll style rhythm section. With songs like "Gravedigger" and "Running Down the Highway," the band showed impressive chops. They also knew how to put on the dog: they played in white tie and tails. No less a figure than Ahmet Ertegun, owner of their record label Atlantic Records, was quoted as saying "You play all the right notes on all the wrong instruments."

He was only half-joking.

In good time, members of the band would find success and acclaim in the music business, Michael Kamen as an award-winning film score composer, and Marty Fulterman in the same role for numerous TV shows. Doran Rudnytsky gained a career as a session cellist and bassist for both film and television.

Their shows at La Cave sparked a little fire of temporary stress relief for Nelson and Larry. Even thought it was the Fourth of July weekend, the most popular outdoor holiday, over eight hundred fans wedged into the weekend that put the period at the end of La Cave's sentence. But no one knew it until the next weekend.

The Winter of Our Discontent

Everyone was jazzed about the upcoming weekend. Johnny Winter was raw white boy blues energy. One reviewer described him as "a rail-thin blues guitarist known for his scorching riffs, flowing white hair and gravelly, hard-times voice." Born with albinism which left him legally blind, Johnny had begun playing guitar early. At age 15 he won a talent contest for his song "School Day Blues," which shot to number eight in his hometown of Beaumont, Texas. In early '69 he jammed onstage at the Fillmore East with Mike Bloomfield and Al Kooper, and when Johnny ripped through B.B. King's "It's My Own Fault," Columbia

Records execs flipped their wigs and gave Johnny the biggest advance in the history of the music industry, a stratospheric $600,000.

Larry pulled out all the stops. He printed up 1,500 tickets and hit the five music stores selling La Cave tickets. They responded by selling over 400 tickets to one of Johnny's six scheduled set over three days. He made sure that Nelson's $1,500 advance check did not bounce.

La Cave
Ph 231-3020
10615 Euclid Ave.
PRESENTS
JOHNNY WINTER
THUR. JULY 10, 7:30 P.M. 1ST SHOW
ADVANCE SALE $4.00
MIDWEST TICKET CO., CLEVE. 5
No 1227

Johnny Winter ticket

Everything was set. Johnny and his band would arrive early on Monday the 7th of July to sound check and rehearse, and was slated to play the 8th through the 10th.

There was only one problem: the band never showed up. Larry recalls, "Johnny Winter was a big gamble for us. We'd agreed to a $3,500 guarantee for three nights, more than we'd ever spent before and, without publicizing it, scheduled them as our last shows. The dates were cancelled for no good reason we could tell except that he seemed to be getting bigger fast."

It's true. Johnny was blowing up. With his brother Edgar on keyboards and the ubiquitous Willie Dixon on electric bass, his album featured songs that would become Johnny Winter classics, such as, "Sonny Boy" Williamson's "Good Morning Little School Girl", and B.B. King's "Be Careful with a Fool." In less than six weeks he would explode into the consciousness of millions of record buyers after a truly incendiary set on the Woodstock stage.

Nelson faced it head-on, filing a suit to collect on the deposit and projected lost profits. In part, his pleading said, "[La Cave] further claims that it had been the intention of the defendants…to cancel this contract and all other club concerts for reasons that defendant, Johnny Winter, suddenly discovered that he could make more money elsewhere."[lxxxv]

Sure enough, as Larry concurred, "[the] Belkins[lxxxvi] announced a concert with him at [the 3,000-seat] Music Hall." This kind of poaching wasn't limited to La Cave. In the lawsuit, Nelson said, "in fact, said defendant did cancel other contracts elsewhere in the United States."

Larry wrapped it up in a tidy bow, writing, "Nelson was outraged, and sued for the contract price, won a judgment, and went with the sheriff and got the Music Hall gate receipts confiscated. We collected."[lxxxvii]

It was a Pyrrhic victory. Aside from a couple of non-publicized, private jam sessions held ad hoc later in July, the joyous sounds of live music never again reverberated off the damp, clammy walls and nicely swept but sticky La Cave floorboards. Never again would young Clevelanders be beckoned by Sue Crutch's dayglo mural to "Feed Your Head." No plots would be hatched, no 3.2 beer guzzled, no furtive joints inhaled, no boy meets girl, and none of the shared glory of impressionable young adults being innocently, or not so much, instilled with a sense of freedom, confidence and activism that wasn't available at home.

And maybe, in the bright light of hindsight, it was all for the best. The world was about to turn mean, and the lessons lived and learned in the basement, far from the prying eyes of those across the gulf of the generation gap, would turn into action in the streets and courtrooms of America. There was a war on, killing other young Americans, to stand up against, and civil rights, voting rights, and gender equality to stand up for. The '60s were a time of growing: less than a year later, on 4 May, 1970, four Kent State students lay dead, with thirteen more injured by the thirty-ought-six cartridges fired at them under the orders of the Governor and possibly the President. Two weeks later, more students lay dead or dying at Jackson State. The time for innocence and growth was over: it was now time to put the lessons learned at La Cave into action, or else the future would become a very dark destination.

The Shortest Epitaph in History

On 11 July, Jane Scott of the *Plain Dealer,* snuck this succinct 18-word announcement in the middle of her "the happening" column: "With La Cave leaving the field, there won't be many places to hear progressive, blues, or folk concerts." But she was a week late with the news. Tom Weigel of the *Cleveland Press* scooped her. On Friday, the 4th, even as the New York Rock and Roll Ensemble was tuning up, Tom's obituary for La Cave graced the better part the paper's page 4-N. He closed by hoping La Cave wouldn't fall into oblivion.

Epilogue

La Cave blasted off a month after fellow Ohioan John Glenn sped into space and circled the fast-shrinking globe, and played its last note during the same month that yet another Ohioan, Neil Armstrong, took his small first step for mankind. The club's story fits neatly between those two achievements. The advances apparent in those two launches reflected just how much the world had advanced technologically in seven years. In the same manner, the La Cave story reflects the sociological revolution that came about in the 1960s. La Cave was a tiny club wedged into a dark basement room that barely held 300 souls, and yet it helped catalyze those social changes in ways much larger and long-lasting than its unimpressive physical appearance dictated. When the newspapers referred to La Cave as a "launching pad," there was no hyperbole in that description. La Cave helped launch dozens of world-shaping musicians into the public consciousness and various Halls of Fame membership. At the same time, it launched into adulthood thousands of young people who found safety, comfort, and some damn good times in a troubled world. Many have gone on to live talented, productive and socially conscious lives. La Cave's importance as a small part of a much bigger sociological awakening cannot be overstated.

Long live La Cave.

References

---

[i] From a typed list of prospective suppliers.
[ii] American Society of Composers, Authors and Publishers, the entity that licenses the public performance of copyrighted material.
[iii] This took place exactly two years prior to Mrs. Mellow being named "*The Plain Dealer's* professional Beatles reporter." http://www.meetthebeatlesforreal.com/2014/09/no-beat- in-beatles-for-teen-reporter.html
[iv] Known to all by his stage name Dean Martin.
[v] Letter from the Ohio State Board of Liquor Control.
[vi] $4,400 in 2021 dollars.
[vii] http://www.usinflationcalculator.com/
[viii] https://www.census.gov/library/publications/1963/demo/p60-041.html
[ix] Motion for Reconsideration dated 9 October 1962.
[x] So claimed the State of Ohio in court documents.
[xi] Not to be confused with the prolific country music singer-songwriter of the same name.
[xii] $23 each per nightly performance!
[xiii] Email from Doug Yeager.
[xiv] Letter dated 28 February 1963 from Nelson Karl to Len Rosenfeld.
[xv] https://www.discogs.com/release/6655429-Oscar-Brand-Jean-Ritchie-George-Britton-Tom-Pasle-Casey-Anderson-3-Charlie-Byrd-Cynthia-Gooding-Mike
[xvi] Not to be confused with Cleveland's present-day WCLV at 104.9 FM.
[xvii] Just over $1,700 in 2021 dollars.
[xviii] In November 1989, as the NBC television cameras chronicled the dismantling of the Berlin Wall, they showed East German school kids singing "Last Night I Had the Strangest Dream" en

masse: "Last night I had the strangest dream I ever had before/I dreamed the world had all agreed to put an end to war…"

[xix] La Cave income and expense statement 1st quarter 1963.

[xx] With permission. https://web.archive.org/web/20140517061355/http://candaceforest.com/

[xxi] Per their signed contracts.

[xxii] Whom Dylan later wrote the song "Mr. Tambourine Man" about.

[xxiii] Spike Lee's father!

[xxiv] https://www.senate.gov/artandhistory/history/common/generic/CivilRightsAct1964.htm

[xxv] $13,200 in 2021 dollars!

[xxvi] https://www.historyplace.com/unitedstates/vietnam/index-1965.html

[xxvii] From the Doors' song "Unknown Soldier" on their album *Waiting for the Sun.*

[xxviii] https://www.historyplace.com/unitedstates/vietnam/index-1965.html

[xxix] The album's name ultimately became "Jim & Jean."

[xxx] "Ringo" won.

[xxxi] $26,300 in 2021 dollars.

[xxxii] In 2022, ezz-thetics released Albert's "La Cave Live, 1966 Revisited" CD.

[xxxiii] 3 February, 1959 was "the day the music died." That's when Buddy Holly's airplane crashed.

[xxxiv] https://case.edu/ech/articles/h/hough-riots

[xxxv] Roberts, Michael D. (2006, June 27). "The Riot and the Bad Address". *Cleveland Magazine*.

[xxxvi] In a revealing slipup, Nelson uses the (at the time) proper business greeting punctuation mark, the colon, as opposed to the "personal" mark, the comma.

[xxxvii] https://www.in2013dollars.com/us/inflation/1967?amount=2500

[xxxviii] Blues, Rags and Hollers: The Koerner, Ray & Glover Story. (1995). *Latch Lake.*
[xxxix] Roth, Arlen (1985). Arlen Roth's complete acoustic guitar. Schirmer Books. p. 47. ISBN 0- 02-872150-0.
[xl] A popular local duo consisting of Jim Murray and Paul Penfield.
[xli] It was 5 and 6 May, 1967.
[xlii] The US Army.
[xliii] The Mindgarden.
[xliv] https://quoteinvestigator.com/tag/brian-eno/
[xlv] With permission. https://www.facebook.com/Mr.Stress/
[xlvi] Today, she is known as Sura Crutch Sevastopolous.
[xlvii] https://daily.redbullmusicacademy.com/2016/12/dwight-burns-j-zone-interview
[xlviii] Federal Bureau of Investigation, "The Doors Part 1 of 1".
[xlix] Schmitz (1979). The Irony of Vietnam. The Brookings Institution, p. 90.
[l] "Tet Offensive". www.u-s-history.com.
[li] With permission. "LINER NOTES FOR THE APPLE PIE MOTHERHOOD BAND'S THE APPLE PIE MOTHERHOOD BAND".
[lii] Larry Bruner's notes.
[liii] Not Gram Parson's Fallen Angels.
[liv] https://ctva.biz/Music/US/Upbeat_04_(1967-68).htm
[lv] "The Mad Hatters Meet the Fallen Angels (2012) CD booklet. Cicadelic Records.
[lvi] "Dock Boggs & Kate Peters Sturgill Festival | Norton, VA - Official Website". Nortonva.gov.
[lvii] https://www.allmusic.com/album/fusion-mw0000856846
[lviii] http://brunoceriotti.weebly.com/blood-sweat--tears.html?fbclid=IwAR2gWnW6sNTmLkqXRyWG01AsW- LdFxsvT9zqwgevX2ofiGSEVV1JQz_yovw
[lix] National Mobilization Committee to End the War in Vietnam.
[lx] https://en.wikipedia.org/wiki/Carl_Stokes
[lxi] https://insheepsclothinghifi.com/album/harumi-s-t/
[lxii] Ibid.

[lxiii] Band accounting for the engagement lists Ross Bushman instead of Roger Sherman.
[lxiv] With permission. A publication that was supported financially by Larry Bruner with La Cave receipts.
[lxv] levy, d.a., (1968, March) unpublished poem.
[lxvi] Written by Michael and Tom's friend Freddy Neil.
[lxvii] Holmes, Robert J. (1968, May 14). "Circle Area LSD Ring Smashed." *The Plain Dealer*, pg.1.
[lxviii] Ibid, pg. 8.
[lxix] Staff writer, (1968, May 14). *The Akron Beacon Journal,* pp. A1 – A2.
[lxx] Ibid.
[lxxi] Witcover, Jules (1988). 85 Days: The Last Campaign of Robert Kennedy. Quill. ISBN 978-0- 688-07859-1.
[lxxii] And at least 28 acts cancelled from January through July, 1969.
[lxxiii] Andrew Gilbert, (2008, August 13). "Loading Zone Reloaded", East Bay Express.
[lxxiv] Joni's manager Elliot Roberts, who signed the contracts.
[lxxv] Larry's ledger reveals 1,488 paid fans for the 4 days.
[lxxvi] https://www.archives.gov/news/topics/1968-a-year-of-turmoil-and-change
[lxxvii] Ibid.
[lxxviii] https://www.allmusic.com/album/la-cave-1968-mw0002437978
[lxxix] "Lisa" was Alan's wife Patti.
[lxxx] $21,000 in today's money!
[lxxxi] The name of a poem by the English poet Christina Rossetti.
[lxxxii] Leopold, Jason, "Inside the FBI's File on The Fugs: The 'Most Vulgar Thing the Human Mind Could Possibly Conceive'". Noisey.vice.com
[lxxxiii] With permission. "Ohio's State Rock Song - Hang On Sloopy". ohiohistorycentral.org.
[lxxxiv] Davis, Jr., Tom (1969, July 4). *The Plain Dealer,* pg. 14.
[lxxxv] Case A-905-429, Cleveland Municipal Court docket.
[lxxxvi] Longtime Cleveland area concert promoters.

[lxxxvii] From Larry Bruner's oral history notes.

Index

D

Made in the USA
Las Vegas, NV
19 December 2024

14923345R00174